Suburban Religion

Churches and Synagogues in the American Experience

by

W. Widick Schroeder, Victor Obenhaus,
Larry A. Jones, and Thomas Sweetser, S.J.

C
S
S
R

Center for the Scientific Study of Religion

Chicago, Illinois

To the Men and Women

Who Serve American

Religious Institutions

and the People

Who Choose to Participate

in Them

This volume is one of the publications in the "Studies in Religion and Society" series, edited by Thomas C. Campbell, W. Alvin Pitcher, W. Widick Schroeder, and Gibson Winter.

Center for the Scientific Study of Religion
5757 University Avenue
Chicago, Illinois 60637

I S B N: 0-913348-05-8

Library of Congress Catalog Card Number: 74-82113

PREFACE

This study had its genesis in various courses dealing with church and community, research methods, and Christian ethics jointly taught by two of the authors. It evolved out of discussions with several generations of theological students about the nature of voluntary religious institutions in the context of American society. It took more definite shape in several seminars with members of a research group interested in furthering the study. In developing the study and in interpreting the findings presented here, the interests and needs of the clergy serving American churches and synagogues and of theological students preparing for professional religious leadership responsibilities were foremost in our minds.

The text is organized around major issues with which American religious leaders are struggling, highlighting the problems and the promises of American religious institutions. Readers interested in particular topics may turn directly to the appropriate chapter.

We were also interested in contributing to the understanding of lay people who choose to belong to American religious institutions, for the future of American churches and synagogues depends substantially upon them. We hope social scientific students of religion and society may find some facets of the work useful to them, even though many of them will not share the presuppositions informing the study.

All who participated in the development of this study are concerned about the contributions of religious institutions to human well-being. We hope the study will assist lay people and clergy to understand the unique situation of American religious institutions and will sensitize them to the unity and diversity of religious expression in the American experience.

We are especially indebted to Edward Bergstraesser, Welton Warkentin, and R. Dean Drayton for their assistance in designing the study, developing questionnaires and interview schedules, and interviewing clergy in the suburban sector on which this study is focused. Their work was a labor of love, for we had only sufficient research funds to pay for their transportation costs.

Peg Strait served as secretary for the entire project, coordinating appointments, preparing interview schedules and questionnaires, supervising the mailing and receiving of lay questionnaires, following up on non-respondents, and competently handling all the other details involved in survey research. We are deeply in her debt for her meticulous care in overseeing this aspect of the work as well as for her assistance with the typing of numerous drafts of the manuscript.

We want to thank Betty Fuerst for her care in typing the final copy. Her interest and helpfulness were far beyond that which one might have reason to expect.

We also want to thank participants in several research seminars held under the auspices of the Center for the Scientific Study of Religion for their assistance in helping us shape the study. We are especially grateful to Professors Thomas C. Campbell, W. Alvin Pitcher, and Gibson Winter for their counsel during this phase of the study. We also want to thank Professor Joseph C. Hough, Jr., Rabbi Robert Marx and Professor Talbert Shaw for their helpful critiques of an earlier draft of the manuscript.

The Chicago Theological Seminary and the General Services Foundation provided funds to defray the costs of transportation, preparation and distribution of questionnaires, coding, and data processing. The Chicago Theological Seminary also provided secretarial assistance, printing facilities, and office space. Those aware of the costs of survey research will appreciate the voluntary contributions of members of the research team, for our total budget was less than $5,000, all of which was used to meet direct expenses.

Finally, we want to thank the clergy and lay people who took the time to respond to our questionnaires and interviews. Without their gracious cooperation, this study could not have been conducted.

W. Widick Schroeder

Victor Obenhaus

Larry A. Jones

Thomas Sweetser, S.J.

TABLE OF CONTENTS

PART I

SUBURBAN CHURCHES AND SYNAGOGUES
IN HISTORICAL AND SOCIAL CONTEXT

PART II

SUBURBAN CHURCHES AND SYNAGOGUES
AS SOCIAL INSTITUTIONS

PART III

SUBURBAN CHURCHES AND SYNAGOGUES AS RELIGIOUS
AND MORAL AGENCIES FOR THEIR LAY PARTICIPANTS

PART IV

SUMMARY AND CONCLUSION

LIST OF TABLES

LIST OF FIGURES

INTRODUCTION

Religious institutions emerge in response to human experiences of the Divine Presence. The shapes and styles of religious institutions are clearly conditioned by their sociohistorical context, but human experiences of the Divine Presence are foundations for their emergence.[1]

All religious institutions are ambiguous, bearing witness to the Divine Presence in human life and reflecting the frailties of human institutions and people's flickering visions of the Divine Reality.[2] The ambiguities of religious institutions are rooted in finitude, human ignorance, and human sloth and lethargy.

Our focus here is on suburban churches and synagogues in the United States. The participants in these churches and synagogues self-consciously belonged to formally constituted religious institutions. We do not deal with inchoate, amorphous, embryonic, and emerging religious institutions nor with groups and institutions whose participants did not self-consciously term religious institutions. These "latent" religious institutions may be more "religious" from some points of view than the religious institutions discussed here, but they are beyond the scope of this volume.

The religious institutions discussed here have been identified by public, corporate acts of worship to God. This central constitutive act of Divine worship distinguishes religious institutions from other social institutions with which they may share other common functions.[3]

The Relation between Religious

Institutions and American Society

The interplay between religious institutions and institutions in the other spheres of the social order must be considered in any investigation of churches and synagogues in American society, for no social institution exists in a social or cultural vacuum. Most members of any given society assume that the arrangement of social institutions within the social order they know in their own society is "natural," but such arrangements are, in fact, the product of the complex interplay of human decisions and historical destiny. Because religious experience is interwoven with societal expressions and intellectual interpretations, it is very difficult and sometimes impossible to sort out religious, societal, and cognitive factors definitively.

1

Religious institutions, such as temples, churches, monasteries, shrines, and synagogues, have been part and parcel of the fabric of social life in all human societies. The modern occidental historical epoch is distinguished from all others by the sharper separation of the religious sphere from the other spheres and by the widespread questioning by people in many social strata of interpretations of life affirming the reality of the Divine Presence in the world.

The crucial notions guiding the relation of American religious institutions to each other and to social institutions in other spheres of American society are the separation of church and state, religious pluralism, religious tolerance, and religious liberty. These notions and the broader cultural values to which they are related did not emerge de novo in America; they are the outgrowth of an historical process during which the United States has evolved from a rural, agrarian, folk society to an urban, industrial, mass society. In this transition from a traditional society to a post-traditional society shifts have occurred in values and forms of social organization that have had a profound impact on traditional religious institutions.

In order to understand the bases for contemporary forms of religious institutions in America, salient historical developments are reviewed in Part One, the focus being upon the broad processes by which America has become a technological society par excellence. In this evolution, religious institutions have been transformed, and the vast majority of members of almost all of them has come to accept or to acquire common overarching societal norms defining church-state relations.

The Contemporary Situation

In the American context, piety and secularity have coexisted for more than 200 years. In a society shaped in its major forms by technical rationalism, that is, reason seeking the most efficient means to attain a given end, churches and synagogues--at least until very recently--have been constantly growing in numbers and in institutional vitality. The United States has been at the same time one of the most secular and one of the most pious of modern societies.[4]

In the past fifteen or twenty years, some evidence of decline in institutional religious life in America has been developing.[5] The proportion of the American people attending religious services in a given week has been decreasing since the early 1960's.

Some clergy and some laymen were leaders in civil rights and anti-war movements in the past decade, reflecting both continuity and discontinuity with earlier periods. Such involvement has produced social conflict within various communions, for not all clergy and laity interpret in the same way political issues related to civil rights and international relations.[6]

Although financial support for America's religious institutions is massive compared to other societies, this support has faltered in the late sixties and early seventies. Some ecclesiastical agencies and instrumentalities have had actual reductions in income; most have not had increases commensurate with the rate of inflation in the period.

As a result of these financial difficulties, directly related to reduced lay support for religious institutions in America, most religious groups have either reduced or curtailed the expansion of ecclesiastical staffs in the past half-decade.

These financial problems have preoccupied the members of ecclesiastical bureaucracies, but they are manifestations of more significant contrasts in religious loyalties, values, and commitments among various segments of the American people. At this level, people's basic values and meanings are most important, for human beings do not commit themselves wholeheartedly to movements and institutions in which they do not believe.

The findings reported in this study focus upon these values which illumine the religious and moral understanding of suburban clergy and lay people in contemporary America.

Suburban styles of religious membership are of special interest to the clergy, for church and synagogue members are disproportionately concentrated among the middle and upper strata of the American population such as those in suburban America. If the religious professional is to minister sensitively to such members, he must be aware of the social and cultural situation in which he finds them.

The Organization of the Study

This volume is organized primarily around problems and issues with which contemporary American religious leaders are wrestling. Part One outlines the social-cultural context in which suburban churches and synagogues are set. It accentuates the importance of the voluntary religious association, for the disestablishment of state churches is one of the most significant events in the history of church-state relations. Religious liberty has decisively affected American religious institutions, for in the final analysis an American is a member of a church or synagogue because he wills to be.

This voluntaryism has accentuated the impact of the new urbanism on religious institutions, for it has contributed to the multiplicity of religious institutions in America and to the identification of given social and ethnic groups with particular religious institutions. The rapid population mobility and the succession of different social and ethnic groups in a given geographical area which is characteristic of the new urbanism complicates the life of religious institutions, for various social and ethnic groups are apt to belong to different religious institutions. The implications of this situation and the ethos of the new urbanism are also considered in Part One.

Part Two, Suburban Churches and Synagogues as Social Institutions, examines the situation of the professional religious leadership serving suburban churches and synagogues and discusses trends in religious institutions.

Part Three, Suburban Churches and Synagogues as Religious and Moral Agencies, explores some critical problems confronting suburban churches and synagogues in the familial, ethnic, status, political, and cultural spheres. The emphases on private morality--particularly familial and interpersonal morality--are explored in Chapter VI.

Partly as a result of religious voluntaryism and partly as a result of cultural, ethnic, and status exclusiveness, members of local suburban institutions are relatively homogeneous in status and ethnic composition. Black-white contrasts are especially sharp. These problems are discussed in Chapter VII.

All the major faith groups in America are concerned with issues of public morality and social justice, but there are significant intra- and inter-faith differences in matters of public morality. These are examined in Chapter VIII.

Earlier the intermingling of piety and secularity in the American context was noted. This interplay and the significance of religious beliefs in the lives of church and synagogue participants are treated in Chapter IX.

Parts Two and Three are designed to highlight issues confronting America's major faith groupings. Those who are interested in particular topics or issues can turn directly to the pertinent sections.

Even though it is ultimately arbitrary to differentiate analytical "factual" matter from evaluative "interpretive" material, the focus in these parts is upon the former. The final chapter summarizes _and_ evaluates the findings elaborated in the preceding parts. It elaborates a constructive understanding of authentic religion and uses this under- standing to evaluate the religion of America and the religions of American suburbia. Every analyst must evaluate his material from _some_ constructive viewpoint; the perspective developed in the concluding chapter, at odds with many contemporary social scientific and theological interpretations of contemporary American religious institutions, evaluates the data from one constructive perspective.

In contrast to almost all social scientific studies, the viewpoint here presupposes the authenticity of religious experience. It affirms the _sui generis_ character of a divine reality undergirding human religious experience and the religious institutions elicited by that experience.

In contrast to many theological studies, the constructive viewpoint developed here interprets in an ambiguously positive way the salient values shaping American social institutions. It also affirms the normative value of the voluntary religious institution, with all the attendant ambiguities for social witness and inclusiveness.

The Sources of the Data

The interpretations developed in Chapters I and II of Part One are based largely on historical and sociological studies made by others. They have been reprocessed and reordered to fit into the interpretive socio-cultural framework elaborated in Part One.

The interpretations and analyses developed in Chapter III of Part One and in Parts Two and Three are based primarily on interview and questionnaire data obtained from approximately 125 clergy and 1500 lay people in a sector of a major metropolitan region in the Midwest. The sampling procedures are discussed in the concluding section of the Introduction.

The Suburban Study Sector

The Suburban Sector

The interview and questionnaire data were gathered in a suburban sector of Midwest City, the fictional name given to a large multiple-industry and financial center in the midwestern part of the United States. The suburban sector had substantial numbers of members in each of the major faith groupings in the United States. It was approximately 55 percent Protestant, 45 percent Roman Catholic and 5 percent Jewish. Between 5 and 10 percent of the Protestants were black. Compared to the nation as a whole, the sector thus had a slightly lower proportion of Protestants, a slightly higher proportion of Jews, a somewhat higher proportion of Catholics, and a somewhat lower proportion of blacks.

The suburbs reflect the same combination of considerable social and ethnic homogeneity in small geographical areas and great social and ethnic heterogeneity in larger geographical areas that is characteristic of large metropolitan areas. Within a relatively small geographical area, the population, as characterized by race, income level, and such highly correlated social factors as status, education, and occupation, is quite homogeneous. One such homogeneous community contrasts markedly with other relatively homogeneous communities of markedly differing ethnic and socioeconomic composition in the suburban sector. For example, one old industrial satellite city and one "new town" established after World War II lay in the sector. Many of the suburbs had older pre-World War II cores and later post-World War II rings.

Based on selected socioeconomic indicators, one of the sector suburbs ranked among the upper 10 percent of the suburbs in the Midwest City Metropolitan Area, and two ranked among the lower 10 percent. The variety of suburban communities in this sector belies a common assumption that suburban communities are exclusively middle status or above.

The Religious Communities Considered

In America, four predominant faith groups have emerged: white Protestant, Catholic, black Protestant, and Jewish. These faith groups constituted the focus of this study.[7]

The questionnaires and interviews used in the study probed salient moral and religious values of lay people and clergy in the four faith groups. Some items focused on areas of potential or actual conflict between these moral communities and some focused on areas of common agreement.

Questionnaires were mailed to a sample of lay people drawn from nine religious institutions in three of the eight sector suburbs. Among Midwest City suburbs, one ranked socioeconomically in the upper 10 percent, one ranked in the central 20 percent, and one ranked in the lowest 10 percent. The institutions included two predominantly black Protestant churches, three predominantly white Protestant churches, three predominantly white Roman Catholic parishes, and one Jewish synagogue.

Budgetary restrictions limited the lay questionnaire to one Protestant institution. The United Methodist Church was selected, for it is the largest and most nearly centralist American Protestant denomination outside the South.[8] As the predominant Protestant church in much of America, the United Methodist Church sets the tone and determines the patterns to which other Protestant groups respond and react. Because of this limitation, intra-Protestant lay contrasts could not be explored.

Limitations of resources and problems of access also prevented an exploration of intra-Jewish contrasts, for the lay sample is confined to one large Reform synagogue.

There was an insufficient number of blacks in the predominantly black United Methodist Church in the suburban sector to draw an adequate sample, so questionnaires were also sent to members of an African Methodist Episcopal Church.

Both these churches were overwhelmingly black (one respondent was white), so these data permitted a comparison between middle status black churches and the middle status United Methodist Church. The data do not permit a comparison between blacks in Baptist churches -- predominant in the black community -- and the United Methodist Church, but the substantial differences in participation and values reported in this study between white Protestants and black Protestants would be accentuated by the inclusion of blacks in the Baptist tradition.

The Suburban Sector as a Microcosm

of the American Suburban Religious Situation

Although the analyses of the factors shaping American religious institutions and the critical problems confronting the lay and clerical leaders of American churches and synagogues developed here are focused on a suburban sector of one major midwestern metropolitan area, they illumine factors and problems present to a greater or lesser degree in most American communities.

In this sense the suburban sector from which these data are drawn is best viewed as a microcosm of America. The religious institutions of this sector portray the religious situation in contemporary America.

To be sure, some of the factors shaping the life of churches and synagogues in America are modified by geography and by community size, but all of the issues considered here emerge in the inner lives of churches and synagogues everywhere in the United States.

Some of the patterns discussed here are modified substantially in the southern states, for this region has maintained the most distinctive subculture of any section of the United States. It is the only large region of the world with a massive preponderance of evangelical Protestants, and this style of Protestantism has given the South's religious life a distinctive tone.[9] Even here, however, America's public religion interplays with the particular religions of America to produce a religious institutional configuration unique in the world.

Sampling Procedures

Introduction

The suburban sector whose religious institutions are considered here included approximately 150,000 people and stretched eighteen to twenty miles from Midwest City's city limits. Since comparable ecological factors shaping urban life affect all suburban sectors, the examination of one of them can illumine the general processes conditioning the evolution of religious institutions in most suburban areas.

The field data were obtained through interviews and questionnaires with over 80 percent of the clergy serving the churches and synagogues in the sector and through questionnaires from some 1500 lay members of religious institutions.

Sampling procedures varied from population to population. The procedures used with the different populations are summarized subsequently. More detailed materials are presented in Appendix A. A lay questionnaire used in the study is reproduced in Appendix B.

Most of the data are presented by individual congregation or parish to emphasize the organic unity of a given religious institution.[10] In this way, one may assess the extent of diversity <u>within</u> as well as between congregations or parishes. Since religious professionals serve particular congregations or parishes, this analysis is more useful to them than would be an analysis combining the findings from several congregations or parishes.

The Communities Selected for the Lay Surveys

Three communities varying markedly in socioeconomic characteristics were selected for the lay surveys. One was an old industrial city near Midwest City, the second a post-World War II middle status suburb at the distant fringe of the suburban sector, and the third an upper status suburb contiguous with the middle status suburb. They are described more fully in Chapter III, but a brief resume is presented here.

Satellite City ranks socioeconomically in the lowest 10 percent of suburbs in the Midwest City metropolitan region. It is about one-third black, and it is the only city studied in which the majority of Protestants belong to churches not affiliated with the National Council of Churches.

Satellite City had more blue collar workers than either of the other two communities from which lay samples were drawn. It had a population of about 35,000. Most of its housing had been built before World War II.

In Satellite City, the following groups of adult lay people were surveyed: members of one of the predominantly white United Methodist churches; those of a racially mixed black-white ethnic Roman Catholic parish; those of a predominantly black United Methodist Church; and those of a predominantly black African Methodist Episcopal Church. There was no synagogue in Satellite City.

New Town was open prairie prior to World War II. Many junior executives were attracted to it during its development in the two decades after World War II, and it became a family-centered town with few single, young adult, or old people. There is now almost no open land left in New Town, and its population has stabilized at about 30,000. It is still a "port-of-entry" for well-educated young married adults, having an above average educational level but a slightly below average income level among Midwest City's suburbs. It has a sprinkling of blacks, but it is primarily a white suburb.

In New Town, lay people of the "United Protestant" church most closely identified with the United Methodist denomination and those of the Roman Catholic parish were surveyed. There was a Reform synagogue and a Conservative synagogue in New Town, but they were not studied. No predominantly black church existed.

Country Club Estates ranked socioeconomically in the upper
10 percent of Midwest City suburbs. Homes were large and expensive, and
zoning restrictions on lot size, land use, and minimum size of homes
were rigidly enforced. Professional people and higher level executives
were concentrated in Country Club Estates. It had an almost entirely
white population of about 12,000. Considerable open space existed, and
the area was growing rapidly at the time the surveys were being conducted.

In Country Club Estates, lay people of a United Methodist Church,
of a Roman Catholic parish, and of a Reform synagogue were surveyed. No
predominantly black church existed.

About half of the Midwest City Metropolitan Area population lived
in the suburbs. The rankings cited here refer only to the suburban population. If the population of Midwest City were considered in making
these rankings, New Town and Satellite City would increase their rankings.
The broad patterns would not change, but the proportion of blue collar
people in the total population would be substantially larger than in the
suburban population.

The Catholic Lay Sample

The Catholic lay sample was taken from three representative
parishes, one parish in Country Club Estates, the higher status parish,
one parish in New Town, the middle status young parish, and one parish
in Satellite City, the lower status, recently ethnic parish. The higher
and lower status parishes have parochial schools. The parish school in
Satellite City is over 50 percent black. The New Town parish closed its
school four years ago due to financial difficulties and now concentrates
on family catechesis and religious youth instruction.

The sampling was drawn from the membership lists of the three
parishes by using a table of random numbers. Because of the large number
of parishioners—the average membership for the three parishes is 1300
families—and the high mobility of the parishioners, a complete and up-
to-date listing of parish members was not available. The best that could
be done was to make a random sample from the list of parishioners who
either received Sunday contribution envelopes or at some time within the
past few years had declared themselves as belonging to the parish.

The procedure of "belonging" to a parish is different for Catholics
than it is for Protestants. The Protestant parishioners formally declare
membership to a particular church, whereas for Catholics the sole criterion
for membership is baptism. The people have been free to attend whichever
Catholic Church they wish. Catholics, however, have always been encouraged
to attend the geographical parish within whose boundaries they live.

Certain sanctions have been imposed to assure their attendance.
Marriages, baptisms, parish school attendance, confirmation, and funerals
have all been under the scrutiny and supervision of the local pastor whose

permission was necessary for any deviation from the geographical parish tradition. But due to the complexity and inner penetration of ethnic parish boundaries, this practice of attending the local parish always had its exceptions and is being ignored more and more in the years of shifting church structures since Vatican II. As an example of this fluidity, when asked whether they went to a church other than that in their own local parish, 20 percent of the respondents replied that they did for one reason or another. This is a sizeable non-conformist minority.

The overall response rate from all three parishes was 69 percent (n=629). This rate included both the extended responses to the question- naire returned by mail (61 percent, n=555) and a more limited response received by telephone (8 percent, n=74) from those not returning the mail questionnaire. The highest response (65 percent) to the mail questionnaire came from the younger, middle status, New Town parish, and the lowest response (50 percent) came from the lower status, ethnic Satellite City parish. Some comparative data on mail and telephone respondents are presented in Appendix A. In the main, differences between the two groups were minimal.

As indicated by this favorable response rate as well as the marginal comments made by the respondents themselves, the survey was well received. The refusal rate was only 14 percent (n=128) while the remaining number (17 percent, n=160) were those who could not be contacted, who said they had returned the questionnaire but it was never received, or who, after promising to return the material, failed to do so.

The White Protestant Lay Sample

The white Protestant sample consisted of members of United Methodist churches in the same communities as the three Catholic parishes just discussed. The United Methodist Church in Satellite City, founded prior to World War I, had been declining in membership for the past twenty years. The churches in New Town and Country Club Estates, both founded after World War II, had experienced steady growth until the middle or late 1960's; they had been relatively stable since then.

The original intent was to select a sample of about 300 names from three churches' membership lists, using a table of random numbers. This procedure was followed in Satellite City, but in Country Club Estates the total membership was just over 300 after members living over fifty miles away and those under eighteen years of age were eliminated, so an exhaustive survey was taken. In New Town the clergyman and lay board made an exhaustive survey a condition of access, which resulted in a population of slightly over 400. After adjusting for persons who had moved, were no longer members, or were too old to be able to respond, 264 persons in Satellite City, 381 persons in New Town and 280 persons in Country Club Estates comprised the final sample.

The overall response rate from the three congregations was 86 percent. This rate included both the extended responses to the questionnaire returned by mail (73 percent, n=678) and a more limited response received by telephone (13 percent, n=119) from those not returning the mail questionnaire. The highest response to the mail questionnaire (78 percent) came from the Country Club Estates church, and the lowest response (71 percent) came from New Town.

Because the Protestant churches were so much smaller than the Catholic parishes, the Protestant clergy were able to provide some background data on those not responding to the telephone interview. Selected data comparing the respondents to the mail questionnaire, respondents to the telephone interview, and the non-respondents are shown in Appendix A.

The percent of explicit refusals was also low among white Protestants. Exactly 10 percent explicitly refused in each of the three United Methodist Churches.

The Black Protestant Sample

As noted earlier, financial limitations and access problems limited the black Protestant sample. Two black churches in Satellite City were surveyed. One was a black United Methodist Church and the other was a black African Methodist Episcopal Church. The two groups have some internal differences, but they were the only ones to which the research team could gain access. The combined adult membership of these two churches was slightly over 300, so questionnaires were mailed to every adult member.

After adjusting for persons who had moved away or were no longer members, the total number surveyed was 265. The overall response rate from these two congregations was 41 percent. This rate included both the extended responses to the questionnaire returned by mail (25 percent, n=67) and a more limited response (16 percent, n=42) received by telephone from those not returning the mail questionnaire. In addition, the pastor of the United Methodist Church provided background data on those not returning the mail questionnaire. Selected data on respondents and non-respondents are summarized in Appendix A.

This return rate was much lower than in any of the other churches. The clergy were very cooperative, and there was no evidence of lay hostility to the study.

The following factors may have contributed to the lower return rate: the absence of a black member of the research team; the somewhat shorter time span between mailing and cut-off dates than for white Protestants or Catholics; the higher proportion of lower middle status and lower status members.

The last factor affected the return rate in two ways. Many more blacks did not have telephone listings, so the only feasible way to contact

non-respondents in the follow-up was by mail. There is also some evidence
that lower status people do not respond as frequently to questionnaires
as middle and upper status people.

The Jewish Sample

The Jewish group consisted of a sample of 300 members of a Reform
synagogue in Country Club Estates, drawn by using a table of random
numbers. Adjusting for persons who had moved or withdrawn from membership,
the total number surveyed was 271. The overall response rate from this
congregation was 63 percent. This rate included both the extended response
to the questionnaire returned by mail (46 percent, n=124) and a more limited
response (17 percent, n=47) received by telephone from those not returning
the mail questionnaire. In addition, a member of the synagogue staff
provided background data on 81 of the 100 (37 percent) who did not respond.
Selected data on respondents and non-respondents are summarized in Appendix A.

The return rate was somewhat lower than those of the white Protestants
or Catholics. The following factors may have contributed to the lower
return rate: the marginal commitments of many synagogue families; the
absence of a Jewish member of the research team; the somewhat shorter
time span between mailing and cut-off date than for white Protestants or
Catholics.

The Clergy Sample

The 125 religious professionals serving the religious institutions
of the eight towns in the suburban sector were sent questionnaires and
contacted for interviews. The interviewer went over the questionnaire
at the time of the interview and collected it.

Data were obtained from 88 percent (22) of the Roman Catholic
priests, 92 percent (35) of the clergy serving Protestant churches affiliate
with the National Council of Churches, 58 percent (33) of the clergy serving
Protestant churches not affiliated with the National Council of Churches,
and 60 percent (3) of the rabbis. A detailed discussion of the clergy
sample is found in Chapter IV.

A Note on Lay Response Rates

As the data in Appendix A indicate, non-respondents generally
were less involved in their religious institutions than were respondents.
As intentionality looms large in voluntary religious groups, it is
reasonable to expect that those most deeply related to their church or
synagogue would more strongly reflect the distinctive moral and religious
values of their group, assuming distinctive values did in fact exist.

Since most of the lay analyses presented here are focused on the four faith groups, selective responses--if they exist--ought to accentuate the differences between the faith groupings.

Statistical Tests

The chi-square statistical test and the related coefficient of contingency have been used to determine the significance of differential responses among lay people in the tables presented in this volume. Since the data are presented by community areas of differing social status, both religious affiliation and social status may contribute to statistically significant differences. The statistical tests do not enable one to assess the relative importance of these two factors. From the point of view of clergy and lay people in a given congregation, this evaluation is of little direct importance to them.

With the exception of white Protestants in Satellite City, the social status of respondents of various faith groups within a specified community is roughly comparable, so those interested in assessing the relative impact of religious affiliation on lay values may do so by comparing responses by faith groups within a specified geographical area.[10]

PART ONE

SUBURBAN CHURCHES AND SYNAGOGUES

IN HISTORICAL AND SOCIAL CONTEXT

CHAPTER I

CHURCHES, SYNAGOGUES, AND THE AMERICAN EXPERIENCE:

THE EMERGENCE OF THE VOLUNTARY RELIGIOUS INSTITUTION

Introduction

A sequence of events that was one of the most significant in
the history of Christianity transpired in the United States in the latter
part of the eighteenth and the early part of the nineteenth centuries;
the federal government and, subsequently all the state governments,
affirmed the principle of religious liberty by disestablishment of all
religious institutions. Some voluntary sectarian Christian groups and
Jewish faith communities had existed in Europe, but the principle of an
officially favored and supported state religion had long been the practice
in Europe. Now, in the Age of Reason, the Bill of Rights to the Constitution of the new republic affirmed the principle of church-state separation.

In human affairs, critical actions of leaders in an epoch-forming
period shape the feelings, customs, habits, social institutions, and
cultural values of succeeding generations, for their decisions become
causal components contributing to the decisions of others both in their
own time and in later historical periods.

This chapter retrieves salient aspects of America's past to
enhance the understanding of contemporary church-state relations and to
illumine the factors shaping the emergence of the voluntary religious
institution to a position of preeminence in the United States.

From Establishment to Voluntaryism

American religious institutions are rooted primarily in Europe,
for the vast waves of European immigrants brought their own religious
institutions with them.[1]

Unable to transplant their social, economic, or political institutions in the New World, they were able to implant their religious institutions with fewer modifications. Some American Indian and some Oriental
religious institutions have resisted assimilation, but the overwhelming
majority of religious institutions in America is related to some facet of

the Christian movement. The most influential minority religion in America
is Judaism, which has some shared history with Christianity and with the
European tradition.[2]

The early post-feudal period during which the first white settlers
migrated from Europe to the New World was scarcely conducive to the idea
of religious liberty. With the notable exceptions of Rhode Island and
Pennsylvania, the early colonists established their versions of established
churches in the colonies they settled. They may have had doctrinal
disputes with the established churches in Europe, but they did not repudiate
the idea of establishment per se.

Social and cultural realities, however, made the maintenance of
the established church difficult in the American colonies. Immigrants to
a given colony came from many different parts of Europe with different
established state churches. This religious diversity made the establishment of one state church difficult and contributed to the trend toward
disestablishment.

This sociological reality was augmented by ideological trends, for
both non-Christian thought forms, particularly French deism and various
forms of naturalism and romanticism, and also various Christian views of
the Believers' Church, rooted in the Left-Wing of the Reformation, led
more and more people in the colonies to question the wisdom of an established church.

The framers of the Constitution were very aware of the potentially
divisive effect of religious sects upon the body politic, and they were
determined to mitigate such possible conflicts by minimizing the involvement
of the government in religious matters. The First Amendment to the United
States Constitution, prohibiting Congress from enacting any law establish-
ing a state church, reflected this concern.

The Supreme Court held the amendment applied only to the federal
government and not to the state governments, but its suasive power was
considerable. By 1833 the last of the states had disestablished the
church, and the separation of church and state in America was substantially
completed.

The importance of this historical development for the style and
shape of contemporary American religious institutions can scarcely be
overemphasized, for it minimized the hostility toward religious institutions
manifested so frequently in Europe. It also reinforced the norms of
religious liberty, religious tolerance, and religious pluralism. It
provided the framework for the mass evangelism of the frontier era and
made the voluntarily gathered congregation the normative form of religious
organization in the United States.[3]

This vision of the intentional gathered church as normative had
been fostered by various Anabaptist groups related to the Left-Wing of the
Protestant Reformation. Neither sixteenth century Lutheran nor Calvinist
churchmen had supported this view of the church; they had sought to

substitute an established Protestant church for the established Catholic one in the nations where they were predominant.

The sociocultural homogeneity of the small European principalities of the late feudal period and the elitism of both state and church made this transition from an established Catholic church to an established Protestant church possible in most European contexts, and Anabaptist groups emphasizing the Believers' Church were subject to various forms of persecution in most of Europe.

The Anabaptist vision of the church as an intentional gathered fellowship of believers was sanctioned politically in the United States, for religious voluntarysim, religious pluralism, and religious liberty were inevitable correlates of the separation of church and state. The denomination, representing an amalgamation of the more inclusive, less evangelical, less intentional, and less demanding church with the more exclusive, more evangelical, more intentional, and more demanding sect, was destined to emerge as the predominant form of religious organization in the United States.[4]

Jews, long subject to various forms of persecution in Europe and already having a voluntary religious association, readily affirmed religious voluntaryism, religious liberty, and religious pluralism. The few Roman Catholics did likewise.

By the time of the Civil War, something of a consensus on this issue had been attained, but the consensus was challenged between 1865 and 1915 by the large numbers of Roman Catholic and Lutheran migrants coming from European lands where these faith groups were established churches.

These migrants altered markedly the religious composition of America. By this time the separation of church and state had become a core, integrative value in American society, a part of the religion of America. Consequently, if the national consensus were to be sustained, the separation of church and state, religious liberty, religious freedom, and religious pluralism had to be accepted by these more recent migrants. Since these notions were alien to many of the migrants, especially Roman Catholics from eastern and southern Europe, considerable disharmony and conflict about church-state relations developed in this period. The continued debates about state aid to church-related schools and some issues of public morality and public policy show that these issues are still not completely resolved, but a consensus has been attained on the basic idea of state neutrality in religious affairs, as Table I-1 reveals.

Only a tiny segment of the respondents in the suburban communities selected for study indicated strong disagreement to the proposition "The government should be neutral toward religious institutions." The exceptionally high Jewish support of state neutrality underscores the strong Jewish commitment to separation of church and state. As the targets of Christian "evangelism" and governmental persecution over the centuries, they are especially committed to a principle protecting them from overzealous evangelists and the government. White Protestants were almost as strongly committed to the principle.

RESPONSE TO STATEMENT

"THE GOVERNMENT SHOULD BE NEUTRAL TOWARDS RELIGIOUS INSTITUTIONS"

IN PERCENT BY COMMUNITY FOR SELECTED RELIGIOUS GROUPS*

| | COMMUNITY | | | | | | | |
| | SATELLITE CITY | | | NEW TOWN | | COUNTRY CLUB ESTATES | | |
Response to Statement	Black Protestant	White Protestant	Catholic	White Protestant	Catholic	White Protestant	Catholic	Jewish
Strongly agree	13	18	13	14	11	15	12	33
Agree	41	61	48	64	61	63	58	50
Mixed feelings	16	6	15	10	8	13	11	7
Disagree	11	5	6	3	7	3	7	5
Strongly disagree	3	0	3	1	2	0	0	1
Depends on circumstances	10	4	2	4	5	3	7	3
No opinion	6	5	13	4	6	2	4	2
N =	63	184	143	264	197	216	203	123

Chi square = 107.40070   p<0.001

Coefficient of Contingency = 0.26755

*See the Introduction for a description of these groups

The separation of church and state precluded the use of governmental monies for the support of religious institutions and their salaried professionals. As a consequence, religious professionals in America have had to be more sensitive to the needs and interests of the members of their institutions than their European counterparts. A simple explanation for the much higher religious institutional involvement of American laity than European laity is impossible, but the long established voluntaryism of American religious institutions is certainly a most significant factor.[5]

In order to sustain their institutions, American clergymen have had to develop much more innovative and often more imaginative programs than their European colleagues. Voluntaryism, coupled with the pragmatism and the lack of intellectualism in the nineteenth century American ethos, accounts for the activistic and programmatic emphases of American religious institutions, looked upon with such disdain by many European religious professionals. The fund-raising aspects of the church socials of American Protestantism, the bingo nights of American Catholicism, and the sisterhood activities of American Judaism all reflect this pragmatism and activism.

The lack of any significant feeling of anti-clericalism in the United States is also related to religious voluntaryism, pluralism, and tolerance, for no ecclesiastical group was able to impose either its teachings on any significant segment of the learned community or its social and economic views on large segments of the country. The dependence of the clergy on voluntary lay contributions has ameliorated potential lay-clergy conflicts, for the lay people can readily withhold their talents and their money. Suasion was the only means by which church people could seek members or pursue matters of public policy.

In relating to their lay people, religious leaders in America have had to pay much more attention to the consensus formation process, for in the United States--regardless of polity or doctrine--a person is a member of a religious institution because he chooses to belong. If a given person finds a particular church or a particular denomination unsatisfactory for any reason, he can probably find some religious institution which will welcome him to membership without undue difficulty. He can also become inactive in his given faith community or he can withdraw from any and all religious institutions at will.

Consequently, most local clergymen focus on adjustive and integrative issues, seeking to attract and to keep members in their fellowship. In this situation it is easier to be a priest than a prophet, for comfort is less disruptive to the life of a religious institution than challenge.

The promises and the problems of the consensus formation process in the voluntary religious institution will be addressed frequently in subsequent chapters. In the present context, the point deserving emphasis is the necessity for this style of leadership in the voluntary church. The only alternative is an established state church, funded by tax monies. Such an alternative is unacceptable to those who think religious liberty is one of the hallmarks of high civilization.

Religious voluntaryism does have other consequences, both positive and negative. People tend to choose to join religious institutions whose constituents reflect their own ethnic and status situation. This self-selection process contributes to the status and/or ethnic exclusiveness of many churches and synagogues. Insofar as this exclusiveness obscures people's visions of the inclusiveness of humankind, it is evil. At the same time, insofar as this exclusiveness enhances novelty and gives rise to contrasts contributing positively to the whole, it is good.

The development of the voluntary religious institution in America was affected by the concomitant emergence of technical rationalism and secular humanism to central positions in the American value complex. The following section explores these developments.

Technical Rationalism, Secular Humanism and

the American Experience[6]

Technical rationalism seeks the most efficient means to attain a given end; secular humanism affirms individual dignity and the value of the human personality. Both motifs have their genesis in elements of the Judeo-Christian tradition. Technical rationalism is a transformation of the inner-worldly asceticism of Calvinism; secular humanism is a truncation of the value of the human personality as a child of God rooted in portions of the Judeo-Christian heritage. The two motifs cannot be perfectly harmonized with each other, and some conflict between them is inevitable. Technical rationalism tends to atomize people and to foster competition, but secular humanism tends to unify them and to foster cooperation.

In spite of this conflict, the two motifs are interrelated, for a person appropriating technical rationalism is apt to challenge traditionalist views of life. Such traditionalist views restrict the potentiality of some groups, such as women, beyond the limits placed by nature. Thus, an uneasy alliance exists between proponents of technical rationalism and secular humanism. They both reject theistic interpretations of life and seek to minimize the limits history and nature place on human life.

In the public realm, secular humanism, technical rationalism, and the public religion of America interplay, partly reinforcing one another and partly conflicting with each other. No strong coherence exists, and the same person may emphasize different motifs at different times and in different contexts.

These secular motifs also intermingle with the particular religions of America. The popularity of various forms of situation ethics and the alliances of various religious and secular groups to promote particular social causes reflect the intermeshing of these diverse motifs in the context of American society.

Technical rationalism has fostered the transformation of America from a folk society to a large scale technological society, for technical rationalism knows nothing of history and of social honor. It asks only "What are the most efficient means to attain a given end?" In this way technical rationalism supports the pragmatism and activism which are part of the American experience.

This transition from a folk society to a large scale technological society has altered the shape of the life of religious institutions, for it contributed to the privatization of the religious sphere and to the development of large ecclesiastical bureaucracies.

From a Folk Society to a Large Scale Technological Society[7]

Over the past two centuries, the scale of social organizations in the United States has increased tremendously. At the time of the first census in 1790, the population was slightly less than 4,000,000. Farm and rural residents comprised 95 percent of the population, and the 200,000 urban dwellers lived in what would now be considered small towns.

At the present time, over two-thirds of the nation's population live in urban areas. They live in a society shaped by big business, big labor, and big government. Without the mind set encouraged by technical rationalism, the large bureaucracy--corporate or governmental--would not have emerged. This emergence was coterminous with the industrialization and urbanization of America. Technical rationalism was the foundational value fostering the vast extension of urbanization, bureaucratization, and industrialization that characterized the transformation of America from a folk society to a large scale technological society.

Prior to this transformation, people knew each other in many different contexts. Churchgoers on Sunday saw the people with whom they dealt every day in social, economic, and political activities. The gradual disestablishment of state churches and the influx of different immigrant groups increased the number of religious institutions. This increase reduced the likelihood that people worshiping together on Sunday would interact with each other in other social contexts during the week, but people still encountered each other in many different circumstances.

The vast extensions of urbanization, industrialization, and bureaucratization in the late nineteenth and twentieth centuries have greatly segmented human social interaction. Today the likelihood that a suburbanite attending a given religious institution will encounter a fellow member in other social contexts during the week is much less than in earlier periods.

This segmentation of social institutions reinforces the privatization of religion discussed in the following chapter. The contemporary suburban parishioner is not as likely as was his earlier counterpart to see others with whom he might discuss his own religious activities in non-ecclesiastical contexts.

The increase in the size of social institutions over the past two centuries, directly related to the extension of industrialization and bureaucratization, has affected the shape and style of religious institutions in two salient ways.

It has accentuated the anonymity of members of a given parish, placing a greater responsibility for integrating and coordinating on the professional staff. The percentage of lay people having major leadership roles declines as the size of the membership increases, for the number of major leadership posts does not increase in direct proportion to increases in size of the institution. As a consequence, a smaller proportion of the membership is deeply involved in the ongoing life of the religious institution.

The increase in size has also accentuated the growth of ecclesiastical bureaucracies, for the need for specialized staffs and coordinating agencies is part and parcel of the vast extension of the influence of technical rationalism manifest in urbanization, industrialization, and bureaucratization. The more specialized staffs are relatively distant from the local parish, and they often do not relate directly to lay people. They provide goods and services for local parishes, and they often evolve a quasi-autonomous life of their own.[8]

The development of the voluntary religious institution, the emergence of technical rationalism and secular humanism to prominent places in America's value complex, and the shift from a folk society to a large scale technological society have changed the American ethos. These factors have all affected the style and shape of religious institutions in American society. They have contributed to the emergence of a public religion and to the privatization of religious institutions.

CHAPTER II

AMERICA'S PUBLIC RELIGION: THE PRIVATIZATION OF

SUBURBAN CHURCHES AND SYNAGOGUES

Introduction

In order for church-state separation to become a reality in the
United States, no doctrine associated with a particular religious group
could hold sway in the public sphere. Religious beliefs became private
matters not directly pertinent in the public realm. This privatization
of religious beliefs contributed to the emergence of the technological
society par excellence in the United States, for it largely freed the
economic sphere from the restraints of religious convictions.[1]

The principle of religious liberty, an aspect of America's public
religion, highlights the intentionality of membership in religious institutions in the United States.[2] Regardless of the particular polity of a
given religious tradition, the congregational principle of a voluntary
fellowship becomes the overarching principle of religious organization
in the American context. People choose to join religious institutions,
and they may withdraw from them with relative ease.

Most Americans share America's public religion and also identify
with one of the major faith groups. This chapter is focused on these
two dimensions, for most suburbanites share facets of the public religion
of America and one of the religions of American suburbia. The relations
of the religions of American suburbia to each other are shaped largely
by the notions of religious pluralism, religious tolerance, and religious
liberty embodied in America's public religion.

The Emergence and Development of a

Public Religion in America

In order for the members of a society to sustain themselves over
any extended period of time, most of them must share some common integrative values. As noted earlier, American society is unique in its

25

religious history, for it encompassed a plurality of faith groups from its beginning. Religious liberty, religious pluralism, and religious tolerance emerged as core integrative values in the religious sphere, for the doctrine of separation of church and state required that most people accept these primary values.

The church-state separation gave impetus to the privatization of particular religious traditions alluded to earlier, for no religious tradition could legitimately claim to speak definitively in the public sphere. To be sure, religious groups continued to influence public policy, but they needed to appeal to values shared with other groups.

Taken together, the need for inclusive commonly shared norms and the privatization of particular religious beliefs fostered the emergence of an American public religion, dominated by Judeo-Christian motifs but not especially identified with any particular religious tradition. This religion of America does not monopolize the faith of the public realm, for it shares this domain with non-theistic secular humanism and technical rationalism. The faith of the public realm, somewhat inchoate and amorphous, is a blending of motifs drawn from these three sources.

The broad contours of America's public religion have been shaped by epoch-making events in American history--the settlement of the country, the Revolutionary War and the unification of the Colonies, the westward expansion and the doctrine of Manifest Destiny, the Civil War and the assassination of Abraham Lincoln, the mass European immigrations between the Civil War and the First World War, and, in the first half of the twentieth century, the emerging consciousness of a national vocation to extend democracy to all people. The contemporary interpretations of these trends is emphasized in the following brief characterization, for the recollection of the past is always selective and interpretative. The analysis is concentrated on major national holidays and the interpretations of major culture heroes, for these events and the interpretations of culture-sharing and culture-bearing elites elucidate the major components of America's public religion.[3]

The analogue between the early colonists and the people of Israel is striking. Old Testament imagery was frequent in public references in the seventeenth and eighteenth century America. The early settlers saw themselves carving new colonies out of the wildernesses of the Atlantic seaboard, for they were a chosen people, freeing themselves from the bondages of Europe and starting afresh in a land which had known no feudal period.[4]

An unduly romantic reading of this historical epoch is clearly unwarranted, for, as we have noted, most leaders intended to found their version of a state church in the American colonies. In addition more people probably were drawn to the New World by economic motives than by religious vision.

In spite of these cautionary observations, the novelty and freshness of the New World were facts of major importance in shaping colonial America and in the subsequent reinterpretations of that period by later generations of Americans.

George Washington, seen as the one who led his people to liberty from the oppressor, is the "Moses" of the American religion. As the "Father" of his country, he helped unify the colonies into a new nation. In these formative years, liberty, equality, and brotherhood, reflecting deistic influences, began to emerge as other central motifs in America's shared and core integrative values.[5]

The notion of Manifest Destiny, giving divine sanction to America's westward movement, emerged between the time of the Revolutionary War and the Civil War. It gave an overarching theological rationale for activities and practices shaped in large part by self-interest and desires for economic betterment, and it contributed to the popularity of the doctrine of progress.

During the fusion of deistic and Christian motifs in the period between the Revolutionary War and the Civil War, the concept of a trans-cendent, creative, and judging God, shorn of Christocentric emphasis, emerged into a central position in America's public religion. This concept was personified in the public theological interpretation of life offered by Abraham Lincoln.

Just as George Washington may plausibly be interpreted analogically as the "Moses" of America's public religion, Abraham Lincoln may plausibly by interpreted as the "Jesus of Nazareth" of that religion. In his December, 1862 Message to Congress, in the Gettysburg Address and in the Second Inaugural Address, he powerfully reinforces the idea of a transcendent creative and judging God in the public realm.[6]

Lincoln's sacrificial death sanctified what he had said and done. His life and death gave impetus to the emergence of the value complex "Liberty, equality, and brotherhood in democracy under God" to a central position in the American moral order.

The great symbolic importance Americans attach to the birthdays of Washington and Lincoln and to Independence Day and Thanksgiving Day give credence to this symbolic interpretation of Washington and Lincoln and of the emergence of America's public religion.

The vast immigration of persons from southern and eastern Europe in the period between the Civil War and World War I engendered considerable internal disharmony in the United States. It produced the "melting pot" vision of American society, for no society in history sought to assimilate so many diverse groups in so short a time span.[7]

As Americans sought to interpret and to adjust to this increasing internal diversity, the Statue of Liberty began to attain symbolic signifi-cance. America was to be the recipient of the poor and oppressed from other parts of the world and to be a model of democracy for all the world.

During the first half of this century, America's sense of a national vocation came to fruition. Earlier America had sought to create a new nation, freed from foreign entanglements. During this period, the notion began to emerge that America was called to extend democracy to all people.

It was during this time that Memorial Day began to achieve the symbolic importance of Independence Day and Thanksgiving Day.

In World War I, Woodrow Wilson proclaimed that America sought to make the world "safe for democracy"; in World War II, Franklin Roosevelt sought to extend the "four freedoms" to all people.

It is too soon to be certain, but the Vietnam War may mark the end of this expansionist era. America may become less expansionist-minded in the last part of the twentieth century.[8]

In this context, presidents serve as high priests of America's public religion. They are especially apt to evoke the religion of America in their inaugural and other highly symbolic addresses and in periods of national crises. The death of major national heroes also evokes aspects of the public religion.

This public religion--vague, diffuse, and only fitfully self-consciously held--is shared by almost all Americans and serves to unify diverse and conflicting values.[9]

The Religions of American Suburbia

The Basic Structure of the Religions of American Suburbia

The notions of religious liberty, religious pluralism, and religious tolerance embodied historically in America's public religion and in some of the religions of America, have shaped the relations between the religions of American suburbia. At the time of the American Revolution, the country was overwhelmingly Protestant; subsequently very substantial numbers of Roman Catholics and considerable numbers of Jews migrated to America. No substantial numbers of any other religious tradition were present.

Under these circumstances, Americans gradually came to consider a basic tri-partite faith grouping rooted in the Judeo-Christian tradition to be normal and natural in the United States. The public religion affirms the legitimacy and appropriateness of being a Protestant, a Catholic, or a Jew. One's social identity is in part defined by one's relation to these three faith groups.[10] One may be a Muslim, Buddhist, Shintoist, Hindu and be an American, but such a person is marginal to American life.

This situation is reflected in the studied suburban sector. Aside from one Bahai temple, all the religious institutions in the sector were churches or synagogues having their historic roots in the Judeo-Christian tradition.

The tri-partite faith structure of American suburbia is qualified by racial segregation and denominationalism. Racial residential segre-gation has resulted in sharp cleavages between black and white Protestant churches.[11] The presence of many subgroups within Protestantism and three

subgroups within Judaism permits lay people and clergy in these traditions
to move from subgroup to subgroup without renouncing their basic identity
as Protestants or Jews.

The persistence of racially segregated residential communities
and the evolution of indigenous black Protestant churches have fostered
racial cleavages in Protestantism. The voluntary church accentuates this
problem, for Protestant churches of many denominations compete for members.
Most lay people will not choose to join a biracial church, even in those
geographical areas where sufficient numbers of both races make such a
church possible.

The multiplicity of subgroups within Protestantism and Judaism
minimizes the importance of doctrinal or liturgical disputes, for people
may readily move from one subgroup to another. If they take substantial
exception to the beliefs or practices of a particular church or synagogue,
they may transfer their affiliation to another church or synagogue in the
same or a different subgroup within Protestantism or Judaism without
rejecting their basic faith identity.

Roman Catholicism is under greater pressure, both theologically
and sociologically, to maintain doctrinal uniformity. The presence of
some nationality parishes, a variety of religious orders, and various
special interest groups in Catholicism permits considerable internal
diversity, but church insistence on the truth of Catholic doctrine puts
pressure on dissidents to leave the church altogether. A Roman Catholic
cannot shift his allegiance from one religious subgroup to another in the
Protestant or Jewish sense and retain his primary allegiance, for comparable
subgroups do not exist in Catholicism.

Black-white cleavages and the multiplicity of subgroups within
Protestantism have resulted in sharp black-white divisions within suburban
Protestantism. Over 90 percent of the Protestant congregations were either
all white or all black.

As a result of these historical, theological, and sociological
factors, four relatively distinct faith communities exist in American
suburbia: white Protestant, black Protestant, Jewish, and Roman Catholic.
Some of the findings presented here and data from other sources suggest
increasing rapprochement between white Protestants and Catholics, but it
is premature to suggest an amalgamation of white Protestantism and
Catholicism into a white Christianity.[12]

Principles of Religious Organization, the Religion

of America and the Religions of American Suburbia

Historically, three types of ecclesiastical organization have been
prevalent in Christianity: congregational, presbyterian, and episcopal.
Local autonomy has been greatest in churches with congregational forms of
polity and least in churches with episcopal forms of polity. Churches with

presbyterian forms of polity have fallen in between.

In the American experience, the congregational principle of organization has become preeminent, for the religious voluntaryism embodied in the public religion and the doctrine of the separation of church and state give powerful support to it. Suasion is the only way religious institutions have to attract and to keep their members, so, as observed earlier, religious leaders of all religious institutions, regardless of polity, have to pay some attention to the desires, interests, and needs of their lay memberships.

Viewed broadly, differing predominant sub-principles of religious organization have evolved in the three major religious institutions of American suburbia. Within Protestantism, the predominant sub-principle is congregational; within Catholicism, it is cultic; within Judaism, it is communal. The voluntary and intentional shape of religious association in America was more readily accepted by Protestants and Jews than by Roman Catholics.

The initial acceptance of the idea of intentional association by significant segments of Protestantism facilitated the transition to the congregation as the predominant principle of religious organization among American Protestants. Theoretically Protestants could distinguish the religious dimension of life from social, ethnic, political, and cultural dimensions so members with a variety of associations could belong to the same church. Practically, because of the voluntaryism particular churches tended to be rather homogeneous.

The Protestant principle of organization is most diffuse, for presbyterian and episcopal principles are also widespread. In no instance, however, does the leadership claim special sacerdotal rights vis-à-vis the laity. In all instances, lay members participate directly in policy-making matters, but their powers are more circumscribed in some denomination: than in others. In any event, the congregational principle embodied in the public religion is quite compatible with American Protestantism.

The situation is more complicated in Judaism, for in principle the religious and communal dimensions are inextricably intertwined. The history of Israel and the Jewish people is an integral part of the religion of the Jew. In spite of this communal focus, a modified congregational principle of religious organization was feasible in the American context. As a non-Christian minority persecuted in much of Europe, most Jews heartily embraced the principle of church-state separation in America, for it offered them a protection from the harassment of people seeking to proselytize them. The autonomy of local Hebrew congregations parallels that of many Protestant congregations.

Roman Catholicism has had the most difficulty in accommodating to church-state separation and to religious voluntaryism. Its historical principle of organization has been cultic, focused on a priesthood who perform religious rites and practices for the laity. The recent emphases on the laity in Roman Catholicism, conflicts about authority, and innovations in the Mass suggest a shift in the direction of a congregational focus, consonant with the dominant cultural values in the United States.[13]

As Table I-1 revealed, the basic idea of state neutrality in religious matters was affirmed by the overwhelming majority of the four faith groups. This affirmation of a facet of America's public religion does not preclude conflicts between the several faith communities, for the various groups sometimes interpret state neutrality differently.

The issue of state aid to public schools, taken in conjunction with the overwhelming support for state neutrality in religious matters, illustrates the blending of religious accommodation and religious conflict in American suburbia. Free secular education was a natural corrollary to the separation of church and state, and America early supported an extensive system of free, public education. Since there is no neutral perspective from which to interpret the world, there is certainly some legitimacy to Catholic concern about an educational system largely committed to technical rationalism and non-theistic humanism. Nonetheless, state aid to "sectarian" education has been rather consistently viewed by the courts as a violation of the First Amendment to the Constitution.

The contrast between Catholic and non-Catholic views on this issue are shown in Table II-1. A majority of Catholics in every studied community felt the government should give money to church-sponsored schools, compared to small minorities of non-Catholics.

In accord with the very strong Jewish commitment to church-state neutrality noted earlier, Jewish opposition is most intense. White Protestant opposition is quite strong, and black Protestant opposition is moderate.

The historical and cultural factors discussed in Chapters I and II have shaped the nature of religious institutions in the American context. In spite of conflicts on specific issues, the vast majority of Protestants, Catholics and Jews agree on the basic principle of church-state separation.

TABLE II-1

RESPONSE TO STATEMENT

"THE GOVERNMENT SHOULD GIVE MONEY TO CHURCH-SPONSORED SCHOOLS"

IN PERCENT BY COMMUNITY FOR SELECTED RELIGIOUS GROUPS

Response to Statement	COMMUNITY							
	SATELLITE CITY			NEW TOWN		COUNTRY CLUB ESTATES		
	Black Protestant	White Protestant	Catholic	White Protestant	Catholic	White Protestant	Catholic	Jewish
Strongly agree	11	2	25	1	14	1	16	2
Agree	22	16	36	14	41	13	42	9
Mixed feelings	20	18	17	17	17	15	16	12
Disagree	19	33	9	37	19	41	13	34
Strongly disagree	16	16	4	19	5	24	7	37
Depends on circumstances	9	6	4	5	3	3	6	4
No opinion	3	8	5	2	3	3	0	2
N =	64	184	142	263	193	217	203	123

Chi square = 403.73022 $p < 0.001$

Coefficient of Contingency = 0.47456

CHAPTER III

THE NEW SHAPE OF URBANISM:

IMPLICATIONS FOR SUBURBAN CHURCHES AND SYNAGOGUES

Introduction

The emergence of the voluntary religious institution, the evolution
of a mass society, and the blending of the religion of America, technical
rationalism, and secular humanism into a public faith have been discussed
in Chapters I and II. The process of urbanization was briefly discussed
in those chapters, but its substantial impact on suburban churches and
synagogues warrants more extended discussion.[1]

Although contemporary American cities are composed of quite hetero-
genous populations, people of similar status and/or ethnicity tend to
cluster in distinctive areas, producing substantial homogeneity in particular parts of the city and its suburbs.

While this combination of homogeneity and heterogeneity is characteristic of major cities in other periods, in modern American cities
the pervasive influence of technical rationalism and the resultant high
technology is so substantial that American cities differ markedly from the
cities existing prior to the Industrial Revolution.

Technological innovations have fostered shifts in scale, making
contemporary cities a new phenomenon. There are many more large cities
and a much larger proportion of the population lives in them. In most
preindustrial cities, a resident could walk from any given point in the
city to any other given point in ten minutes or less. There was no need
for elaborate transportation systems to convey city residents great
distances as they went to and from work. The homogeneous areas of preindustrial cities were relatively small compared to the sprawling homogeneous areas of contemporary cities. Today a resident can walk ten
minutes in many American cities and detect almost no change in the ethnic
or social status of the inhabitants.

The contrasts between the very rich and the very poor were perhaps
greater in preindustrial cities than in contemporary cities, but the size
and variety of the homogeneous areas comprising a metropolitan region are
greater in contemporary cities.

The contemporary urban complex also differs from preindustrial
cities in that its residents are much more mobile, moving with great

frequency both from one geographical area within a given metropolitan area to another and also from one metropolitan area to another.

Contemporary American urban residents are mobile socially as well as geographically. High social mobility is also related to technical rationalism, for technical rationalism is anti-traditional. People are more apt to be evaluated by what they can do rather than by who they are. (In sociological terms, high industrial societies foster social stratification by achievement, and traditional societies foster social stratification by ascription.)

Both social and geographical mobility affect suburban religious institutions, for their voluntary nature makes membership recruitment very important. This situation is especially salient in Protestantism, for many churches are seeking to recruit members from the same basic potential constituency.

The implications of these population movements for churches and synagogues are examined in this chapter. The following section describes in detail the suburbs that were briefly mentioned in the Introduction to illumine the new shape of urbanism. The concluding section examines the effects of this development on the life cycles of suburban churches and synagogues. All persons seeking to understand, to serve, or to formulate policy for religious institutions should be aware of these life cycles, for they provide most significant insights about the future of particular religious institutions.

The Sector Suburbs

The suburban sector selected for study is representative of much of American suburbia, but the Midwest City Standard Metropolitan Statistical Area is larger than most. As a result the patterns of suburban development are magnified in this metropolitan area, but the basic patterns are repeated--usually on a smaller scale--in all American suburbs.

The suburban sector begins at the border of Midwest City and extends some twenty miles beyond to the edge of the area of high population density on the fringe of the Midwest City metropolitan area. The geographical relation of the sector suburbs is shown in Figure III-1.

Each of the communities has been designated here by a number as well as by a fictional name. Number 1 has been assigned to the suburb closest to Midwest City, and number 8 to the suburb farthest from Midwest City. Thus Waterside (1) is the suburb contiguous to Midwest City, Satellite City (2) is the next closest to Midwest City, and so on to Germantown (8), the suburb farthest from Midwest City.

As Figure III-1 shows, the suburban sector was served by three major expressway systems and a suburban railroad. Convenient rail transportation to Midwest City's central business district, a major commercial and financial center, had contributed to the concentration

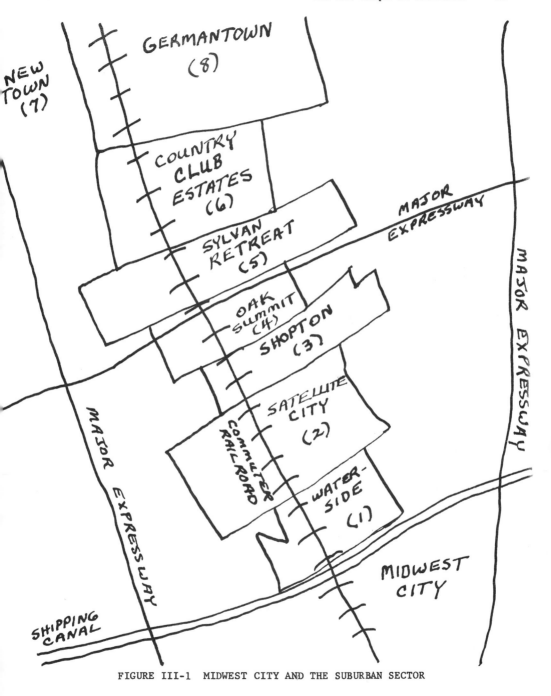

FIGURE III-1   MIDWEST CITY AND THE SUBURBAN SECTOR

of white collar workers in the sector, for the suburban railroad line
passed through all the communities studied.

In the following subsections, a brief historical introduction of
the area and a summary of pertinent socioeconomic data are developed to
acquaint the reader with the communities studied and to permit him to
compare them with others. As noted in the Introduction, Satellite City,
Country Club Estates, and New Town are of special interest, for lay
surveys providing the data subsequently discussed were conducted in these
communities.

An Historical Overview

Fathers Marquette and Joliet were the first European explorers to
chart the territory where Midwest City is now located. They traversed
the lakes and rivers which later determined the location of Midwest City
and contributed to its growth.

Founded in the first half of the nineteenth century, Midwest City
was a bustling metropolis by the time of the Civil War. As is true of so
many large cities located near waterways, Midwest City also became a
railroad center. With the railroads came immigrants by the hundreds of
thousands. Many chose to remain in the new, sprawling, burgeoning metropolis.
Others went on to the north, the west, and the south. Industrialists and
merchandisers soon recognized the potential of Midwest City and its hinter-
lands, so they located there, augmenting its growth.

Midwest City and its environs became the object of a vast land
rush. New England Yankees were the first to arrive in substantial numbers.
Soon thereafter came Northern Europeans, then Southern Europeans, and then
Eastern Europeans. Each new wave of immigrants pushed its predecessors
toward and beyond the city's external limits. Small, quiet independent
communities became thriving towns and eventually suburbs.

Low land costs and proximity to a fast evolving city drove the
new migrants into the "rural" part of the county in which Midwest City
was developing. Newcomers were attracted from other parts of America and
from abroad to the suburban sector studied here. The larger contingents
of natives came from North Carolina, Vermont, Ohio, New York, Connecticut,
Pennsylvania, and Kentucky. Those coming from abroad originally occupying
the sector communities came predominantly from Ireland, Scotland, France,
Germany, Bohemia, and Switzerland.

The pattern of suburban development in this sector does not differ
greatly from those in other areas. The evolving pattern of coach roads,
street cars, railroads, buses, highways, and expressways parallels transportation developments in many American metropolitan regions.

Up until World War I many of the communities remained small,
independent villages. About that time, industrial and real estate development accelerated, and the great burgeoning of the suburban sector began.

Black migrants from the south came in increas'ng numbers after World
War I. By World War II, no one ethnic group predominated in any of these
communities.

Five of the eight suburbs [Waterside (1), Satellite City (2),
Oak Summit (4), Sylvan Retreat (5) and Germantown (8)] were founded in the
nineteenth century and three [Shopton (3), Country Club Estates (6) and
New Town (7)] were founded in the twentieth century. New Town, founded
after World War II, was the most recent.

German immigrants were prominent among the settlers of the nineteenth
century villages. Dutch, Irish, Scotch, and English settlers were also in
evidence. Later, eastern and southern European migrants began to settle
in some of the villages.

The construction of a major railroad after the Civil War fostered
the development of many of the communities. Waterside, Satellite City,
Shopton, Sylvan Retreat, and Germantown were all substantially influenced
by the construction and expansion of the railroad.

The presence of Lutheran and Catholic churches in the area is
evidence of the early settlement patterns in these communities. By the
time of World War II, the ethnic flavor of most of these communities had
been diminished by the influx of diverse groups.

Two of the communities--Waterside (1) and Satellite City (2)--
have some heavy industry, such as steel foundries and forging mills, but
none of the other suburbs has any heavy industry. Satellite City is the
major manufacturing city in the sector. There is some light industry in
Oak Summit (4) and New Town (7) but the rest of the suburbs are primarily
residential.

A Summary of Socioeconomic Data on the Sector Suburbs

Midwest City had its major growth between 1880 and 1930. It has
fewer people in it today than it did in 1930.

During the 1930-1970 period the population of the Midwest City
Standard Metropolitan Statistical Area has almost doubled, dramatically
increasing the population of the suburban area around Midwest City. By
1970 over half the population (52 percent) in the Midwest City Standard
Metropolitan Statistical Area lived in the suburbs. While middle and upper
status people left Midwest City and relocated in the surrounding suburban
towns, black, Indian, Puerto Rican, Chicano, and southern white migrants
seeking better jobs and improved living standards have been lured to
Midwest City. The resulting population movements have markedly affected
the character of religious institutions, for rarely do immigrants and
emigrants share common religious traditions.

Because of the voluntary character of religious membership in
America religious institutions were most vigorous in middle and upper

status communities. As data presented subsequently will show, the higher the social status of a suburb, the higher the proportion of its residents who were members of religious institutions. Lower status people, less able to contribute financially to religious institutions, participated in them less frequently.

The suburban sector studied here had a 1970 population of about 150,000. It was about five or six miles wide and eighteen to twenty miles long. Within the sector, there was marked socioeconomic and ethnic heterogeneity. Country Club Estates (6) ranked in the upper 10 percent of suburbs in socioeconomic status in the Midwest City Standard Metropolitan Statistical Area, and Satellite City (2) and Shopton (3) ranked in the lower 10 percent. The others fell between these two extremes. Waterside (1), Oak Summit (4), New Town (7) and Germantown (8) were "average" amongst Midwest City's suburbs, ranking between the fortieth and sixty-fifth percentile. Sylvan Retreat (5) was in the upper third. Selected socioeconomic data are summarized in Table III-1.

Since the suburban area had higher proportions of middle and upper status residents than Midwest City or the total United States population, the sector was biased in the direction of over-representation of middle and upper status people. For the purposes of this study, such a bias is not serious for two reasons. Because middle and upper status members of religious institutions are culture-bearing and culture-creating elites, their participation patterns and value orientations give more salient clues about the emerging shape of institutional religious life in America than do the participation patterns and value orientations of lower status people. In spite of this middle status bias, the sample also included a sufficient number of lower status members of religious institutions and lower status communities to permit statistical analyses and to correlate types of religious institutions with types of communities.

Every community in the sector had more than doubled in population since 1940. In some of the communities farthest from Midwest City, the population has tripled, quadrupled, or quintupled since 1940. Typically, the suburbs have a central area developed between 1900 and 1945, surrounded by a ring of newer dwelling units and shopping complexes built since World War II.

Satellite City (2), which has had the least post-World War II growth, had a cluster of downtown religious institutions and a few newer outlying ones. In most of the other communities, the large majority of the religious institutions had been built since 1945. Some were located near the city center; others were situated on the peripheral ring.

As Table III-2 shows, the greatest population increases between 1960 and 1970 occurred in the communities farthest from Midwest City. The single exception was New Town (7), a planned community developed after World War II and now completely built up. A new and larger planned community was being developed beyond New Town when the study was under way, and it will most likely go through a cycle comparable to that of New Town in the next two or three decades.

TABLE III-1

SELECTED SOCIOECONOMIC DATA FOR MIDWEST CITY,

MIDWEST CITY SMSA, AND SUBURBAN COMMUNITIES IN THE SECTOR

Geographical Area	Median Years School Completed Persons 25 and over	Median Family Income	Percent Labor Force Professional and Kindred Workers	Socioeconomic Rank among Midwest City Suburbs
Midwest City SMSA	12.1	11,900	15.1	
Midwest City	11.2	10,200	12.6	
Waterside (1)	12.3	12,500	18.4	Medium
Satellite City (2)	11.7	11,000	10.1	Low
Shopton (3)	12.0	12,000	10.1	Low
Oak Summit (4)	12.5	14,100	19.6	Medium
Sylvan Retreat (5)	12.8	15,800	24.8	Upper Medium
Country Club Estates (6)	14.8	26,400	33.6	High
New Town (7)	13.1	14,000	31.4	Medium
Germantown (8)	12.5	14,000	21.1	Medium

Source: United States Bureau of the Census, Census of Population, 1970.

TABLE III-2

SELECTED POPULATION DATA FOR MIDWEST CITY,

MIDWEST CITY SMSA, AND SUBURBAN COMMUNITIES IN THE SECTOR

Geographical Area	Approximate 1970 Population	Percent Change 1960-70	Rank in Percent Change 1960-70	Percent Black	Percent Female	Median Age
Midwest City SMSA		12		18	51	28.4
Midwest City		-5		33	52	29.6
Midwest City Suburban Area		35		4	50	26.3
Waterside (1)	16,000	32	6	*	52	31.1
Satellite City (2)	35,000	19	7	31	51	26.2
Shopton (3)	16,000	37	5	50	50	20.2
Oak Summit (4)	12,000	58	3	*	50	25.3
Sylvan Retreat (5)	19,000	41	4	*	51	33.9
Country Club Estates (6)	11,000	83	1	*	50	31.5
New Town (7)	31,000	2	8	2	50	25.6
Germantown (8)	7,000	76	2	2	51	24.8

Source: United States Bureau of the Census, Census of Population, 1970.

*Less than ½ of 1 percent.

Among the outlying suburbs, the relatively more affluent Sylvan
Retreat (5) and Country Club Estates (6) had the highest median ages.
Such a finding is hardly surprising, for young married couples with small
children cannot afford the housing being developed in these communities.
At the time this study was being made, almost no new single dwelling
housing units under $50,000 were being built in these communities.

Waterside (1), bordering Midwest City on one side and Satellite
City (2) on the other, had the highest proportion of its residents over
sixty-five, the lowest under eighteen, and the fewest persons per house-
hold. Satellite City's white population was also relatively old. Both
these communities have tripled in population since 1950, but the greatest
absolute and percentage increases occurred between 1950 and 1960. Consequently, their populations had higher proportions of older people. Such
age distributions are typical of communities in transition from one ethnic,
status, or racial group to another.

As Table III-2 also shows, the residential segregation of blacks
and white manifest throughout the nation, especially in the north and west,
was reflected in the suburban sector. The black segment of the population
was overwhelmingly concentrated in two communities, the heavy industry
community of Satellite City (2) and Shopton (3), contiguous to Satellite
City. The black population of Satellite City was considerably younger
than the white population. This age composition implies a continued
decline in the white population and a continued increase in the black
population in Satellite City.

The presence of a substantial black population in this particular
suburban sector was one of the factors leading to the decision to study
the area, for it permitted an exploration of black-white religious institution relations and some comparisons of black-white value orientations
among Protestants.

Fashionable shops and small shopping centers of high quality were
concentrated in and near Country Club Estates, the most prestigious
community in the suburban sector, one that ranked socioeconomically in the
top 10 percent of Midwest City suburbs. Regional shopping centers were
located in Satellite City (2), New Town (7), and Germantown(8).

New Town had the distinction of having one of the first suburban
shopping centers developed in the United States after World War II.
Midwest City's most prestigious department store had a branch store in
New Town, and a major national merchandising chain also had a large store
there. The regional shopping center in Germantown, constructed after
1970, was on the fringe of the area in the path of new growth. It offered
substantial competition to the New Town complex, but the sharp population
growth of the area made both economically viable. Two of Midwest City's
better department stores and two major national merchandising chains had
large outlets there. There were also many high fashion and specialty
shops.

Reflecting status differences, the "anchor" stores in Satellite
City's shopping center, built about 1960, were two major national mass

merchandise department store chains. It also had fewer high fashion
shops than its counterparts in New Town and Germantown.

Religious Institutions and

the Shape of Suburban Development

Introduction[2]

The shape of suburban development inextricably links institutional
religious life with ethnicity, socioeconomic status, and population movements. This section highlights the consequences of suburban population
distribution patterns for churches and synagogues.

Selected membership data are summarized in Tables III-3 and III-4.
Table III-3 delineates membership by major faith groups and indicates the
ratio of members to residents eighteen years and over by community.
Table III-4 enumerates the number, type, and membership of Protestant
institutions by community.

The marked internal diversity of American Protestantism made
necessary the more detailed analysis shown in Table III-4. Membership
data on three basic groups are presented in that table.

The first group consists of churches in the thirty-three denominations affiliated with the National Council of the Churches of Christ in
America. (These denominations have an inclusive membership of 42,000,000.)
This council includes all the large Protestant denominations with the
exception of some Baptist groups (the Southern Baptist Convention is the
largest of these), the Church of Jesus Christ of Latter-day Saints (Mormons),
and some Lutheran denominations. The council also includes twenty or so
smaller denominations.

The second group is the Lutheran Church Missouri Synod. The concentration of Missouri Synod churches in the communities studied is a
consequence of the heavy German migration to the area in the latter part
of the nineteenth century. This denomination has combined biblical
literalism, ethnic identification, and liturgical emphases to produce a
unique configuration not easily categorized.

The third group includes all other Protestant churches, including
such diverse groups as Southern Baptists, Church of Christ, Christian
Scientists, Church of God, and similar groups. This group is eclectic,
but it is comprised largely of an evangelical, literalistically inclined
group of churches whose historic roots are either southern or frontier
America.

TABLE III-3

RELIGIOUS INSTITUTION MEMBERSHIP DATA BY SUBURBAN COMMUNITY

	Waterside (1)	Satellite City (2)	Shopton (3)	Oak Summit (4)	Sylvan Retreat (5)	Country Club Estates (6)	New Town (7)	Germantown (8)
Number of residents eighteen years and over*	11,500	Total: 21,900 White: 16,100 Black: 5,800	Total: 8,500 White: 4,500 Black: 4,000	7,300	12,000	6,700	17,700	4,500
Number of members of religious insti- tutions in community *	6,100	10,100	2,600	3,500	9,500	8,600	12,300	3,200
Percent Protestant in membership	39%	Total: 72% White: 55% Black: 17%	Total: 50% White: 37% Black 13%	39%	58%	45%	58%	65%
Percent Catholic in community	61%	Total: 28% White: 24% Black: 4%	Total: 50% White: 40% Black: 10%	61%	39%	30%	32%	35%
Percent Jewish in membership	0%	0%	0%	0%	4%	20%	10%	0%
Percent "other" in membership**	0%	0%	0%	0%	0%	5%	0%	0%
Ratio of number of church members to number of residents eighteen years old and older	.53	Total: .46 White: .50 Black: .37	Total: .31 White: .55 Black: .15	.48	.79	1.28	.69	.71
Social status of community in rank order	3	7	8	6	2	1	4	5

*Numbers rounded to closest hundred
**Greek Orthodox and Unitarian

TABLE III-4 SELECTED PROTESTANT CHURCH MEMBERSHIP DATA BY SUBURBAN COMMUNITY

Suburban Community	National Council of Churches Affiliated					Missouri Synod Lutheran					All Other Protestant				
	Number of churches	Total membership	Average membership per church	Percent of Protestant total	Percent of all faiths	Number of churches	Total membership	Average membership per church	Percent of Protestant total	Percent of all faiths	Number of churches	Total membership	Average membership per church	Percent of Protestant total	Percent of all faiths
Waterside (1)	2	1672	836	71	28	0	0	0	0	0	5	673	135	29	11
Satellite City (2)	9	2776	308	38	28	1	75	75	1	1	23	4380	190	61	44
White:	7	2370	339	33	24	1	75	75	1	1	10	3135	314	43	31
Black:	2	412	206	6	4	0	0	0	0	0	12	1245	104	17	13
Shopton (3) Total:	2	280	140	21	11	1	550	550	42	21	6	479	80	37	18
White:	2	280	140	21	11	1	550	550	42	21	2	137	68	10	5
Black:	0	0	0	0	0	0	0	0	0	0	4	342	86	26	13
Oak Summit (4)	2	765	382	56	22	1	470	470	34	13	2	135	66	10	4
Sylvan Retreat (5)	4	3357	839	61	35	1	1200	1200	22	13	5	909	182	17	10
Country Club Estates (6)	4	3666	916	95	42	0	0	0	0	0	1	206	206	5	3
New Town (7)	7	4919	703	69	40	1	1450	1450	20	2	7	785	112	11	6
Germantown (8)	3	1358	453	66	43	1	340	340	17	11	4	362	90	18	11

Churches and Synagogues in the Sector Communities:

An Interpretative Overview

Viewed broadly, the farther the suburb from Midwest City, the higher the socioeconomic level of the population and the lower the median age of the population. Status gradients were discernible, with a lower status concentration around Satellite City (2) and Shopton (3) and an upper status concentration around Country Club Estates (6).

Satellite City and Shopton had the vast majority of blacks in the suburban sector and ranked lowest on all socioeconomic indicators. The upper status community of Country Club Estates is surrounded by upper middle status communities. Though less affluent than Country Club Estates, Sylvan Retreat (5), New Town (7) and the newer portions of Germantown (8) are relatively affluent suburbs.

Oak Summit (4) functions as somewhat of a buffer between Shopton (3), ranking in the lowest 10 percent socioeconomically among Midwest City suburbs, and Sylvan Retreat, ranking in the upper third. Sylvan Retreat in turn, blends into upper status Country Club Estates. Not coincidentally, lower quality housing is concentrated in the heavy industrial complex in and around Satellite City.

The data on religious membership reported in Table III-3 and summarized in the preceding sub-section may be interpreted in light of these social status patterns. Roman Catholics and relatively lower status whites were concentrated on both sides of the black ghettoes of Satellite City (2) and Shopton (3). Waterside (1), an aging community, has attracted Catholics moving out of areas being occupied by blacks in both Midwest City and Satellite City. The Protestant population was aging, and there is little likelihood that enough Protestants will come into Waterside as Protestants die or move away to replace the Protestant population.

Consequently, the large Roman Catholic parish in Waterside has been growing and was relatively well supported. At the same time, all the Protestant churches were in difficulty. Two small sectarian Protestant churches reported a substantial percentage increase (over 35 percent) in the past decade, but the actual numerical increase in membership was less than 100. The large Protestant churches reported losses in membership and had predominantly middle-aged or elderly congregations, so the future does not seem very promising for these institutions.

The Roman Catholic parish displayed much greater vigor than any of the major Protestant churches, growing by 50 percent in the past decade. It also had a somewhat disproportionate number of middle-aged and elderly in the parish. If past patterns persist, in due course the Roman Catholic whites in Waterside will begin to die and to move away disproportionately. At that time, perhaps a decade or two from now, other ethnic groups, most likely blacks, will move into Waterside, and the Catholic parish will experience the declines now visible in Satellite City.

Two of the three Roman Catholic parishes and every major NCC-affiliated Protestant church in Satellite City and in Shopton were suffering from a marked decline in membership. Two of the Satellite City Roman Catholic parishes and all the predominantly white NCC-affiliated churches reached their peak membership about 1960. Since then, the NCC-affiliated Protestant churches have had membership declines ranging from 20 to 35 percent. The current age-sex composition of those churches suggests further membership declines, for the congregations were all predominantly middle-aged to old white. In Satellite City, this population is being replaced by young to middle-aged black populations.

The almost insoluble problem of maintaining integrated local religious institutions over a period of time in a society characterized by residential racial segregation is illustrated by the data for Satellite City and Shopton, the two suburban communities in the study area with substantial proportions of blacks in their population. The only integrated Protestant churches were declining in membership and in a period of transition to all black churches.

The three Roman Catholic parishes in Satellite City were also affected by the shifting racial composition of the suburb. The declines in membership in two of the parishes were proportionately greater than in the Protestant churches, for they reported drops of more than 50 percent in the past decade or so. In each instance, this overall decline was accompanied by an increase in the percentage of blacks in the parish. These parishes are also in transition to all black parishes.

The other Satellite City parish was the beneficiary of white Catholics moving out of areas of black influx, and it reported a membership increase of more than 40 percent in the past decade, with no substantial increase of black parishioners.

The primary reason for the more rapid rate of decline of the Catholic parishes is socioeconomic. Roman Catholic parishes in Satellite City had higher proportions of blue collar workers than did NCC-affiliated Protestant churches. In the main, these blue collar workers lived in areas in which the housing stock was older and less expensive. Consequently blacks, who also were disproportionately blue collar workers, were more likely to move into Catholic areas than into areas with higher proportions of members of NCC-affiliated Protestant churches.

The patterns within Satellite City reflected on a small scale the broad mobility patterns in Midwest City and in the larger suburban sector. Due to historical circumstances related to the patterns of migration and urbanization discussed earlier, the broad succession of ethnic groups in Midwest City has been from whites of northern and western European origin to whites of southern and eastern European origin, to blacks of urban and southern origin, qualified by the immigration of southern whites, Chicanos, and Puerto-Ricans.

Religious institutional life is powerfully conditioned by these broad population movements, for the groups of northern and western European origin are a mixture of Protestants and Catholics; those from eastern and southern Europe are largely Roman Catholic; the southern whites are largely Protestant; the blacks are largely Protestant, and those of Chicano and Puerto-Rican origin are largely Roman Catholic.

The Protestant situation is further complicated by its internal divisions, blue collar and white collar, white and black, for Protestants in these various groups are attracted to different religious institutions. As the data in Table III-4 show, Satellite City and Shopton are the only suburbs in which the majority of Protestants belonged to churches not affiliated with the National Council of Churches. (Broadly speaking, NCC churches are less exclusive theologically, less prone to literalist or quasi-literalist interpretations of Scripture, and less moralistic than non-NCC-affiliated institutions. Because the almost 12,000,000 people related to the Southern Baptist Convention do not belong to the NCC, non-NCC churches have a distinctively southern character, for southern Baptists constitute almost half of the membership of non-NCC churches. As southerners have migrated north and west, non-NCC groups have spread throughout the nation.)

Even though they were quite small, both black and white non-NCC-affiliated churches have been growing in Satellite City and Shopton. As noted earlier, this growth was due in large measure to the shifting racial and socioeconomic status of the residents of these two suburbs. The data do not suggest large absolute increases in non-NCC church membership. In many instances the percentage increases have been substantial because the churches were so small that the addition of a few members caused a large percentage increase in membership.

Not surprisingly, the black churches were generally reporting membership gains, but they were not proportional to the percentage increase in the black population of Satellite City in the past two decades.

Blue collar workers participate less frequently in voluntary associations of all types than do white collar workers, so it is not surprising to find the lowest proportion of church members per 1,000 population in Satellite City and Shopton. As Table III-3 shows, even in these lower status communities, black participation was much lower than white participation.

Waterside (1) and Oak Summit (4), suburbs with Catholic majorities, had fewer members per 100 adult population than did higher status Sylvan Retreat (5), Country Club Estates (6), New Town (7) and Germantown (8). These latter suburbs, farthest from Midwest City, had Protestant majorities or pluralities. In the past decade, however, the Catholic churches and synagogues in this outer region have been growing more rapidly than the Protestant churches, reflecting the shifting composition of the inflowing population. Moving from Midwest City and/or the suburbs closer to Midwest City, Jews and Catholics have come to this outer region in higher proportions than Protestants.

Viewed broadly then, the more distant the suburb from the central city, the more Protestants and Jews in its population. The Protestant

majorities in many of the outlying suburbs, related to the historical
preponderance of Protestants in these villages and earlier Protestant
movements to these outlying suburbs from the central city and suburbs
closer to the central city, are being modified.

A significant difference between Roman Catholic and Jewish migration
patterns is discernible. When one ethnic group succeeds to another ethnic
group's turf, most lower and lower middle status populations tend to move
a few blocks or a few miles, depending on the size of the metropolitan
area. As the persistence of nationality-identified Catholic parishes in
Midwest City and its suburbs reveals, this pattern is manifest among the
Catholic population.

Jews, however, have skipped many suburbs in their move from Midwest
City. Due to the paucity of lower status Jews, there are no synagogues
in Waterside (1), Satellite City (2), Shopton (3) or Oak Summit (4). They
are concentrated in upper status Country Club Estates (6) and contiguous
Sylvan Retreat (5) and New Town (7), some ten miles from the border of
Midwest City.

These broad population movements, so markedly affecting the life
cycles of local religious institutions, have persisted in Midwest City
and other metropolitan areas for over seventy-five years.

Two factors may emerge in the forthcoming decades to modify the
impact of shifting populations on local religious institutions. The first
and least likely factor would be some significant restrictions on mobility
by the federal government. The second and somewhat more likely factor
would be changes in the forms of religious institutions and the values and
types of participation by laity. Data presented in subsequent chapters
provide some clues about these possibilities.

While some shifts may be anticipated--particularly closer relations between Roman Catholicism and NCC-affiliated Protestant churches--
the tripartite structure of religious identity--Protestant, Catholic,
Jew--is apt to persist in the foreseeable future. Within Christianity,
Protestant-Catholic rapprochement might well result in predominantly
white and predominantly black religious identity, for there is minimal
evidence to suggest the possibility of widespread interracial local Christian
churches in America in the foreseeable future.

A third factor affecting the life cycle of religious institutions
in American suburbia is the age structure of the population. Changes in
the birthrate affect both the internal life of religious institutions and
mobility patterns in the suburbs.

The number of births per year has declined by about a third during
the past decade. This decline is attributable in part to the decline in
numbers in the thirty-five to forty-nine age group and in part to the
limitations on childbearing voluntarily effected by young adults.

If women in the younger age group (twenty to thirty-four) were to
reduce markedly the number of children they bore, there would be less

need for new space and new residences. Such a situation could conceivably
slow population mobility and reduce the rate of community change in the
longer run, but not in the next decade or so.

Even if the people currently in the nineteen to twenty-nine age
group decided to have fewer children, the sheer number of people in this
age group means that the number of births per year will almost assuredly
increase substantially in the next decade. Such a situation is apt to
increase the number of people participating in religious institutions.
In some respects the period from 1980 to 1990 may resemble the 1950's
so far as institutional religious life is concerned.

The current age distribution of the suburban population is reflected
in the age distribution of religious institutions in the suburbs. The
white religious institutions in the suburbs close to Midwest City have
higher than average proportions of old people, and the ones farther from
Midwest City have higher proportions of young and middle-aged people.
The black churches in Satellite City and Shopton have high proportions
of young and middle-aged members.

Another pattern of geographical mobility also affects the internal
life of suburban churches and synagogues. The movement of people of
approximately the same social status from one community to a comparable
one in another geographical area is commonplace in American society.
White collar workers are especially likely to make such moves, for national
and multi-national companies frequently transfer their employees from one
metropolitan area to another.

Because of these movements, communities retaining the same status
and ethnic flavor experience substantial turnovers in population. The
pastor of one large suburban church in Country Club Estates observed that
in a five-year period his church had taken in 1500 members and had lost
1500 members. With minor variations this story was repeated by many clergy.

As a result of this high rate of membership turnover, the clergyman
assumes a central role in integrating the life of the church or synagogue.
Even in Protestant churches with congregational polity and in synagogues
the clergy become central administrative persons. In many instances the
clergyman remains, and his constituency changes. This situation contrasts
with rural parishes where the clergyman is likely to move and his constituency to remain.

Size of Religious Institutions and

Principles of Ecclesiastical Organization

The data highlight the large size of Roman Catholic parishes
compared to Protestant churches. Even the smallest Roman Catholic church
in the suburban sector was larger than the majority of Protestant institutions. The size of these institutions accentuates priest-laity distance,
for it is not possible for a priest to know well more than a small proportion

of the laity. Only one of the Catholic parishes reported fewer than 1,000
members; only 10 percent of the Protestant churches reported more than
1,000.

The cultic principle of organization historically associated with
Roman Catholicism has minimized the significance of the relative anonymity
of the Catholic priest in these large parishes, for the objectivist
emphases do not place a strong premium on close interpersonal and intergroup relations. The congregational principle of organization historically
associated with American Protestantism accentuates the importance of lay
direction and control and of close interpersonal relations. As a concomitant, Protestant clergy serving relatively large churches must possess
substantial adjustive and integrative skills to administer and to coordinate
the activities of the institution and to sustain primary group relations.

In Protestantism, the average size of predominantly white collar
NCC-affiliated churches is greater in every community than the average
size of predominantly blue collar non-NCC-affiliated churches. The capacities of white collar workers to participate in relatively large and
complex social organizations is probably greater than that of blue collar
workers, for they are more accustomed to coordinating and integrating
activities. Consequently, they are better able to feel comfortable with
the greater anonymity inevitably associated with larger social institutions.

The communal principle of organization in Judaism is associated
with an emphasis on the teaching function of the synagogue. The meaning
of the term "rabbi" itself underscores this teaching function. This central
teaching function of the synagogue is modified in the American context,
for all religious institutions in America must sustain a range of ancillary
social activities. Nevertheless, the focus on religious and communal
education in Judaism is greater than in Catholicism or Protestantism. In
a certain sense, the local rabbi is expected to be more "learned" than the
Catholic priest or the Protestant minister.

Conclusion

Religious professionals mindful of the population patterns traced
in this chapter will be able to assess the stage of the life cycle in which
a given religious institution finds itself. Though these implications
of the broad population patterns for religious institutions were first
publicly developed by Samuel C. Kincheloe almost a half-century ago, many
ecclesiastical executives and more local clergy still seem unaware of them
as they plan institutional expansion and/or programs.[3]

As sociological entities, religious institutions in America are
necessarily affected by the broad population movements traced in this
chapter. High population mobility and voluntaryism present unique problems
for religious leaders, for no other geographically based social institution
in America having professional leadership has to rely so heavily on suasion
and is so dependent on local funding.

Significant as these broad population movements are for the life
of religious institutions, they are nevertheless somewhat secondary; for
religious institutions are concerned primarily to bear witness to the
Divine Presence in the world. They seek to cultivate and to manifest
religious, cultural, and moral values.

Part II and Part III of this volume explore facets of the inner
life of religious institutions. This exploration is based on interviews
with most clergy serving the religious institutions of the suburban sector
and on questionnaires returned by lay members of United Methodist, Roman
Catholic, and Jewish religious institutions in Satellite City, Country
Club Estates, and New Town. It seeks to illumine selected aspects of the
complex relation of religion to American culture in the lives of clergy
and lay people in American suburbia.

PART TWO

SUBURBAN CHURCHES AND SYNAGOGUES AS SOCIAL INSTITUTIONS

CHAPTER IV

THE RELIGIOUS PROFESSIONAL: JEW-PROTESTANT-CATHOLIC

The Tripartite Faith Structure of American Suburbia

Introduction

As noted earlier, all the religious institutions in the suburban sector examined in this study fit a tripartite pattern. This basic faith division is fundamental in America, but there are significant subdivisions within Judaism and Protestantism.[1]

American Judaism

Three major divisions exist within American Judaism: Orthodox, Conservative, and Reform. Statistics on current memberships of the various groups are not very precise, but there are more families affiliated with Reform synagogues than with either of the other groups. Perhaps half of the Jews belonging to synagogues belong to Reform congregations. Orthodox congregations have perhaps a third of Jews belonging to synagogues, and Conservative congregations perhaps a sixth.[2]

Although it is beyond the scope of this study to detail the inner differences within the major faith groups, a brief note is appropriate. Viewed broadly, Orthodox Judaism is most traditional, and Reform Judaism is least traditional, with Conservative Judaism falling between the two.

Jews may move from one branch to another and still affirm their basic Jewishness. Such internal mobility is akin to that within Protestantism. This internal pluralism prevents the establishment of a doctrinal or liturgical orthodoxy and insures some legitimate variety in belief and practice.

National Jewish agencies, such as the American Jewish Committee, transcend these divisions and seek to represent Judaism--synagogue member and non-member alike--on many issues. These agencies play an important role in American Judaism, for they symbolize Jewish unity beyond its internal diversity.

This symbolic unity was also reflected in the studied suburban sector. The five rabbis in the area often participated publicly in Jewish

55

ceremonial occasions, and group pictures of most or all of them appeared regularly in the suburban newspaper circulated in the area where their synagogues were located. These public symbolic events in which the rabbis participated transcended the "Reform" and "Conservative" traditions to which they were related.

American Protestantism

Protestantism is much more variegated than Judaism.[3] Almost 200 Protestant denominations reported their membership data to the Editor of the Yearbook of American Churches, 1972, and there are probably fifty or so small denominations not reporting. Protestantism is not as fragmented as these data might suggest, however, for almost 60,000,000 of the approximately 72,000,000 Protestants in America belonged to the eighteen denominations having memberships of 1,000,000 or more.[4]

A broad distinction within American Protestantism may be made between denominations belonging to the National Council of the Churches of Christ in the U.S.A. (NCC) and those not belonging to the National Council of Churches of Christ in the U.S.A. (non-NCC). In the main, churches belonging to the National Council are less traditional, less exclusive, and less evangelical than churches not belonging to the National Council.

Of the eighteen Protestant denominations with memberships of 1,000,000 or more, the following ten belong to the National Council: African Methodist Episcopal Church (1,166,000); American Baptist Convention (1,472,000); Christian Church (Disciples of Christ) (1,424,000); Episcopal Church (3,286,000); Lutheran Church in America (3,107,000); National Baptist Convention of America (2,669,000); National Baptist Convention, U.S.A., Inc. (5,500,000); United Church of Christ (1,961,000); United Methodist Church (10,672,000); and United Presbyterian Church (3,087,000). Their combined membership of almost 35,000,000 is over 80 percent of the total membership of the thirty-three denominations belonging to the National Council of Churches.

The following eight denominations with memberships of one million or more do not belong to the National Council of Churches: American Lutheran Church (2,543,000); Assemblies of God (1,065,000); Christian Church and Churches of Christ (1,021,000); Church of Jesus Christ of Latter-Day Saints (2,073,000); Churches of Christ (2,400,000); Lutheran Church Missouri Synod (2,789,000); National Primitive Baptist Convention, Inc. (1,523,000); and Southern Baptist Convention (11,628,000).

Biblically conservative or fundamentalist groups predominate in this non-NCC group. The southern influence is strong, for almost half of this group belong to churches affiliated with the Southern Baptist Convention. In addition, the only denominations in the group not having strong southern ties historically are the Mormons and the two Lutheran denominations.

Members or clergy who switch denominations across the NCC--
non-NCC line are typically doing so in conjunction with a rise or fall
in their socioeconomic status. Such distinct social differentiations are
accompanied by clear and sometimes sharp divergence on religious, moral,
and sociopolitical matters, as data subsequently presented will show.[5]
Such changes in one's life situation have great psychic importance, of
course, and therefore one is unlikely to re-cross the NCC - non-NCC line.
The constant re-affiliating of Protestant Americans is primarily within
each group of denominations.

In spite of these cleavages within Protestantism, members of both
these major groups consider themselves to be Protestant. If such an
affirmation means little else, it does mean they are neither Catholic nor
Jewish.

American Catholicism

Catholicism, in contrast to both Protestantism and Judaism, has
no formal internal divisions; indeed, its claim to unity, verity, and
universalism make such internal divisions impossible in the Protestant
and Jewish sense. The only Catholic analogue to the internal variety of
Protestantism and Judaism is its multiplicity of religious orders and
special interest groups. This variety gives considerable leeway for the
expression of diverse beliefs and practices, but such beliefs and practices
are always subject--at least in principle--to control by ecclesiastical
authority. The result is greater internal tension within Catholicism as
a whole than within Protestantism or Judaism. Dissident Protestants or
Jews can always move from one group to another within Protestantism or
Judaism, but dissident Catholics confront more forcefully the possibility
of leaving the Church.

Tradition and Innovation

It is significant that in the American experience more conservative and more innovative groups emerge in each of the major faith groups.
Such patterns are manifest in many contexts, but the nature of the American
experience makes them more intense. Such diversity is a direct consequence
of religious disestablishment, for no faith group has special support--
financial or legal--from the state.

In different ways each major faith group is struggling with the
general problems of the relation of the individual to and his participation
in his religious group, the relative importance of tradition and past
theological formulations to the present and current theological formulations, and the relation between the individual's freedom of religious
expression and his dependence upon the historical community from which he
came.

In Judaism, the struggle centers on the authority of tradition and
the historical Jewish community; in Protestantism, on the authority of

Scripture; in Catholicism, on the authority of tradition and the Church, particularly its ecclesiastical representatives, culminating in the authority of the Pope.[6]

Clergy Associations and the American Experience

Local clergy associations symbolize both the unity of the public religion and the diversity of the particular religions of America. The public presence of NCC-affiliated and non-NCC-affiliated ministers, priests, and rabbis in a common religious association symbolizes both the reality of the Divine Presence and the importance of religious pluralism and religious tolerance in American life. By their very existence, interfaith associations of Protestant, Catholic, and Jewish clergy attest to public religious values surpassing the more specific values of any particular religious group in America. For this reason, local ministerial associations are most apt to sponsor interfaith events related to public observances of Memorial Day, Independence Day, and Thanksgiving. These three holidays embody much meaning and feeling associated with the public religion, and clergy of all faiths can participate in ceremonies sanctifying them.

Religious Professionals in the Suburban Sector

The clergy of the major faith groups in the studied suburban sector all have special responsibilities in the conduct of public worship and public ceremonial events especially associated with birth, puberty, marriage, and death. They give concrete expression to the theological and sociohistorical motifs characteristic of their traditions.

They are highly visible members of their faith groups, and they have special responsibilities for member recruitment and organizational maintenance. They oversee the collection and distribution of funds and the maintenance of facilities in which to conduct their activities.

In spite of the differences noted subsequently, the suburban clergy all were looked upon as leaders of religious institutions. In the American context, they were leaders of "legitimate" faith groups, for almost all of them were Protestant, Catholic, or Jewish. The "marginal" clergy included the minister of a small Unitarian church in Country Club Estates and the leadership of a Bahai Temple in New Town.

The Clergy Sample

Clergy responses were categorized into four major faith groupings: NCC-affiliated Protestants; non-NCC-affiliated white Protestants; black Protestants; and Roman Catholic. Three of the five rabbis serving synagogues in the suburban sector were interviewed. This small number has prevented their inclusion in the statistical profiles, but a brief summary of their situation is presented below.

The separate analysis of the black clergy is undertaken because of the very sharp cleavage between white Protestant churches and black Protestant Churches. As the findings in Chapter III indicated, only a very small proportion of predominantly black Protestant churches had any white members and vice versa.

Because graduation from a theological school was required for ordination, all the rabbis and priests in the studied suburban sector were college and theological school graduates.

The non-NCC-affiliated white Protestants group includes both the clergy of diverse groups that insist on seminary education for their religious leaders, such as the Unitarians and the Lutheran Church Missouri Synod, and the clergy of fundamentalist groups that have minimal educational requirements for ordination.

Overall, it was estimated the 40 to 45 percent of the clergy serving both black and white non-NCC-affiliated churches in the sector were college graduates. It was further estimated that 20 to 30 percent of the black Protestant clergy in the sector were college graduates.

All of the Protestant clergy serving NCC-affiliated churches were college graduates, and 25 percent of them had done graduate work outside the field of theology. All but one had graduated from a theological school requiring at least three years of work beyond college.

There were approximately 125 clergy serving religious institutions in the sector. Questionnaires were sent to all of them, and the research team attempted to contact them. Questionnaires and interviews were obtained from three of five rabbis in the sector, twenty-two of twenty-five priests, thirty-five of thirty-eight ministers serving Protestant churches affiliated with the National Council of Churches, and thirty-three of approximately fifty-seven ministers serving Protestant churches not affiliated with the National Council of Churches.

Of the twenty-four refusals by Protestants serving churches not affiliated with the National Council of Churches, fourteen were white clergy, and ten were black. It was estimated that fewer than ten of these non-NCC clergy served congregations of more than 100 members. With one notable exception--a black Baptist church of about 400 members-- none of the black churches had more than 100 members.[7] The vast majority of those refusing to answer questionnaires served fundamentalist and strongly evangelistic churches.

The tabular materials have not been subjected to statistical tests of significance, for the small number of cases does not permit detailed statistical analyses. The enumeration of NCC-affiliated Protestant ministers and priests in the sector was almost exhaustive, so these data most accurately represent _all_ NCC-affiliated Protestant and Roman Catholic clergy in the suburban sector. Assuming a relative degree of coherence between non-NCC-affiliated white Protestant respondents and refusals, the responses do permit the development of profiles of the various groups and the elaboration of salient commonalities and differences. Such an assumption is entirely reasonable, for the non-respondents were rooted in the same ethos as the respondents.

The non-respondents came disproportionately from small religious institutions, so the responses reported reflect the views of clergy serving religious institutions having over 90 percent of Protestant church members in the suburban sector.

Comparative data on clergy views on aspects of religious institutional life, selected religious beliefs, personal and public morality, and social justice are discussed in the following sections of this chapter. Some of these data are compared with lay views in Part Three.

Jewish Clergy in the Suburban Sector

Reflecting the high standards of education required of all rabbis, the three rabbis interviewed were literate and learned men, deeply rooted in their theological and historical tradition. As the spiritual leaders of their congregations, they conducted worship services and supervised the educational programs of the synagogues. Classes in Hebrew and Jewish history were very important in the educational programs of all the synagogues.

Each rabbi interviewed displayed some anguish about the indifference and insensitivity of many people in their congregations to the spiritual values of their tradition. As subsequent data will show, this concern was based on fact, for Jewish lay people were the most "secular" of the lay people in any of the faith groups included in this study.

According to a Gallup Poll conducted in 1971, six out of ten rabbis under forty considered leaving their profession, compared with four out of ten Roman Catholic priests and Protestant ministers.[8] The findings reported here shed some light on the ethos contributing to this higher Jewish dissatisfaction, for the rabbi encounters greater skepticism and indifference among members of his congregation than his Catholic or Protestant counterparts.

In general, the interviewed rabbis overestimated somewhat the extent of the coherence between their own moral and religious values and those of their congregations.

All were very aware of the significant Jewish contributions in the quest for social justice in the United States; the rabbis had a clearer sense of the principles of liberty and equality and the contribution of contemporary Judaism to those principles than did Protestant or Roman Catholic clergy. Old Testament emphases and Christian injustices to Jews over the centuries have undoubtedly heightened Jewish sensitivity to the role of high religion in the quest for social justice.

At the same time, they commented on the increasing numbers of families in their congregations who had left Midwest City as blacks moved

into their neighborhoods. Such new families, they observed, were often
strongly anti-black, primarily because they felt blacks had forced them
out of their old neighborhoods.

The interviewed rabbis felt there would be increased rapprochement
and eventual merger of the Reform and Conservative branches of Judaism in
America, but they saw little likelihood of a merger with Orthodox Judaism
in the foreseeable future. All emphasized the distinctiveness of Judaism,
but they enthusiastically supported interfaith activities and were active
in local associations of religious professionals.

This interfaith involvement is consistent with an aspect of America's
public religion: interfaith pluralism, in which all religious groups seek
to attain harmonious relations with each other, is a goal to be sought.

In sum, the rabbis were articulate, sensitive, and highly educated
clergy, alert to their own heritage and its role in contemporary American
life. They were seeking to minister to the members of their congregations--
members who were more deeply attuned to the communal than to the theological
aspects of their tradition.

Protestant and Catholic Clergy in the Suburban Sector

Introduction

Leaders of churches and synagogues may not consider membership
recruitment, building maintenance, and financial management central to
their calling, but in the American context all clergy must pay some heed
to these matters. Churches and synagogues are both religious fellowships
and social institutions.[9]

In these circumstances, the religious professional seeks to foster
meaningful patterns of worship and education to sustain various age, sex,
and interest differentiated social groups, and to promote appropriate
social witness and public service. Since the members will participate
only in those things that interest them, the vast majority of churches
and synagogues in the suburban sector support a wide range of programs
and activities.

This section examines Protestant and Catholic clergy questionnaire
responses to profile their attitudes toward their work and their church
program, their relations with officials in ecclesiastical bureaucracies,
their sermonic emphases, and their religious and moral perspectives.

The Clergy and Their Churches

Clergy Attitudes toward Their Work

As Table IV-1 reveals, the large majority of religious professionals
in the suburban sector had favorable attitudes toward their work. Only

among Roman Catholic priests did anyone indicate unfavorable attitudes
toward their present parish work. Such attitudes are consonant with
other findings in this study and with many varieties of evidence indicating increasing job dissatisfaction among American priests.[10]

TABLE IV-1

CLERGY ATTITUDES TOWARD PRESENT PARISH WORK

BY SELECTED FAITH GROUPINGS IN PERCENT

Faith Groupings

Attitudes toward Present Parish Work	NCC-Affiliated Protestants N=35	Non-NCC-Affiliated White Protestants N=30	Black Protestants N=8	Roman Catholic N=22
Strongly favorable	46	47	88	18
Favorable	34	40	12	46
Mixed feelings	20	13	0	18
Unfavorable	0	0	0	9
Strongly unfavorable	0	0	0	9

The relatively greater freedom of clergy placement within Protestantism is reflected in these findings; Protestant clergy with negative
attitudes toward suburban parishes are freer to leave than Catholic clergy.
Furthermore, clergy attitudes become more positive over time. As Table
IV-2 indicates, most of the clergy reported either a more favorable inclination toward the parish work now than a few years ago or no change in
attitude. Less than one in five reported a less favorable attitude now,
partly because those feeling less favorable are more likely to leave.

About 90 percent of the clergy reported the majority of their
parishioners held "very favorable" or "favorable" attitudes toward them.
A small proportion (20 percent of NCC-affiliated Protestants, 10 percent
of non-NCC-affiliated white Protestants, 12 percent of black Protestants,
and 5 percent of Roman Catholics) reported they felt the majority of their
members had less favorable attitudes now than earlier. Not surprisingly,
no one reported a majority of members holding "unfavorable" or "very
unfavorable" attitudes toward them or their work. In light of the controversies at the national and regional levels about religious institutional
involvement in political issues, such shifts seem quite modest.[11]

TABLE IV-2

CHANGES IN CLERGY ATTITUDES TOWARD PARISH WORK

BY SELECTED FAITH GROUPINGS IN PERCENT

Faith Groupings

Change in Attitudes in Last Few Years	NCC-Affiliated Protestants N=35	Non-NCC-Affiliated White Protestants N=29	Black Protestants N=8	Roman Catholic N=22
More favorable now	40	31	75	41
Less favorable now	14	14	12	18
No change	46	55	12	41

Clergy Views of Church Activities

All the Catholic parishes and the vast majority of Protestant churches in the studied suburban sector sponsored a variety of programs and activities related to the various aspects of parish life--economic, political and administrative, educational, recreational, service, and worship. They usually had both lay and clergy participation.

The clergy questionnaire sought to assess clergy attitudes by seeking their views on nine different program areas, activities, or groups. Respondents were asked to express their feelings toward a particular area, group, or activity, ranging from "very favorable" at one extreme of a five-point scale to "very unfavorable" at the other extreme.

The activities, groups, or programs enumerated were: administrative and policy making groups, such as board of trustees, board of Christian education, board of social action, etc.; fund raising, such as bake sales, paper sales, etc.; experimental personal growth group, such as marathons, encounter groups, sensitivity groups, etc.; prayer and devotional groups; recreational and social groups, such as bridge groups, couples clubs, etc.; religious education, such as Bible study, adult education, etc.; service groups, such as deacons, deaconnesses, altar societies, etc.; social action groups, such as community education, peace groups, civil rights groups, etc.; and choir and liturgy groups.

Clergy in all groups were nearly unanimous in their support of groups supporting worship, education, and administrative activities.

At least 88 percent of the respondents in each clergy grouping reported "strongly favorable" or "favorable" feelings toward religious education and choir or liturgy activities. More than 70 percent of the respondents in each clergy grouping reported "strongly favorable" or "favorable" attitudes toward administrative and policy-making groups.

The vast majority of all the Protestant groups reported "strong favorable" or "favorable" feelings toward parish service groups. The percentages reporting "very favorable" or "favorable" attitudes toward devotional groups were as follows: Non-NCC affiliated white Protestant, 93 percent; NCC-affiliated Protestant, 77 percent; black Protestant, 62 percent; and Roman Catholic, 52 percent.

Such near-unanimity is not surprising, for any voluntary religious institution in contemporary America needs lay support in administrative, educational, service and choir and liturgical activities.

The predominantly adjustive and integrative stance of local clergy was reflected in their responses to this item. The only areas in which substantial proportions of clergy reported "unfavorable" or "very un-favorable" feelings were fund-raising, experimental personal growth groups, and social action groups.

The actual percentages reporting "unfavorable" or "very unfavorable" feelings on fund raising activities were: NCC-affiliated Protestants, 49 percent; non-NCC-affiliated white Protestants, 79 percent; black Protestants, 38 percent; Roman Catholic, 36 percent.

These responses reflect an "anti-institutional" bias and some uneasiness about the economic side of institutional life.

The other activities or groups about which more than 30 percent of the respondents of any clergy group reported unfavorable feelings were personal growth groups and social action. These distributions are shown in Tables IV-3 and IV-4.

TABLE IV-3

CLERGY ATTITUDES TOWARD PERSONAL GROWTH GROUPS IN LOCAL CHURCHES

BY SELECTED FAITH GROUPINGS IN PERCENT

Faith Groupings

Clergy Attitude	NCC-Affiliated Protestants N=35	Non-NCC-Affiliated White Protestants N=29	Black Protestants N=8	Roman Catholic N=21
Very favorable	6	3	0	14
Favorable	31	10	25	14
Mixed feelings	34	38	25	24
Unfavorable	17	17	0	29
Very unfavorable	6	21	0	10
No opinion	6	10	50	10

TABLE IV-4

CLERGY ATTITUDES TOWARD SOCIAL ACTION GROUPS IN LOCAL CHURCHES

BY SELECTED FAITH GROUPINGS IN PERCENT

Faith Groupings

Clergy Attitude	NCC-Affiliated Protestants N=35	Non-NCC-Affiliated White Protestants N=29	Black Protestants N=8	Roman Catholic N=22
Very favorable	29	14	25	32
Favorable	46	21	50	23
Mixed feelings	23	24	25	27
Unfavorable	3	17	0	14
Very unfavorable	0	24	0	4

As Table IV-3 reveals, there was wide spread clergy negativity toward church-sponsored personal growth groups. About 40 percent of the non-NCC-affiliated white Protestants and Roman Catholics had unfavorable feelings about personal growth groups. Half the black clergy had not heard of them. The bi-modal nature of this distribution, with substantial numbers supporting such groups and substantial numbers opposing them, reflects the general controversy about these groups.

It is revealing that more clergy had unfavorable feelings toward personal growth groups than toward social action groups. The fact that personal growth groups deal with interpersonal relations within the religious association is probably significant. Personal growth groups may alter social relations within the church, but social action groups usually deal with social service and social justice concerns beyond the parish. There was substantial opposition to social action groups only among non-NCC-affiliated white Protestant clergy, as Table IV-4 shows. About two-fifths of them expressed unfavorable feelings toward these groups. Such views cohere with the opposition to direct church involvement in the public sphere characteristic of many non-NCC-affiliated Protestant churches. The antipathy of non-NCC-affiliated white Protestant clergy for social action is further reflected in Table IV-5.

Respondents were asked to select the ways in which they thought local churches should relate to social, economic, and political issues. The responses, as Table IV-5 indicates, were categorized from "no response" to "high response." Five possible responses were enumerated:

1. Encourage individuals to form church discussion groups on public policy issues.

2. Take official stands on public policy issues.

3. Allow church facilities to be used by community action groups.

4. Encourage individuals to form unofficial church action groups.

5. Encourage individuals to participate in community action groups.

6. None of the above.

Response number 6 was categorized as "no response" in Table IV-5. Responses 1, 4, and 5 or any combination of them were categorized as "Low Response," response 3 (with or without any other except response 2) was coded "Medium Response" and response 2 with or without any other response was coded "High Response."

TABLE IV-5

CLERGY VIEWS OF PROPER RESPONSE OF LOCAL CHURCH TO SOCIAL ISSUES

FOR SELECTED FAITH GROUPINGS IN PERCENT

Faith Groupings

Clergy View	NCC-Affiliated Protestants N=35	Non-NCC-Affiliated White Protestants N=29	Black Protestants N=7	Roman Catholic N=21
No response	6	28	0	0
Low response	14	45	0	10
Medium response	54	17	14	5
High response	26	10	86	85

As Table IV-5 shows, non-NCC-affiliated white Protestants were strongly negative on church involvement in social, economic, and political issues. Almost three-fourths of them minimized direct church involvement in the public sphere.

At the other extreme, Roman Catholic priests and black Protestant clergy gave strong support to direct church involvement in the public sphere. The views of the black clergy cohere with the historic expectation that black clergy should "promote the race."[12]

The views of the Roman Catholic priests cohere with the historic involvement of the Catholic church in the public sphere when its clergy think matters of faith and morals are involved.

The NCC-affiliated Protestant clergy contrasted sharply with non-NCC-affiliated white Protestants. Though not as strongly supporting official stands on public policy issues as Roman Catholic priests or black clergy, they did support church involvement in the public sphere much more strongly than non-NCC-affiliated white Protestants.

Clergy attitudes toward position statements on issues of public policy advanced by denominational and interdenominational bodies were not as sharply distinguished as their attitudes toward local church involvement, but comparable patterns emerge. As Table IV-6 indicates, few clergy reported "very favorable" attitudes, but few reported "very unfavorable" attitudes.

TABLE IV-6

CLERGY ATTITUDES TOWARD POSITION STATEMENTS ON ISSUES OF PUBLIC

POLICY ADVANCED BY DENOMINATIONAL AND INTERDENOMINATIONAL BODIES

BY SELECTED FAITH GROUPINGS IN PERCENT

	Faith Groupings			
Clergy Attitude Toward Policy Statements	NCC-Affiliated Protestants N=34	Non-NCC-Affiliated White Protestants N=29	Black Protestants N=8	Roman Catholic N=20
Very favorable	6	0	0	5
Favorable	35	24	50	35
Mixed feelings	41	41	25	40
Unfavorable	9	10	12	10
Very unfavorable	6	17	0	10
No opinion (or no denomination)	3	7	12	0

NCC-affiliated Protestant, black Protestant, and Roman Catholic clergy
had a positive bias toward such statements, and non-NCC-affiliated white
clergy had a negative bias.

These data on clergy attitudes toward social action groups and
denominational pronouncements on public policy issues are considered
further in Chapter VIII.

Local Clergy Relations with Ecclesiastical Bureaucracies

In recent years, there has been a marked decline in the financial
support of ecclesiastical bureaucracies in many denominations. In addition,
largely lay-inspired critics of some church mission and social issue projects
have attracted attention.[13]

These facts and data to be discussed subsequently in Chapter VIII
suggest some lay hostility toward ecclesiastical bodies and officials. To
assess the extent to which such public events reflected clergy sentiments,
clergy were asked to express their attitudes toward their ecclesiastical
officials and to report any changes in attitudes over the past few years.

As Table IV-7 shows, most clergy in most groups were supportive of
the members of their ecclesiastical bureaucracies, but substantially more
NCC-affiliated Protestant clergy reported "mixed feelings" toward the
members of their ecclesiastical bureaucracies than clergy of any other group.

TABLE IV-7

CLERGY VIEWS TOWARD ECCLESIASTICAL OFFICIALS OF HIS CHURCH

BY SELECTED FAITH GROUPINGS IN PERCENT

	Faith Groupings			
Clergy Attitude	NCC-Affiliated Protestants N=35	Non-NCC-Affiliated White Protestants N=26	Black Protestants N=7	Roman Catholic
Very favorable	11	12	14	
Favorable	37	54	29	Comparable Data Not Available
Mixed feelings	46	19	29	
Unfavorable	0	8	0	
Very unfavorable	3	0	0	
No opinion (or no officials)	3	8	29	

The disenchantment of local clergy serving NCC-affiliated churches was
real and suggests continued restraint on regional and national budgets in
these groups. Trend data indicate that clergy have become increasingly
disaffected with ecclesiastical officials over time. Thirty-seven percent
of the NCC-affiliated Protestant clergy and 36 percent of the non-NCC-
affiliated white Protestant clergy reported less favorable attitudes toward
ecclesiastical officials now compared to a few years ago. In contrast,
only 20 percent of the NCC-affiliated Protestant clergy and 4 percent of
the non-NCC-affiliated white Protestant clergy reported more favorable
attitudes now.

In the early 1970's, denominational officials began to respond to
local pressure and disaffections by developing programs to support local
churches and down playing social action.

Sermonic Emphases

The most important single facet of the typical Protestant worship
service is the sermon. Though not as important in Catholicism, most priests
do offer a homily in the context of most public celebrations of the Mass.
It was not possible to examine the substance of sermons preached by clergy
in the suburban sector, but it was feasible to determine the degree of
emphasis on a range of sermon topics. Clergy were asked to indicate the
degree of emphasis on five topics: personal prayer life, theological
matters and explication of Scripture, familial and marital problems,
political and social issues, and business and job morality and ethics.

"Theological Matters and Explication of Scripture" was the only
topic on which all four groups had a majority of respondents reporting
"much emphasis." Eighty-three percent of non-NCC-affiliated white
Protestants, 75 percent of black Protestants, 68 percent of NCC-affiliated
Protestants, and 59 percent of the Catholic priests reported "much emphasis
on this topic.

The vast majority of the clergy also reported "much emphasis" or
"some emphasis" on direction in personal prayer life and discussions of
familial and marital problems. There were negligible differences between
the groups reporting "much emphasis" on familial and marital problems
(about one-third in all groups) and "some emphasis" (about 60 percent in
all groups).

The proportions of respondents reporting "much emphasis" on
providing direction for personal prayer life did highlight differences
in personal piety between the various faith groups. Sixty-three percent
of the black Protestants, 52 percent of the non-NCC-affiliated white
Protestants, 21 percent of the NCC-affiliated Protestants, and 18 percent
of the Roman Catholics reported "much emphasis" in sermons on direction in
personal prayer life.

Consonant with the lay expectation that black clergy should
"promote the race," 38 percent of the black Protestants reported they gave

"much emphasis" to political and social issues, compared to 18 percent
for Roman Catholics, 12 percent for NCC-affiliated Protestants, and 3
percent for non-NCC-affiliated white Protestants. A higher proportion
of respondents reported "little emphasis" or "no emphasis" on this topic
than on any other. Fifty-nine percent of the non-NCC-affiliated white
Protestants, 38 percent of the black Protestants, 36 percent of the Roman
Catholics, and 29 percent of NCC-affiliated Protestants so reported.

The personal pietism and the avoidance of "political" issues
among non-NCC-affiliated white Protestants was striking. The black
Protestants were pulled in opposite directions on this issue, reflected
in the bimodal distribution of their responses. On the one hand, their
rootage in forms of biblical fundamentalism and personal piety characteristic of facets of southern religion pushed some of them away from
theological reflection on public issues. Others (two of those reporting
"much emphasis" were NCC-affiliated Protestant clergy) were seeking to
address social and economic issues.

More than 75 percent of the respondents reported "much emphasis"
or "some emphasis" on business and job morality and ethics. For reasons
that are not evident, almost twice as many Roman Catholic priests (41
percent) as any other group reported "little emphasis" or "no emphasis"
on business and job morality and ethics.

Overall, all the clergy gave greater emphases to theological and
biblical interpretation, personal prayer life, and interpersonal morality
than to intergroup morality. The non-NCC-affiliated white Protestants
and black Protestants were distinguished by their strong emphasis on
personal prayer life and theological matters and explication of Scripture.
The non-NCC-affiliated white Protestants were also distinguished by their
relatively less emphasis on political and social issues; black Protestants
were distinguished by their polarization on this issue. (The small number
of black respondents suggests caution in interpreting this finding. Considering the likely orientations of those black clergy not included, the
proportion of black clergy giving "much emphasis" to political and social
issues was probably no higher than the other groups.)

Religious and Moral Perspectives of the Clergy

Introduction

Religious professionals are bearers of the meanings and feelings
of their particular religious traditions, for their training and full-time
involvement have sensitized them to their heritages in a special way.
Questionnaire data cannot probe the depths and complexity of religious
experience and theological understanding, but they can point to tendencies
and configurations, permitting one to discern major contrasts between
clergy in the four faith groupings.

Clergy response to five items in the questionnaire have been
selected to probe the religious and moral perspectives of the suburban

clergy: views on the Ten Commandments; the role of the church in enforcing standards of personal conduct; personal religious experience; the role of the church in offering peace and security; and attitudes toward Scripture.

Views of the Ten Commandments

Table IV-8 outlines the respondents' attitudes toward the statement "There are times when it might be all right to break one of the Ten Commandments."   This item obviously cannot probe the full complexity of the respondents' understandings of the "principled"-"contextualist" controversy in Christian social ethics, but it does illumine the general direction of clergy views in the various faith groupings.[14]

TABLE IV-8

CLERGY RESPONSES TO STATEMENT "THERE ARE TIMES WHEN IT MIGHT

BE ALL RIGHT TO BREAK ONE OF THE TEN COMMANDMENTS"

FOR SELECTED FAITH GROUPINGS IN PERCENT

Faith Groupings

Clergy Attitudes Toward Statement	NCC-Affiliated Protestants N=34	Non-NCC-Affiliated White Protestants N=29	Black Protestants N=7	Roman Catholic N=21
Strongly agree	12	3	14	0
Agree	24	7	14	5
Mixed feelings or depends on circumstances	26	14	14	14
Disagree	21	21	14	57
Strongly disagree	18	55	43	24

The contrasting responses to this item are striking.   The NCC-affiliated Protestant clergy group had far more respondents sustaining a "contextualist" social ethic than any other group.   (The two black clergy strongly agreeing or agreeing with the statement were clergy of NCC-affiliated churches.)

The Roman Catholic priests and the non-NCC-affiliated white Protestant clergy have very similar profiles.   In both instances, formal dimensions of experience are accentuated, and dynamic dimensions are minimized.

The distribution of the NCC-affiliated group is bimodal, reflecting diffuse and conflicting perspectives among the members of this group.

Views on Enforcement of Strict Standard of
Moral Conduct Among Church Members

Clergy views on the binding nature of the Ten Commandments are paralleled by their views on the church's role in enforcing a strict standard of personal conduct among its members.

Historically, the church in both its Protestant and Catholic forms has often sought to enforce specific standards of moral conduct among its members. The post-traditional character of American society has resulted in the weakening of many traditional norms, and this weakening is reflected in clergy expectations on moral codes among members.

As Table IV-9 shows, only among non-NCC-affiliated white Protestants and black Protestants did a majority of clergy think the church should enforce a strict standard of moral conduct among its members. The contextualist and non-principled stance of NCC-affiliated clergy was striking; only 6 percent of them thought the church should enforce a strict standard of moral conduct among its members.

TABLE IV-9

CLERGY ATTITUDES TOWARD STATEMENT "THE CHURCH SHOULD ENFORCE A

STRICT STANDARD OF MORAL CONDUCT AMONG ITS MEMBERS"

BY SELECTED FAITH GROUPINGS IN PERCENT

	Faith Groupings			
Clergy Attitudes Toward Statement	NCC-Affiliated Protestants N=33	Non-NCC-Affiliated White Protestants N=30	Black Protestants N=7	Roman Catholic N=22
Strongly agree	3	27	57	10
Agree	3	30	0	30
Mixed feelings or depends on circumstances	30	23	29	25
Disagree	46	17	14	15
Strongly disagree	18	3	0	15
No Opinion	0	0	0	5

These responses are undoubtedly conditioned by the views of lay people, for the diversity of moral values held by members of large suburban NCC-affiliated Protestant churches and families in suburban Catholic parishes make such enforcement impossible, even if desired.

The post-traditional nature of American society, as noted earlier, has resulted in fragmented social relations and limited informal means of social control. The separation of church and state has further weakened the possibility of church direction of lay morality, for the only way the church can exercise such control is by suasion.

Religious Experience of Clergy

Religious experience has always been considered a foundation of Christianity. It has been more important in Protestantism than in Roman Catholicism, for a corollary to the doctrine of justification by grace through faith, basic in most of Protestantism, is the notion that intellectual analysis cannot lead humans to an awareness of the Divine Presence.

In Roman Catholicism, the experiential dimension has been balanced with intellectual and cultic ones, for Catholicism has held that intellectual analysis may lead humans toward an understanding of God. The presence of the Divine in the Mass has an objectivist emphasis for which there is no strong counterpart in Protestantism.

The relative emphases on experience and on intellectual and objectivist factors in Protestantism and Roman Catholicism cohere with the responses to the question "As an adult, have you ever had a personal experience of the Divine Presence?" As Table IV-10 shows, the overwhelming majority of clergy in every faith grouping reported a personal experience of the Divine Presence, but the level of certitude was higher among Protestant clergy than among Catholic clergy.

Views on Church as Place of Peace and Security

For many, the church ought to be a place where one can go to find peace of mind and security. Both Protestantism and Catholicism have traditionally held that the church bears witness to God's Spiritual Presence. Though many churches have held that the substantial manifestation of the Divine is fragmentary and anticipatory under the conditions of existence, the churches have historically affirmed that the truly free are those who have experienced and are bound to the substantial presence of the Divine. In a profound way, such an experience of Spiritual Presence ought to provide a measure of security and peace of mind.

As Table IV-11 indicates most priests and most NCC-affiliated Protestant ministers affirmed this view in only a qualified way. The majority of non-NCC-affiliated white Protestant clergy and black clergy agreed. In part these distributions probably reflect rejection of a "pie in the sky by-and-by" view of peace and security. Nonetheless, it is certainly worth noting that only a minority of NCC-affiliated Protestant

TABLE IV-10

CLERGY RESPONSES TO QUESTION "AS AN ADULT, HAVE YOU EVER HAD A

PERSONAL EXPERIENCE OF THE DIVINE PRESENCE?"

BY SELECTED FAITH GROUPINGS IN PERCENT

Faith Groupings

Clergy Attitudes Toward Statement	NCC-Affiliated Protestants N=35	Non-NCC Affiliated White Protestants N=33	Black Protestants N=7	Roman Catholic N=19
I'm sure I have	86	88	86	42
I think I have	11	6	14	42
I don't think so	3	3	0	16
I'm sure I have not	0	3	0	0

TABLE IV-11

CLERGY ATTITUDES TOWARD STATEMENT "THE CHURCH SHOULD BE A PLACE

WHERE ONE CAN GO AND FIND PEACE OF MIND AND SECURITY"

BY SELECTED FAITH GROUPINGS IN PERCENT

Faith Groupings

Clergy Attitudes Toward Statement	NCC-Affiliated Protestants N=33	Non-NCC-Affiliated White Protestants N=29	Black Protestants N=7	Roman Catholic N=21
Strongly agree	9	34	86	14
Agree	18	28	0	33
Mixed feelings or depends on circumstances	43	17	14	29
Disagree	24	21	0	19
Strongly disagree	6	0	0	5

and Roman Catholic clergy affirmed this classical understanding. (As data on laity expectations subsequently will show, clergy and laity views on this issue contrasted sharply.)

Interpretations of the Bible

According to Roman Catholic understanding, the Christian tradition as interpreted by the Church is normative in matters of faith and morals. In Protestantism, two competing views of Scripture are predominant in the American scene.

According to one view, Scripture is literally true, not only bearing witness to God's revelation but also accurate in matters of physical and biological detail. Such views are associated with biblical fundamentalists in the United States. Concentrated in the South but present throughout all the country, members of such groups are often outspoken in their defense of the veracity of "The Word of God," usually identified with Scripture.

According to the other view, Scripture is interpreted as a vehicle through which God speaks, but its spiritual truth is not dependent on the veracity of its scientific world view.[15] The vast majority of clergy in such Protestant denominations as Episcopal, Lutheran Church in America, United Church of Christ, United Presbyterian, and United Methodist entertain this view.

The responses delineated in Table IV-12 reveal a broad grouping of responses in line with the perspectives on Scripture just outlined. Two-thirds of the non-NCC-affiliated white Protestant clergy were biblical literalists, and only 12 percent of the NCC-affiliated Protestant clergy were biblical literalists. This differential highlights the great contrast in theological understanding between these two Protestant groups. NCC-affiliated Protestants were biblically centered, for two-thirds of them felt the Bible was the most important way of knowing about God, but they rejected a literal interpretation.

A plurality of Roman Catholic priests responded that the Scripture is one of many equally important ways of knowing about God, and none responded that Scripture is literally true. This wording of the question was unfortunate, for it did not reflect sensitively Roman Catholic understanding of the role of tradition in the development of theological truth.

In spite of this inadequacy, the responses did reveal substantial differences between the major faith groupings. So far as the Bible is concerned, the contrast between priests and NCC-affiliated Protestant ministers seems less marked than the contrast between these groups and non-NCC-affiliated white Protestant clergy.

Due to the over-representation of NCC-affiliated black clergy in the sample, the data for black Protestant clergy certainly did not reflect

TABLE IV-12

CLERGY ATTITUDES TOWARD SCRIPTURE

BY SELECTED FAITH GROUPINGS IN PERCENT

Faith Groupings

Clergy Attitude Toward Statements	NCC-Affiliated Protestant N=34	Non-NCC Affiliated White Protestant N=31	Black Protestant N=8	Roman Catholic N=21
Scripture is literally true	12	68	50	0
Scripture is not literally true, but it is the most important way of knowing about God	65	13	12	38
Scripture is one of many equally important ways of knowing about God	21	6	38	48
Scripture is less important than other ways of knowing about God	0	0	0	0
Scripture is of very little importance	0	0	0	0
Other	3	13	0	14

the situation in the black churches as a whole, for all the non-NCC-affiliated black clergy were biblical literalists. As noted earlier, churches of this type constitute about 80 percent of the predominantly black churches in the sample area.

Contrasts in world views between Protestant biblical fundamentalists, classical Roman Catholics, and Protestant non-fundamentalists are striking. The first two views presuppose an authoritative statement of true theological propositions, but they differ on the locus of that authority. The latter view focuses on a foundational religious experience, but it refuses to make absolute particular propositional formulations related to that experience.

The Private Sphere:

Personal and Interpersonal Morality of the Clergy

Introduction

In order to relate general perspectives to particular issues, the clergy were asked their opinions about specific modes of behavior as well as about more general principles of morality. This section explores clergy attitudes about sexual and familial issues and about the consumption of alcoholic beverages. The latter item was selected because historically it has been a major issue of personal morality among many groups in American Protestantism.

Familial Values

The family items focus on areas of known historical and contemporary controversy: premarital sexual relations, extramarital sexual relations, divorce, and abortion. This area is one in which substantial shifts in norms and behavior have been developing in the past half-century. The post-traditional values sustaining the high technology of the American economic order have undercut or challenged traditional values in the family, particularly in premarital sexual relations, divorce, and abortion. The commitments and ambiguities shown by clergy about these values permit an assessment of the blending of traditional and post-traditional values among suburban clergy.

Clergy attitudes toward the statement, "It is wrong for people to have premarital sexual relations" are shown in Table IV-13. The majority of the clergy in each group agreed with the statement, but fewer of the NCC-affiliated Protestant clergy did so than in the other groups.

The vast majority of the clergy in each group agreed with the statement "It is wrong for married people to have sexual relations with persons other than their husbands and wives." The patterns were similar to those in Table IV-13, except for the overwhelming proportion of Roman Catholic priests (96 percent) who strongly agreed with the statement. The comparable percentages for the other groups were: NCC-affiliated Protestants, 65 percent "strongly agree," 18 percent "agree"; non-NCC-affiliated white Protestants, 83 percent "strongly agree," 10 percent "agree"; and black Protestants, 57 percent "strongly agree," 14 percent "agree." Nine percent of the NCC-affiliated Protestant clergy responded "depends on circumstances," reflecting the contextual ethical orientation mentioned earlier.

Non-NCC-affiliated white Protestant and Roman Catholic clergy were most opposed to divorce on moral grounds, as Table IV-14 shows. NCC-affiliated Protestants were sharply divided on this issue. About a quarter agreed that divorce is wrong, about a third disagreed, and about a third took a contextualist stance. The black Protestant distribution was similar to the NCC-affiliated Protestant group.

TABLE IV-13

CLERGY ATTITUDES TOWARD STATEMENT "IT IS WRONG FOR

PEOPLE TO HAVE PREMARITAL SEXUAL RELATIONS"

BY SELECTED FAITH GROUPINGS IN PERCENT

Faith Groupings

Clergy Attitudes Toward Statement	NCC-Affiliated Protestants N=34	Non-NCC-Affiliated White Protestants N=29	Black Protestants N=7	Roman Catholic N=22
Strongly agree	35	79	71	59
Agree	21	14	0	23
Mixed feelings or depends on circumstances	38	7	29	14
Disagree	3	0	0	0
Strongly disagree	3	0	0	4

TABLE IV-14

CLERGY ATTITUDES TOWARD STATEMENT "DIVORCE IS WRONG"

BY SELECTED FAITH GROUPINGS IN PERCENT

Faith Groupings

Clergy Attitudes Toward Statement	NCC-Affiliated Protestants N=33	Non-NCC-Affiliated White Protestants N=29	Black Protestants N=7	Roman Catholic N=21
Strongly agree	9	34	29	38
Agree	18	21	0	19
Mixed feelings	6	7	0	10
Disagree	15	7	14	10
Strongly disagree	18	0	29	0
Depends on circumstances	33	31	29	24

Probably the most controversial current issue in the area of familial values in America is abortion. Catholic and NCC-affiliated Protestant differences were sharper on this item than on any other in the study. As Table IV-15 indicates, 85 percent of the Roman Catholic priests agreed with the statement "It is wrong for a woman who wants an abortion in the first three months of pregnancy to have one," but only 18 percent of NCC-affiliated Protestants concurred with that statement. A majority (52 percent) of the non-NCC-affiliated white Protestant clergy agreed with the statement, and only 6 percent disagreed. Reflecting the nature of the black sample, black Protestants were split on the issue.

TABLE IV-15

CLERGY ATTITUDES TOWARD STATEMENT "IT IS WRONG FOR A WOMAN WHO WANTS AN

ABORTION IN THE FIRST THREE MONTHS OF PREGNANCY TO HAVE ONE"

BY SELECTED FAITH GROUPINGS IN PERCENT

Clergy Attitudes Toward Statement	Faith Groupings			
	NCC-Affiliated Protestants N=34	Non-NCC-Affiliated White Protestants N=29	Black Protestants N=7	Roman Catholic N=21
Strongly agree	15	35	29	76
Agree	3	17	14	10
Mixed feelings or depends on circumstances	41	41	14	5
Disagree	18	3	0	5
Strongly disagree	24	3	43	5

Consumption of Alcoholic Beverages

The final item selected to portray dimensions of personal morality focused on the consumption of alcoholic beverages. The piety and moralism associated with Puritanism and frontier evangelical Protestantism of the nineteenth and early twentieth century have left their marks on American Protestantism, for a moralistic motif is still widespread in the folk understanding of Protestant morality.

As Table IV-16 indicates, this expression of pietistic moralism was concentrated among non-NCC-affiliated white Protestant clergy and black clergy. About 60 percent of the respondents in these two groups agreed with the statement "drinking is wrong." Only 18 percent of the NCC-affiliated Protestant clergy and 9 percent of the Catholic clergy agreed with that statement. Over a third of the Catholic clergy gave a circumstantial response to this statement.

TABLE IV-16

CLERGY ATTITUDES TOWARD STATEMENT "DRINKING IS WRONG"

BY SELECTED FAITH GROUPINGS IN PERCENT

Faith Groupings

Clergy Attitudes Toward Statement	NCC-Affiliated Protestants N=34	Non-NCC-Affiliated White Protestants N=29	Black Protestants N=8	Roman Catholic N=22
Strongly agree	12	45	50	9
Agree	6	17	12	0
Mixed feelings or depends on circumstances	29	10	25	41
Disagree	32	21	12	27
Strongly disagree	21	7	0	23

Summary

        The overall pattern emerging from the analysis of the responses to the familial value items illumines the extent to which the clergy in the various faith groups supported traditional familial values. At one extreme, the Roman Catholic clergy were the most principled and traditional; at the other, NCC-affiliated Protestant clergy were most contextual and contemporary. The non-NCC-affiliated white Protestant clergy pattern was close to that of the Roman Catholic one; black Protestants were between this group and the NCC-affiliated Protestant clergy.

        The convergence between Catholic priests and non-NCC-affiliated white Protestant clergy on familial values was not apparent on the issues of the consumption of alcoholic beverages. Largely immune to this emphasis of American evangelicalism, Roman Catholic priests saw no moral issue directly involved in the consumption of alcoholic beverages.

        On this issue, the responses of NCC-affiliated Protestants and Roman Catholic priests paralleled each other. Moral objections to drinking are concentrated among non-NCC-affiliated white Protestants and black Protestants.

NCC-affiliated white Protestants generally take a more contextual and less principled approach to both familial values and drinking; non-NCC-affiliated white Protestant clergy are more principled and moralistic on both issues. Roman Catholic priests, cohering with their church's teachings and traditions, take a strong principled and supportive moralistic stance toward traditional familial values and a circumstantial approach to drinking.

The Public Spheres:

Social and Intergroup Morality of the Clergy

Introduction

Clergy are concerned with intergroup morality as well as with interpersonal morality. Clergy attitudes toward selected social issues and toward structures of American society are profiled here. Since these interests reflect themselves through political parties in the United States, clergy political preferences are also profiled.

Clergy Views on Selected Social Issues

To highlight differences and commonalities between the various groups being examined here, items dealing with each of the trilogy of social issues persistent in American life and its religious institutions-- race, poverty, and war--are discussed in this section. The items are concrete and specific. A fourth item dealing with an emergent controversy-- the legalization of the sale of marijuana--is also discussed. This item was selected to profile the groups within religious institutions on the innovative and conserving sides of a controversial legal and political issue. The final issue discussed focuses on church-state relationships, the use of government monies to help fund church-sponsored schools.

As Table IV-17 shows, the overwhelming majority of NCC-affiliated Protestant clergy, black Protestant clergy, and Roman Catholic clergy believed the suburbs should be racially integrated. The non-NCC-affiliated white Protestant clergy were less clear on this matter. Only 17 percent disagreed with the statement, but more than one-third of the respondents in this group indicated "mixed feelings," "depends on circumstances" or "no opinion."

Comparable patterns emerged on the poverty item, "Able-bodied welfare recipients should be put to work," except for the fact that the small black sample had the highest proportion of respondents strongly agreeing with the statement. As Table IV-18 shows, 90 percent of the

TABLE IV-17

CLERGY ATTITUDES TOWARD STATEMENT

"THE SUBURBS SHOULD BE RACIALLY INTEGRATED"

BY SELECTED FAITH GROUPINGS IN PERCENT

Faith Groupings

Clergy Attitudes Toward Statement	NCC-Affiliated Protestants N=34	Non-NCC-Affiliated White Protestants N=29	Black Protestants N=7	Roman Catholic N=22
Strongly agree	38	17	86	36
Agree	53	31	0	41
Mixed feelings or depends on circumstances	6	21	14	18
Disagree	0	10	0	4
Strongly disagree	3	7	0	0
No opinion	0	3	0	0

TABLE IV-18

CLERGY ATTITUDES TOWARD STATEMENT

"ABLE-BODIED WELFARE RECIPIENTS SHOULD BE PUT TO WORK"

BY SELECTED FAITH GROUPINGS IN PERCENT

Faith Groupings

Clergy Attitudes Toward Statement	NCC-Affiliated Protestants N=31	Non-NCC-Affiliated White Protestants N=29	Black Protestants N=7	Roman Catholic N=22
Strongly agree	16	45	71	18
Agree	39	45	0	54
Mixed feelings or depends on circumstances	42	7	14	27
Disagree	3	0	0	0
Strongly disagree	0	3	14	0

non-NCC-affiliated white Protestants agreed with the statement. The majority of the respondents in all the faith groupings concurred with the statement, but NCC-affiliated Protestant and Roman Catholic clergy had the highest proportions responding "depends on circumstances."

Though the non-NCC-affiliated white Protestant clergy were least responsive to suburban racial integration and most insistent on work by able-bodied welfare recipients, a majority or plurality of clergy in each faith grouping agreed with both statements. Responses to the item dealing with war did not follow this pattern.

As Table IV-19 shows, in the NCC-affiliated Protestant and black Protestant clergy faith groupings the majority of the respondents agreed with the statement "American involvement in the Vietnam War has been immoral." A substantial minority of Roman Catholic priests agreed (37 percent), but only 10 percent of the non-NCC-affiliated white Protestant clergy agreed. They were the only group in which a large minority (42 percent) disagreed with the statement.

TABLE IV-19

CLERGY ATTITUDES TOWARD STATEMENT

"AMERICAN INVOLVEMENT IN THE VIETNAM WAR HAS BEEN IMMORAL"

BY SELECTED FAITH GROUPINGS IN PERCENT

Faith Groupings

Clergy Attitudes Toward Statement	NCC-Affiliated Protestants N=34	Non-NCC-Affiliated White Protestants N=29	Black Protestants N=7	Roman Catholic N=22
Strongly agree	41	7	57	14
Agree	32	3	0	23
Mixed feelings or depends on circumstances	9	38	14	41
Disagree	6	21	14	9
Strongly disagree	6	21	0	9
No opinion	6	10	14	4

As Table IV-20 indicates, no faith group had a majority of respondents supporting the legalization of the sale of marijuana. Catholic priests seemed to be most receptive to the idea, but only 13 percent of them supported legalization. Non-NCC-affiliated white Protestants were least receptive.

Most groups were neutral to negative on the idea. Certainly, no group was
in the vanguard of those advocating legalization.

TABLE IV-20

CLERGY ATTITUDES TOWARD STATEMENT

"THE SALE OF MARIJUANA SHOULD BE LEGALIZED"

BY SELECTED FAITH GROUPINGS IN PERCENT

Faith Groupings

Clergy Attitudes Toward Statement	NCC-Affiliated Protestants N=34	Non-NCC-Affiliated White Protestants N=29	Black Protestants N=7	Roman Catholic N=22
Strongly agree	0	0	0	4
Agree	24	10	29	9
Mixed feelings or depends on circumstances	15	17	28	32
Disagree	32	7	14	23
Strongly disagree	26	62	29	18
No opinion	3	3	0	13

Protestant-Catholic contrasts were very sharply drawn on the issue
of government financial aid to church-sponsored schools, as Table IV-21
shows. Seventy-three percent of the Catholic priests agreed with the statement "The government should give money to church-sponsored schools," but
less than 10 percent of the Protestant clergy agreed. The black Protestant
clergy were more ambivalent than the white Protestant clergy, possibly
reflecting the fact that the government had given nursery school grants to
some of these black churches. Consistent with previously considered patterns, NCC-affiliated Protestant clergy were less adamant in their opposition than non-NCC-affiliated white Protestants. In this instance, however,
very substantial majorities of both groups opposed the use of government
monies to fund church-sponsored schools.

TABLE IV-21

CLERGY ATTITUDES TOWARD STATEMENT

"THE GOVERNMENT SHOULD GIVE MONEY TO CHURCH-SPONSORED SCHOOLS"

BY SELECTED FAITH GROUPINGS IN PERCENT

	Faith Groupings			
Clergy Attitudes Toward Statement	NCC-Affiliated Protestants N=34	Non-NCC-Affiliated White Protestants N=29	Black Protestants N=7	Roman Catholic N=22
Strongly agree	3	0	14	32
Agree	9	0	14	41
Mixed feelings or depends on circumstances	29	14	57	9
Disagree	21	21	0	9
Strongly disagree	32	66	14	5
No opinion	6	0	0	4

Attitudes Toward Structures of American Society

Introduction

Data drawn from several broad questions designed to explore the respondent's general stance toward the major structures of American society are examined here. The following areas are considered: attitudes toward America's future and the direction of change in the past few years; attitudes toward the American economic system; attitudes toward America's political system; and attitudes toward the principle of separation of church and state.

Views of America's Future

Clergy views of America's future are shown in Table IV-22. The clergy in those groups most central in American society, NCC-affiliated Protestant and Roman Catholic clergy, had majorities expressing some optimism about America's future. Black clergy, whose constituents have been marginal in American society, and non-NCC-affiliated white Protestant clergy, some of whom lament a decline in morals and some of whom have an apocalyptic pessimism about the future of the world in general, had the highest proportion of respondents pessimistic about America's future.

TABLE IV-22

CLERGY VIEWS OF AMERICA'S FUTURE

BY SELECTED FAITH GROUPINGS IN PERCENT

Faith Groupings

Clergy View	NCC-Affiliated Protestants N=33	Non-NCC-Affiliated White Protestants N=29	Black Protestants N=8	Roman Catholic N=22
Very optimistic	6	3	0	14
Somewhat optimistic	48	31	25	46
Mixed feelings or confused and uncertain	36	34	50	36
Somewhat pessimistic	9	21	25	4
Very pessimistic	0	10	0	0

Over the past few years a higher proportion of clergy have become less optimistic about America's future than have become more optimistic. About half reported they were less optimistic now, and only about 10 percent reported they were more optimistic now. Clearly, the events of the past decade have disturbed the clergy's confidence in the American future. However, as Table IV-22 indicates, less than 10 percent of the NCC-affiliated Protestant clergy and Roman Catholic clergy held a pessimistic view toward America's future. Somewhat shaken by the events of the past decade, the bulk of the clergy still had a relatively positive view of America's future.

Broad View of American Political and Economic
Systems and Principles of Church-State Separation

Three items in the clergy questionnaire explored the respondents' broad feelings about America's political and economic systems and the principle of church-state separation, a central doctrine of the religion of America. These items obviously did not permit respondents to give reasoned specific affirmations or critiques of American society, but they did permit an assessment of the "feeling tone" of the respondents toward the broad structures of American society.

Tables IV-23, IV-24 and IV-25 portray the responses of clergy toward these three areas. The statements were worded so that mild critics of the American social order could be expected to respond "mixed feeling" and stronger critics could be expected to respond "disagree" or "strongly disagree."

As Table IV-23 indicated, only the non-NCC-affiliated white Protestants gave reasonably strong support to the statement "Our present economic system is the best form of economic organization." Fifty-eight percent of the respondents in this faith grouping agreed with this statement, compared with 23 percent of the Roman Catholic clergy, 15 percent of the NCC-affiliated Protestants, and 14 percent of the black Protestants.

TABLE IV-23

CLERGY ATTITUDES TOWARD STATEMENT

"OUR PRESENT ECONOMIC SYSTEM IS THE BEST FORM OF ECONOMIC ORGANIZATION"

BY SELECTED FAITH GROUPINGS IN PERCENT

Faith Groupings

Clergy Attitudes Toward Statement	NCC-Affiliated Protestants N=34	Non-NCC-Affiliated White Protestants N=29	Black Protestants N=7	Roman Catholic N=22
Strongly agree	6	10	14	0
Agree	9	48	0	23
Mixed feelings or depends on circumstances	62	28	57	41
Disagree	9	10	14	18
Strongly disagree	6	7	14	4
Don't know	9	3	0	14

The evidence suggests the vast majority of the other clergy were "moderates," envisaging reform rather than radical change, for only a tiny minority "strongly disagree" with the statement.

The clergy were relatively more supportive of the American political system, as Table IV-24 reveals. In this instance, nonetheless, only the non-NCC-affiliated white Protestant clergy had a majority of respondents agreeing with the statement "Our present political system is the best form of political organization." None of these respondents disagreed with the statement.

TABLE IV-24

CLERGY ATTITUDES TOWARD STATEMENT

"OUR PRESENT POLITICAL SYSTEM IS THE BEST FORM OF POLITICAL ORGANIZATION"

BY SELECTED FAITH GROUPINGS IN PERCENT

	Faith Groupings			
Clergy Attitudes Toward Statement	NCC-Affiliated Protestants N=34	Non-NCC-Affiliated White Protestants N=29	Black Protestants N=7	Roman Catholic N=22
Strongly agree	0	14	14	4
Agree	26	45	29	36
Mixed feelings or depends on circumstances	47	38	28	14
Disagree	18	0	29	18
Strongly disagree	6	0	0	9
No opinion	3	3	0	18

About a quarter of the NCC-affiliated Protestant, black Protestant, and Roman Catholic clergy disagreed with the statement, but only a tiny proportion strongly disagreed. Such a pattern again indicates the predominance of societal "reformists" among the suburban clergy.

As Table IV-25 indicates, the overwhelming majority of all clergy groups shared the core societal value of separation of church and state. As noted earlier, this common affirmation, an important aspect of the religion of America, is critical for the survival of religious liberty, religious tolerance, and religious pluralism in the American context.

Clergy ambivalence about the meaning of separation of church and state is probably reflected in the preponderance of "agree" responses over "strongly agree" responses. As the data reported earlier on the use of government monies to help support church-sponsored schools indicate, not all respondents interpret state neutrality in the same way. In spite of this ambiguity of interpretation, the strong clergy support of this principle points to one area in which these clergy groups, diverse in many areas, can speak with one voice.

TABLE IV-25

CLERGY ATTITUDES TOWARD STATEMENT

"THE GOVERNMENT SHOULD BE NEUTRAL TOWARD RELIGIOUS INSTITUTIONS"

BY SELECTED FAITH GROUPINGS IN PERCENT

Faith Groupings

Clergy Attitudes Toward Statement	NCC-Affiliated Protestants N=33	Non-NCC-Affiliated White Protestants N=29	Black Protestants N=7	Roman Catholic N=22
Strongly agree	24	31	71	27
Agree	61	55	29	50
Mixed feelings or depends on circumstances	6	10	0	9
Disagree	6	3	0	14
Strongly disagree	0	0	0	0
Don't Know	3	0	0	0

Summary

In almost all of the areas explored in this section, NCC-affiliated white Protestant clergy and Roman Catholic clergy expressed views at variance with the views of their lay people, as data in Part III will show.[16] This contrast in perspectives results in some conflict in the minds of the clergy, for their understanding--often more implicit than explicit--of the implications of the Christian faith in the public realm differs from that of their lay people.

A substantial contrast exists between non-NCC-affiliated Protestant clergy and the other clergy on most items. This theologically conservative group is also conservative socially and politically.

Political Preference of Clergy

Though there is not a one-to-one relationship between societal value orientations and political parties in the United States, a crude pattern of relations does exist. In the main, the Republican party has

more participants seeking to conserve existing forms of social and economic
organization and the Democratic party has more participants seeking to
reform or transform existing forms.

As Table IV-26 indicates, the political preferences of the members
of the various faith groupings cohered with the societal value orientations delineated in Tables IV-23 and IV-24. The overwhelming majority of
priests and black Protestant clergy and a plurality of NCC-affiliated
Protestant clergy indicated a preference for or an inclination toward the
Democratic party. The only clergy grouping in which the majority of
respondents indicated a preference for or an inclination toward the
Republican party was the non-NCC-affiliated white Protestant group.

TABLE IV-26

POLITICAL PREFERENCE OF CLERGY

BY SELECTED FAITH GROUPINGS IN PERCENT

Faith Groupings

Political Preference	NCC-Affiliated Protestants N=34	Non-NCC-Affiliated White Protestants N=29	Black Protestants N=8	Roman Catholic N=21
Democrat	9	3	38	19
Independent leaning toward Democrats	35	14	38	62
Strictly independent	15	14	12	10
Independent leaning toward Republicans	29	31	0	0
Republican	3	31	0	5
No political preference or other	9	3	12	5
American Independent Party (Wallace)	0	3	0	0

In light of the rootage of many non-NCC-affiliated white Protestant
groups in the South, the preponderance of clergy with Republican party
inclinations among this group is especially interesting. It is highly
likely that participants in such groups outside the South find the Republican party more congenial than the Democratic party, for its less
activist role for the government fits the view that the church should not
deal directly in the public realm. Such a conjectural interpretation of

these data is consistent with the known conservatism of the southern
segment of the Democratic party and its frequent rapprochement with the
national Republican party. Some non-NCC-affiliated white Protestant
groups have also risen in the agrarian sections of the Midwest, traditionally a politically conservative area. In such an ethos, more conserving views of the economic and political systems may have influenced
those clergy.

Summary of Clergy Findings

The majority of the respondents in all four clergy groups were
relatively well-satisfied in their parish work. They all affirmed foundational religious experiences, were favorably inclined toward most of the
group activities involved in the life of the parish, were moderately
supportive of ecclesiastical bureaucracies, and accepted the core integrative value of government neutrality in the religious sphere.

The clergy were critical of some aspects of American life, but
they were moderately supportive of existing forms of economic and social
organization. In general, they were more critical of the economic order
than of the political order. The black clergy were most critical, and
the non-NCC-affiliated white clergy were most supportive.

Within Protestantism, there was a major contrast between clergy
who served churches affiliated with the National Council of Churches and
clergy who served white churches not affiliated with the National Council
of Churches. The NCC-affiliated clergy group had many fewer biblical
literalists. They were less moralistic, less evangelical, more critical
of existing American social, economic, and political institutions, and
more likely to prefer the Democratic political party than non-NCC-
affiliated white Protestant clergy. The latter group combined theological
and social conservatism.

Reflecting common historical roots, the majority of both black
Protestants and non-NCC-affiliated white Protestants were biblical
literalists. The black clergy were much more willing to promote directly
social, economic, and political causes than the non-NCC-affiliated white
Protestants. In this area, the black Protestants had more in common with
NCC-affiliated Protestants.

Both Roman Catholic priests and the non-NCC-affiliated white
clergy were strongly supportive of traditional family values and a principled social ethic. This predominance of formal components gave them both
a conserving bias. In the case of the Catholic group, the church and
its tradition was the explicit locus of authority; in the case of the
non-NCC-affiliated white Protestant clergy, the Bible was the explicit
locus.

Even though these two groups resembled each other in some ways,
there were major differences between them. The Roman Catholic priests

were better educated, less moralistic in many ways, more attuned to major currents in the broader culture, and associated with much larger local religious institutions.

All the Protestant groups differed sharply with Catholic priests on the issue of the use of public funds to support church sponsored schools and on the question of the morality of abortion in the first trimester.

In general, NCC-affiliated Protestant clergy were less formalistic on issues of personal and social morality than clergy in any other group. They were more critical of the Vietnam war, more supportive of racial integration of the suburbs, more critical of existing forms of economic and political organization in the United States, more permissive on premarital sexual relations, and more supportive of first trimester abortion than clergy in any other group.

CHAPTER V

TRENDS IN SUBURBAN INSTITUTIONAL RELIGIOUS LIFE:

VOLUNTARYISM, MEANING, AGE COHORTS, AND THE FAMILY LIFE CYCLE

Introduction

From the time of the founding of the Republic until the latter part of the 1950's, a steadily increasing proportion of the American population associated with religious institutions.[1] Since that time these long-term trends have been modified, for decreasing proportions of Catholics and Jews have been attending divine services. In Protestantism, the situation has been diffuse; some Protestant groups have been gaining in membership, others have been about stable, and some have been losing slightly in membership.

Observers differ in their interpretations of this situation. Some have stressed the continuity of belief and behavior, projecting modest changes in the coming decades.[2] Others have envisioned an emerging age of secularity, in which people radically alter their beliefs, and religious institutions atrophy[3] and/or become marginal to American society. Still others discern the selective growth of some groups and interest themselves in the emergence of new and sometimes esoteric movements.[4]

The murkiness of religious membership statistics, the dynamic dimension of religious experience, the high social and geographical mobility of the American people, the pervasiveness of the public religion of America, the voluntary nature of religious associations in America, and the changing age composition of the American population combine to make projections hazardous. Nonetheless, religious leaders making policy decisions that affect the shape of religious institutional life in the future must seek to assess current and projected trends.

The discussions developed in this chapter seek to contribute to an assessment of these trends. The data suggest modest declines in suburban Protestantism in the past decade--largely related to changes in the family life cycle--and more substantial declines in Catholicism and Judaism. The long-term increase in the proportion of the American population joining religious institutions is probably at an end, but there is little reason to anticipate a substantial decline in the proportion of the American population affiliating with religious institutions. Indeed, substantial increases in the absolute number of members of churches and probably of synagogues are likely in the coming two decades, for the large number of

post-World War II babies will be moving into the period of family formation
and child-rearing. Unless all past patterns are changed, people in this
stage of the family life cycle are most likely to affiliate with religious
institutions, for they want their children to receive some religious
instruction. In the voluntary church and synagogue, members affiliate
and disaffiliate at will. The high mobility of suburbia facilitates this
process, for social pressures to maintain church or synagogue membership
are minimized when disaffiliation is accompanied by a geographical move.

Emerging Religious Movements in the Suburban Sector

Emerging religious movements are necessarily difficult to identify
and to assess, for by their very nature they are amorphous and relatively
inchoate. They are likely to develop in subcultural groups that are not
very widespread in American suburbs, that is, in specialized communities
in the metropolitan area. The leaders initiating such movements generally
attract coteries of followers in areas with higher proportions of young
adults than are found in the American suburbs. Among upper and upper
middle status groups, religiously-based communes and house churches illustrate such movements. Among lower middle and lower status groups, "Jesus
people" and emergent fundamentalist sectarians are illustrative.

The broad significance of such emerging movements is apt to be
overemphasized by persons in theological institutions, for seminaries also
deal with and are populated by young adults. Similarly, persons in
positions of innovative leadership in ecclesiastical bureaucracies are
apt to overestimate the importance of novel programming and new styles of
religious life, for they are promoters as well as evaluators. Unless
innovations have broad support throughout an institution, such as the
reforms initiated in the Roman Catholic Church by Vatican II, their impact
on local religious institutions is diffuse and problematic.

For example, in spite of the widespread interest in many Protestant
theological schools in the human potential movement and the various group
activities associated with it, such as encounter groups, sensitivity training
groups, and house churches, it had had only minimal direct appropriation
in the suburban religious institutions studied here. Only a tiny minority
of lay people had ever been involved in any program directly informed by
the movement.

Such minimal direct impact must be balanced by the indirect influence
of innovative efforts, for in a qualified and modified way some novel ideas
and practices diffuse throughout the component parts of a religious subculture. Pastoral counseling, clinical education, and contemporary worship,
now commonplace in the life of religious institutions, were in their day
looked upon by many as esoteric and whimsical.

Aside from the Young Life Movement (which actually emerged more
than a decade ago) and the Jesus movement, attracting a small proportion
of the young people in the area, there was little visible evidence of
emerging new forms of religious expression independent of existing religious

institutions in the suburban area studied here.   Even these movements have
ties with some established denominational or interdenominational groups.

The Young Life Movement and the Jesus movement were concentrated
primarily among junior high and high school age young people. One know-
ledgeable high school administrator estimated that at the very most only
5 percent of the high school students in the study area were involved in
any way with the Young Life Movement and not more than one or two percent
were involved in the Jesus movement. The relatively higher Young Life
involvement was largely the result of participation by high school students
in very inexpensive weekend recreational trips sponsored by Young Life.

In both instances, the groups had some relations with local churches.
The Jesus movement people related primarily to non-NCC-affiliated conserva-
tive Protestant churches, and the Young Life group to NCC-affiliated
Protestant churches.

Some of the churches and synagogues, particularly in upper middle
status Sylvan Retreat and New Town and in upper status Country Club Estates,
were experimenting with novel forms of religious expression and of service.
In all these instances the emerging and experimental forms were fostered
by established institutions. Without institutional support, new forms of
religious expression and service are evanescent; they either die or they
eventually develop institutional support.[5]

Clergy Assessment of Trends of Institutional Religious Life

Table V-1 summarizes the trend reported by clergymen serving the
churches in the suburban sector. In the main, the trends were toward decline
in most facets of the churches' program. The one major exception was counseling by Protestant clergy. The proportion of NCC-affiliated Protestant
clergy reporting a decline in attendance at Sunday services was especially
high.

Consistent with the national picture, a higher proportion of Catholic
priests reported declines in all activities except public worship. Data
presented in Part III will explore this situation in more detail.

Part of the decline in involvement in all faith groups can be
attributed to the changing age composition of the American population,
for the under fifteen population has been decreasing for almost a decade.
During the same period, the fifteen to twenty-nine age group has been
expanding sharply and the thirty-five to forty-nine age group has been
contracting.

In the American context, parents of preteen age children are disproportionately involved in Christian education activities in local religious
institutions. As this age group contracts, the number of participants
necessarily declines.

TABLE V-1   TRENDS IN FACETS OF CHURCH LIFE BY SELECTED FAITH GROUPINGS IN PERCENT

Facet of Church Life	NCC-Affiliated Protestants N=33				Non-NCC-Affiliated White Protestants N=29				Black Protestants N=8				Roman Catholic N=22			
	Yes	Perhaps	No	DK	Yes	Perhaps	No	DK	Yes	Perhaps	No	DK	Yes	Perhaps	No	DK
Decline in involvement of young people	27	21	46	6	21	17	62	0	0	38	50	12	59	18	23	0
Decline in attendance at Sunday worship	73	15	12	0	31	21	48	0	12	12	62	12	32	27	36	4
Growing disenchantment among members with church renewal efforts*	21	46	27	6	26	30	37	7	12	12	25	50	27	41	18	14
Decline in adult participation in church activities	27	18	54	0	28	24	48	0	38	38	25	0	50	18	32	0
Fewer people coming to clergyman for advice and consultation	9	9	76	6	7	14	79	0	12	0	88	0	54	14	27	4

*For Non-NCC-Affiliated White Protestants, N=27 for this item.

It appears that ideological alienation plays a less significant role in the decline of lay participation in American Protestantism than in the decline of lay participation in American Catholicism.

Interesting differences emerged between NCC-affiliated Protestant churches and non-NCC-affiliated Protestant churches. Forty percent of the NCC-affiliated churches reported increases in membership in the past five years, and 62 percent reported increases in budget. The comparable figures for non-NCC-affiliated churches were 64 percent and 77 percent.

These data suggest the more rapid growth of conservative churches in the suburban sector, but such an interpretation must be qualified.

First of all, membership statistics can be very unreliable. In churches with strong outside denominational ties, which tend to be NCC-affiliated churches, various assessments may be levied on the local church based on its claimed membership. Such assessments encourage pastors to cull the deadwood from their membership roles.

Second, non-NCC-affiliated churches are considerably smaller than NCC-affiliated churches. Fifty-seven percent of the non-NCC-affiliated churches had fewer than 250 members, compared with 18 percent of the NCC-affiliated churches. Substantial percentage increases are easier to come by when the population base is smaller. This phenomenon is probably related to a firmer insistence on orthodoxy as the group defines it among non-NCC-affiliated churches, for in the voluntary church it is easier to obtain doctrinal consensus in a small church than in a large one.

Third, the non-NCC-affiliated churches have substantially more blue collar workers in their memberships than white collar workers.[6] Blue collar workers tend to be less mobile than white collar workers and to form families somewhat earlier. These social factors encourage involvement in church activities at a somewhat earlier age. An economic factor is probably also at work, for more blue collar workers can now afford the contributions expected of members of the voluntary church than in earlier times.

Finally, the ecological succession discussed in Chapter III contributes to the relative picture of strength of non-NCC-affiliated Protestant churches in this sample, for declining non-NCC-affiliated white Protestant churches are not found primarily in the suburbs but within Midwest City near the edge of the expanding ghetto. The lower status suburbs next to Midwest City contain the declining NCC-affiliated churches, for their higher status members are moving farther out.

This interpretation does not preclude somewhat more rapid growth of non-NCC-affiliated white Protestant churches, but it does suggest that the more publicized claims of conservative church growth are exaggerated.

Trends in Lay Participation

As noted earlier, participation in religious institutions in the United States has tended to decrease since the late 1950's. Since 1964, the falloff has been largely among Catholics. In this faith group, the decline is concentrated among those in their young adult years. According to Gallup poll data, the overall percent of adults attending religious institutions in 1970 was 42 percent. For Protestants the rate was 38 percent, having remained fairly constant since 1964. For Catholics, the rate was 60 percent, compared to 71 percent in 1964.

Not surprisingly, participation rates among the suburban sample were uniformly higher than the national averages, as Table V-2 indicates. The Gallup data cited earlier were based on interviews with a random sample of the U.S. population, and the data reported here are based on the voluntary responses of members who have chosen to belong to a particular religious institution. Nonetheless, the trends and patterns within and between these groups can be used to illumine the general patterns, for these lay people are also responding to the general cultural ethos.

The only striking finding in Table V-2 is the extremely high proportion of Catholics in upper status Country Club Estates who attended Mass at least every week. Consistent with the findings of other studies, increased socioeconomic status of Catholics was positively correlated with church participation.[7]

The trend data shown in Tables V-3, V-4, and V-5 reveal somewhat conflicting patterns. All groups had higher proportions of respondents reporting less frequent attendance at worship services (see Table V-3) and less frequent participation in religious activities and programs (see Table V-4). At the same time substantially more respondents indicated they had increased their contributions than indicated they had reduced them. Data on the budgets of the religious institutions showed the majority had increases in the past five years, but they were nominal when adjusted for the effects of inflation during the same period.

Overall, these findings suggest modest declines in institutional involvement by the members of these suburban religious institutions over the past five years. Among these groups, Catholic declines have been less than those of Protestants or Jews. The relatively high proportion of Jews reporting declines is related to the substantial number of young adults in the Jewish sample.

Since these findings are contrary to nationwide patterns, a conjectural interpretation is required. It seems plausible to assume more nominal Catholics than nominal Protestants drop out of their church rather than remain on the church rolls, for Protestants are not under the moral obligation to attend church as Catholics are to attend Mass. It is also possible higher proportions of nominal Catholics failed to respond because of the guilt associated with failure to attend Mass regularly. Finally,

TABLE V-2

FREQUENCY OF ATTENDANCE

IN PERCENT BY COMMUNITY FOR SELECTED RELIGIOUS GROUPS

Community

Frequency of Attendance	Satellite City			New Town		Country Club Estates		
	Black Protestant	White Protestant	Catholic	White Protestant	Catholic	White Protestant	Catholic	Jewish
Almost every week or more	40	48	60	35	68	43	86	6
About two or three times a month	26	18	12	21	7	25	2	11
About once a month	19	11	10	17	6	10	3	21
About two or three times a year	9	13	7	18	6	14	5	52
Almost never	6	10	11	8	12	8	3	10
N=	65	183	148	268	200	218	204	124

Chi square = 397.09180   p<0.001

Coefficient of Contingency = 0.46902

TABLE V-3

WORSHIP ATTENDANCE NOW vs FIVE YEARS AGO

IN PERCENT BY COMMUNITY FOR SELECTED RELIGIOUS GROUPS

| | Community | | | | | | | |
| | Satellite City | | | New Town | | Country Club Estates | | |
Worship Attendance vs Five Years Ago	Black Protestant	White Protestant	Catholic	White Protestant	Catholic	White Protestant	Catholic	Jewish
More or much more now*	28	17	17	14	9	23	14	18
About same	41	52	60	47	63	44	71	44
Less now	25	18	10	19	12	16	8	22
Much less now	6	13	13	20	16	18	8	16
N=	64	185	148	269	199	217	204	123

*Separated in statistical tests

Chi square = 105.04327   p<0.001

Coefficient of Contingency = 0.26349

TABLE V-4

ATTENDANCE AT RELIGIOUS ACTIVITIES AND PROGRAMS NOW vs FIVE YEARS AGO
IN PERCENT BY COMMUNITY FOR SELECTED RELIGIOUS GROUPS

Attendance Now vs Five Years Ago	Community							
	Satellite City			New Town		Country Club Estates		
	Black Protestant	White Protestant	Catholic	White Protestant	Catholic	White Protestant	Catholic	Jewish
More or much more now*	42	18	8	15	10	29	15	16
About the same	14	41	39	36	43	32	49	39
Less now	36	26	20	28	20	20	20	19
Much less now	8	14	34	22	27	19	16	25
N=	64	181	146	270	199	218	202	122

*Separated in statistical tests

Chi square = 133.69870   p＜0.001

Coefficient of Contingency = 0.29525

TABLE V-5

CONTRIBUTIONS NOW vs FIVE YEARS AGO

IN PERCENT BY COMMUNITY FOR SELECTED RELIGIOUS GROUPS

Community

Contributions Now vs Five Years Ago	Satellite City			New Town		Country Club Estates		
	Black Protestant	White Protestant	Catholic	White Protestant	Catholic	White Protestant	Catholic	Jewish
Much more or more now	56	49	41	54	43	57	64	63
About the same	30	33	34	23	36	21	24	24
Less now	9	12	14	10	10	12	5	5
Much less now	5	6	12	13	12	11	6	7
N=	64	185	148	265	197	217	202	112

Chi square = 93.06210   p<0.001

Coefficient of Contingency = 0.25058

the underrepresentation of young adults in the Catholic sample contributes to this situation.

There were sufficient numbers of white Protestants and Catholics in the sample to examine participation patterns for these groups in more detail. Though overall Jewish participation was much lower than Protestant participation, Jewish trends were similar to Protestant ones.

Tables V-6 and V-7 portray the participation patterns for white Protestants and Catholics by age. The Index of Church Participation summarizes the responses to the items concerning a person's level of church attendance now compared with five years ago, involvement in church activities now compared with five years ago, and size of contributions now compared with five years ago. The index was weighted so that the item on contribution levels had only half the weight of the other two items, since it was not considered as strong a measure of church participation as the other two items.

Consistent with the family life cycle rhythm discussed earlier, many white Protestants under twenty-five were drifting away from church involvement. Some drifted back in the family formation stage, only to drift away after their children had completed Sunday School and were confirmed as members. Reflecting ideological conflicts in the Catholic Church, more Roman Catholics than Protestants under thirty-five reported less participation than earlier.

The Catholic dilemma is depicted in Table V-8, where church participation trends are correlated with attitudes toward changes in the church. Catholic respondents were asked their views toward the changes transpiring in the Church since Vatican II. In the table those responding that changes were occurring too rapidly are characterized as "conservative," those responding that changes were occurring at about the right speed are characterized as "status quo," and those responding that changes were not taking place rapidly enough are characterized as "liberal." Those responding that they are "confused and uncertain" by the changes are so reported in Table V-8.

Only a plurality of less than 40 percent were satisfied with the present rate of change. About 25 percent felt the church was changing too fast and about 20 percent felt it was changing too slowly. About one-third of the members in all the groups except the "status quo" group were moving toward less participation. Under these circumstances, church leaders are caught in a dilemma, for no course of action is going to satisfy everyone. In some manner, pluralism in style is going to be necessary to accommodate the expectations of lay people. Without such pluralism, significant segments of the Catholic laity are likely to reduce their involvement in parish life. Because some changes involve challenges to predominant church teachings, they will not come--if they come at all--without substantial inner turmoil.

TABLE V-6

WHITE PROTESTANT PARTICIPATION PATTERNS BY AGE IN PERCENT

Index of Church Participation	N=	Age			
		Under 25	25 to 34	35 to 54	55 and over
Toward greater participation	45	3	17	6	2
Same amount	415	43	66	64	67
Toward less participation	140	27	12	19	28
Toward absenteeism	73	27	6	11	3
N=	673	97	119	318	139

$x^2 = 74.94775$ $p < .00001$

Coefficient of Contingency = 0.31655

TABLE V-7

CATHOLIC PARTICIPATION PATTERNS BY AGE IN PERCENT

Index of Church Participation	N=	Age			
		Under 25	25 to 34	35 to 54	55 and over
Toward greater participation	18	0	5	2	5
Same amount	374	65	62	72	69
Toward less participation	103	26	16	19	21
Toward absenteeism	50	9	17	7	6
N=	545	23	129	287	106

$x^2 = 19.0209$ $p < 0.03$

Coefficient of Contingency = .18364

TABLE V-8

CATHOLIC PARTICIPATION PATTERNS

BY ATTITUDES TOWARD CHANGES IN THE CHURCH IN PERCENT

| | | Attitudes toward changes | | | |
Index of Church Participation	N=	Conservative	Status Quo	Liberal	Confused and Uncertain
Toward greater participation	16	4	4	1	2
Same amount	346	62	82	62	60
Toward less participation	95	23	13	22	21
Toward absenteeism	45	12	0	15	16
N=	502	131	186	94	91

$X^2 = 39.40924$ $p < .0001$

Coefficient of Contingency = 0.26980

The Future of the Religions of the American Suburbs

Declines in attendance, decreases in financial support for regional and national ecclesiastical bodies, and considerable internal dissension within both Protestantism and Catholicism in the latter part of the 1960's have raised doubts about the future of religious institutions in America.

The widespread popularity in intellectual circles of interpretations of life denying, ignoring, or explaining on non-sui generis grounds the Divine Presence in the world is a further factor contributing to questions about the future of religious institutions. The pervasive influence of technical rationalism also conceivably could affect adversely the future of religious institutions in America.

The changing age composition of the American population has had a major impact on religious institutions, for involvement in religious

institutions is closely associated with the family life cycle. Involvement
in religious institutions is substantial in childhood and early adolescence,
drops off markedly in late adolescence and early adulthood, and increases
markedly after new family formation and the birth of children. In the United
States, the marked numerical increase in the young adult population and the
numerical decrease in the middle-aged population in the past decade has
contributed significantly to the declines in attendance at religious services.

As young adults age, both the absolute number and the proportion
of people in the thirty-five to forty-nine age group will increase dramatically in the next three decades. Even if substantially fewer young adults
reaffiliate with religious institutions in the next thirty years than has
been the case historically, the very large increase in numbers in the
thirty-five to forty-nine age group will have a substantial positive impact
on religious institutional membership.[8] At the same time, the mood of the
larger society will probably become more conservative, for middle-aged
people are not generally in the vanguard of those promoting rapid social
change.

National data and the data reported here both suggest Catholicism
is going through a period of greater inner turmoil than either Protestantism
or Judaism. The longer isolation of Catholicism from the mainstream of
America's cultural and social life and the greater contrasts between its
traditional beliefs and its form of ecclesiastical organization and the
public religion of America have accentuated the disharmonies arising from
Catholic acculturation.

Such a situation is related to the timing of migration patterns.
As noted earlier, the great wave of Catholic immigration occurred between
1865 and 1920, and especially between 1885 and 1920. Second and third
generation American Catholics, having internalized some of the values
associated with the public religion of America, found themselves at odds
with much of traditional Catholicism. (Significantly, it is the younger
Catholic priests who are in the vanguard of those pressing for change
within the Catholic church.) Changes in the Catholic church have produced
difficulties for both the more traditional and the more innovative people
in the church. The conservatives think things are changing too fast, and
the liberals don't think they are changing fast enough.

There is no evidence to suggest any drastic short term contraction
of the Catholic Church in America, but a continued decline in participation and continued inner struggles seem very likely in the foreseeable
future. Changes in the age composition of the population just noted will
enhance prospects for increases in membership between 1980 and 2000. The
young adults renewing their participation will be more attuned to non-
authoritarian styles, accentuating some of the changes now occurring in the
Catholic church.

At the same time, the reaction of the Vatican toward the changes
since the Second Vatican Council will determine the shape of the relations
between the American Church and the Vatican. Too many young priests and
lay people have appropriated salient values associated with the American
experience to return easily to the style of the traditional Roman Catholic

Church. If the Vatican reacts too sharply against the changes of the past two or three decades, schismatic moves will most likely develop in the American Church.[9]

Judaism has also experienced very rapid transformation in the context of the American experience, for the large Jewish immigrations coincided with the large Roman Catholic influxes. The response of the Jews to the American experience was initially quite different, for they enthusiastically affirmed the values of religious liberty, religious tolerance, and religious pluralism associated with the religion of America. In that context they also developed their own social institutions.

At the same time, Jews made remarkable strides culturally and educationally. In this process, as Part III will show, they encountered considerable difficulty with the theological side of their religio-ethnic tradition. The intense secularity that made possible substantial accomplishments in education, science, and business could not be easily harmonized with the predominant theological interpretation of Jewish life and history.

As a result of these interrelated factors, Jewish involvement in the synagogue is quite low. There is no evidence to suggest a substantial decline in Jewish religious institutions, however, for the synagogue continues to be a primary focus of Jewish history and lore. Participation may be low, but the symbolic significance of the synagogue is great indeed. The presence of Orthodox, Conservative and Reform Judaism in the United States permits Jews to adjust some issues by intragroup movement without dissociating themselves from Judaism.

If the educational levels and economic conditions of the blacks continue to improve--absolutely if not relatively--the black Protestant church seems likely to persist, but some changes in style are apt to develop. The authority of the pastor seems destined to diminish, and the consensus-forming pastoral director style, now prevalent in many NCC-affiliated white Protestant churches, will, in all likelihood, increase. Greater rapprochement between some black Protestant churches and some white Protestant churches may evolve with an increase in the number of middle status blacks, for the cleavages between white Protestants and black Protestants are due to status as well as race. In all probability, a contrast comparable to the NCC-non-NCC cleavage in predominantly white Protestantism will become more salient in black Protestantism.

White Protestantism has already adapted most fully to the congregation principle of religious organization regnant in America, and nation-wide there has been little overall fluctuation in attendance in the past decade. (The suburban data do suggest modest declines in the past five years.) Because of its marked internal diversity, persons may move readily from one group to another and still consider themselves to be "Protestants." Such possibilities permit varying emphases to be carried on in spite of the variety within as well as between denominations.[10]

Protestantism seems likely to persist in suburban America in the major forms it now manifests. The Protestant lay respondents did not evidence substantial alienation from their churches; reported declines in involvement were due primarily to indifference and to the demographic factors just cited.

Aside from the racial cleavage, the most salient contrast in Protestantism is between NCC-affiliated churches and non-NCC affiliated churches. Because of the isolation of many non-NCC clergy from the intellectual and cultural center of American life, rapprochement between these two groups (except for the Missouri Synod Lutherans) seems unlikely. Missouri Synod Lutherans, as is evidenced by the doctrinal battles now raging there, are partially acculturated; and some of their clergy are appropriating the fruits of modern biblical scholarship.

The persistence of the predominant institutional forms of suburban religion does not preclude the continued inner transformation of the substance of religious understanding, for institutional persistence will undoubtedly continue to be accompanied by changes in beliefs and attitudes resulting from the interplay between the experiences of people in the broader American society and the experiences within the life of the religious institutions. Authentic religion, the religion of America, and the religions of American suburbia will continue to interact with each other as people experience, interpret and bear witness to the Divine Presence in their lives.

Part III explores these values and assesses the extent to which the traditional beliefs of the various faith communities have been modified, qualified, and transformed in the context of the American experience.

PART III

SUBURBAN CHURCHES AND SYNAGOGUES AS RELIGIOUS AND MORAL

AGENCIES FOR THEIR LAY PARTICIPANTS

CHAPTER VI

PRIVATE MORALITY: A CENTRAL FOCUS

OF SUBURBAN CHURCHES AND SYNAGOGUES

Introduction

Earlier it was noted that in the past century family and religious institutions have been largely relegated to the private sphere, separated from the economic and political spheres. This relegation has accentuated the historic close relations between the family and religious institutions, for neither families nor religious institutions have substantial direct involvement in the public spheres. The strong family emphasis is enhanced by the voluntary nature of the church and the synagogue, for leaders of religious institutions have to respond--at least in part--to the expectations of their members.

Most NCC-affiliated Protestant churches, some non-NCC-affiliated Protestant churches, all Catholic parishes, and most synagogues promote a wide range of social, cultural, and religious activities designed to appeal to different age, sex, and interest groups. These many and diverse activities emphasize interpersonal relations and provide one means by which geographically mobile suburbanites may make new friends and acquaintances.

Historically, all of these religious communities supported values sustaining the life-long monogamous family, but such values have been modified markedly in the twentieth century as the general cultural ethos has shifted. The sharp increase in the divorce rate, the widespread acceptance of premarital sexual relations, the increasing explicit public attention to sexual matters, the legalization of abortion and the growth of women's and homosexual "liberation" movements all point to changing familial values.

This post-traditional cluster of values, part and parcel of technical rationalism and an altered understanding of the meaning of human freedom, has modified traditional familial values in all the religious communities. Technical rationalism leads to the questioning of all traditional values and to the objectification of the person. Secular humanism fosters the respect of individuals and the enrichment of life opportunities. Taken together, the mind set supporting these changing values fosters a contract view of marriage, greater premarital sexual freedom, and liberalized abortion laws. The concomitant enhancement of expectations for personal satisfaction in marriage puts great pressures on the ideal of the life-long monogamous marriage.

111

Familial Values and Suburban Churches and Synagogues

Lay respondents were asked to evaluate the helpfulness of their
church or synagogue in providing guidance on family and marital matters.
They were also asked to indicate their attitudes toward four items dealing
with family values--pre-marital sexual relations, extra-marital sexual
relations, divorce, and abortion--by responding on a five point scale,
ranging from "strongly agree" to "strongly disagree." In addition they
could reflect an implicitly contextual ethic by responding "depends on
circumstances," and they could indicate "no opinion."

Responses on these items for the various faith groups in the three
suburban communities are discussed in this section. In addition, data
correlated with an "Index of Familial Traditionalism" are examined. The
responses serve as an indicator of the degree to which lay people in the
various suburban faith groups have appropriated familial values consonant
with technical rationalism and secular humanism.

Helpfulness of Church or Synagogue in

Providing Guidance for Family and Marital Relations

As Table VI-1 indicates, the majority of respondents in most groups
reported their religious institution had been helpful in providing guidance
for family and marital relations. The exceptions were the black Protestant
and Jewish respondents, groups whose members scored lowest on the Index of
Familial Traditionalism to be discussed subsequently.

In the introductory section of this chapter the privatization of
the religious sphere was underscored. The responses to this item, taken
in conjunction with responses to similar items dealing with respondents'
assessments of the guidance provided by their church or synagogue for
decisions connected with their work and on social and political issues
presented in Chapter VIII, confirm this observation, for a much higher
proportion of white Protestants and Catholics reported their church had
been helpful in the familial sphere than in the economic or political
sphere. (The black Protestant and Jewish situations are somewhat different.
They will be discussed in Chapter VIII.)

Sexual and Familial Values

A plurality of the members of all the religious groups except
black Protestants and Jews agreed that it was wrong for people to have
premarital sexual relations, as Table VI-2 shows. A majority of both
Protestant and Catholic respondents in lower status Satellite City and
upper status Country Club Estates agreed that premarital sexual relations

TABLE VI-1

HELPFULNESS OF RELIGIOUS INSTITUTION FOR

GUIDANCE FOR FAMILY AND MARITAL RELATIONS

IN PERCENT BY COMMUNITY FOR SELECTED RELIGIOUS GROUPS

Degree of Helpfulness	Community							
	Satellite City			New Town		Country Club Estates		
	Black Protestant	White Protestant	Catholic	White Protestant	Catholic	White Protestant	Catholic	Jewish
Very helpful	16	26	15	10	11	17	14	11
Helpful	24	37	42	39	41	38	37	22
Of little help one way or another	43	32	29	45	33	37	35	51
Somewhat unhelpful	6	2	2	1	6	2	6	4
Very unhelpful	10	2	8	2	7	2	4	7
Other	2	2	4	2	2	4	4	5
N=	63	165	132	249	195	210	198	121

Chi square = 91.94453   p<0.001

Coefficient of Contingency = 0.25402

TABLE VI-2

RESPONSE TO STATEMENT "IT IS WRONG FOR

PEOPLE TO HAVE PREMARITAL SEXUAL RELATIONS"

IN PERCENT BY COMMUNITY FOR SELECTED RELIGIOUS GROUPS

Community

Response to Statement	Satellite City			New Town		Country Club Estates		
	Black Protestant	White Protestant	Catholic	White Protestant	Catholic	White Protestant	Catholic	Jewish
Strongly agree	9	35	29	17	24	29	30	7
Agree	17	28	31	29	22	23	33	16
Mixed feelings or depends on circumstances	45	25	24	36	35	35	27	38
Disagree	11	7	7	11	11	9	6	23
Strongly disagree	9	3	7	4	6	4	2	16
No opinion	8	2	1	2	1	0	1	0
N=	64	182	141	265	199	216	200	123

Chi square = 174.51306   p<0.001

Coefficient of Contingency = 0.33398

were wrong, but only a plurality in New Town agreed. The ambiguity of
lay attitudes is reflected in the fact that, Jews excepted, less than
20 percent of the respondents disagreed with the statement.

The data are not reported in tabular form here, but further
comparisons were made holding age and status constant. These comparisons
indicated age was more strongly correlated with attitudes toward premarital
sexual relations than was status. This finding agrees with the results
by community shown here, for the churches in New Town had more people
under thirty-five than did the churches in the other surveyed communities.

The black Protestant and Jewish respondents were more tolerant and
permissive about the legitimacy of premarital sexual relations. The Jewish
pattern was especially striking, for only 23 percent of the Jewish respondents agreed it was wrong for people to have premarital sexual relations.
Thirty-nine percent disagreed, and 23 percent felt it depended on circumstances. When controlled for age, the same pattern prevailed.

Clergy responses on the same item, discussed in Chapter IV,
indicated that they were more staunch in their support of premarital
chastity than were their lay people. In this instance, NCC-affiliated
Protestant clergy differed less with NCC Protestant lay people than did
clergy in the other groups. The percentage of clergy agreeing with the
statement were: NCC-affiliated Protestants, 56 percent; non-NCC-affiliated
white Protestants, 93 percent; black Protestants, 71 percent, and Roman
Catholics, 82 percent (Table IV-13).

Very substantial majorities of respondents in all the faith groups
thought extramarital sexual relations were wrong, but the pattern of
responses was similar to the ones on premarital sexual relations. Sixty-
nine percent of the black Protestants, 73 percent of the Jews, and over
80 percent of the white Protestants and Catholics agreed or strongly
agreed with the statement "It is wrong for married people to have sexual
relations with persons other than their husbands or wives."

Even though traditional norms regarding premarital sexual relations
may have eroded among members of suburban churches and synagogues, marital
fidelity is still the predominant norm among suburbanites belonging to
churches and synagogues.

Clergy responses were just as supportive on this issue as were lay
responses, suggesting a mutual reinforcement on the issue of marital fidelity.

Attitudes toward the statement, "Divorce is wrong" showed expected
contrasts between Catholic respondents and the other faith groupings.
Between a quarter and a third of the Catholic respondents felt divorce was
wrong, but less than 15 percent of any other faith grouping responded in
this way. Only 3 percent of the Jewish respondents felt divorce was wrong.

Substantial clergy-lay disagreement on this issue existed in the
Catholic Church, for 57 percent of the Catholic clergy held divorce was
wrong. Twenty-seven percent of the NCC-affiliated Protestant clergy, 29
percent of the black clergy, and 55 percent of the non-NCC-affiliated white
clergy so responded (Table IV-14).

A much sharper faith difference appeared on attitudes toward abortion, as Table VI-3 reveals.

TABLE VI-3

RESPONSE TO STATEMENT "IT IS WRONG FOR A WOMAN WHO WANTS AN

ABORTION IN THE FIRST THREE MONTHS OF PREGNANCY TO HAVE ONE"

IN PERCENT BY COMMUNITY FOR SELECTED RELIGIOUS GROUPS

	Community							
	Satellite City			New Town		Country Club Estates		
Response to Statement	Black Protestant	White Protestant	Catholic	White Protestant	Catholic	White Protestant	Catholic	Jewish
Strongly agree	17	9	29	2	27	4	27	2
Agree	9	7	17	4	10	6	15	2
Mixed feelings or depends on circumstances	38	49	37	44	40	44	42	11
Disagree	22	18	6	25	14	27	10	22
Strongly disagree	9	13	8	24	7	18	3	63
No Opinion	5	4	3	0	2	1	1	0
N=	65	182	142	262	197	217	201	123

Chi square = 469.99121   p<0.001

Coefficient of Contingency = 0.50281

Opposition to abortion is concentrated among Catholics, but even on this issue, on which Catholic Church teaching is strong and unequivocal, less than half of the Catholic respondents agreed it was wrong for a woman who wants an abortion in the first three months of pregnancy to have one. Protestant opposition is negligible, and Jewish opposition practically nonexistent. Catholic clergy-lay contrasts on this issue were especially sharp, for 82 percent of the Catholic clergy agreed with the statement (Table IV-15).

Forty-five percent of Catholic women and 38 percent of Catholic men felt abortion in the first trimester was wrong. There was somewhat more support for abortion among these under thirty-five, but the differences by age were not dramatic. About a third of the respondents under thirty-five felt that first trimester abortion was wrong, compared with about 45 percent of those between thirty-five and fifty-four and slightly over 50 percent of those fifty-five and over. This shift with age suggests it is only a matter of time until suburban Catholic lay people agreeing with their Church's teaching on abortion will be in a small minority.

The sharp lay-clergy disparity among Catholics suggests this issue could become an issue of major dispute between clergy and lay people.

An Index of Familial Traditionalism was constructed by combining responses to the preceding four items. Persons agreeing that premarital and extramarital sexual relations, divorce, and abortion were wrong scored "high" on the index, and persons disagreeing scored "low." Persons responding differently to the several items or responding largely with the responses "mixed feelings" and "depends on circumstances" scored "medium."

As Table VI-4 shows, Catholic respondents scored highest on the Index, white Protestants were second, black Protestants third, and Jews lowest. There was a generational contrast in familial attitudes. When controlled by age, the contrasts were enhanced, for younger people of all faith groupings held less traditional familial attitudes.

In sum, lay respondents were equivocal in their attitudes toward traditional norms of family life. The majority of respondents rejected the immorality of divorce and first trimester abortion. The respondents equivocated on the immorality of premarital sexual relations, for a substantial minority did not feel premarital sexual relations were immoral. The only traditional norm strongly adhered to was the admonition against extramarital sexual relations.

This pattern of responses is very suggestive, for it reflects the strong efforts of lay people to retain the monogamous family amid substantial societal pressures tending to undercut it. Many accept both the prevalence of divorce and premarital sexual relations, but they still insist on the norm of marital fidelity within the monogamous marriage framework. This conjugal family places a premium on intentionality, for the cluster of norms supporting the life-long monogamous family has eroded.

TABLE VI-4

INDEX OF FAMILIAL TRADITIONALISM

IN PERCENT BY COMMUNITY FOR SELECTED RELIGIOUS GROUPS

	Community							
	Satellite City			New Town		Country Club Estates		
Score on Index	Black Protestant	White Protestant	Catholic	White Protestant	Catholic	White Protestant	Catholic	Jewish
High	29	47	61	29	50	35	66	6
Medium	53	41	29	58	39	53	28	54
Low	18	12	10	13	11	12	6	40
N=	56	168	126	252	185	208	192	121

Chi square = 207.60703   p<0.001

Coefficient of Contingency = 0.37011

Among clergy respondents, non-NCC-affiliated white Protestant and Roman Catholic clergy were most supportive of traditional familial values, and black Protestants were intermediate. NCC-affiliated Protestants were most critical of facets of the value complex associated with traditional family life, and Roman Catholic clergy were at sharpest variance with the values of their lay people.

Morality and the Index of Familial Traditionalism

Persons scoring high on the Index of Familial Traditionalism tended to be more moralistic in general than those scoring medium and low. There were sufficient numbers of white Protestant and Roman Catholic respondents to permit statistical analyses of some of these correlations.

Three items were selected to illumine these tendencies: attitudes toward drinking, attitudes toward the notion that the church should enforce a strict standard of moral conduct among its members, and attitudes toward the proposition that there are times when it might be all right to break one of the Ten Commandments. These responses are summarized in Table VI-5.

The findings reveal that persons scoring "high" on the Index of
Familial Traditionalism had higher proportions agreeing that drinking is
wrong and desiring the church to enforce a strict standard of moral
conduct among its members. They also had fewer respondents who agreed
that there are times when it might be all right to break one of the Ten
Commandments. People who affirm the rightness of moral principles in one
sphere thus tend to support principles in other spheres.

TABLE VI-5

SUMMARY OF CORRELATES BETWEEN SCORES ON INDEX OF FAMILIAL

TRADITIONALISM AND SELECTED MORAL ATTITUDES FOR

WHITE PROTESTANTS AND CATHOLICS IN PERCENT

Score on Index of Familial Tradi- tionalism	Percent strongly agreeing or agreeing that drinking is wrong				Percent strongly agreeing or agreeing that the church should enforce a strict standard of moral conduct among its members				Percent strongly agreeing or agreeing that there are times when it might be all right to break one of the Ten Commandments			
	White Protestant		Catholic		White Protestant		Catholic		White Protestant		Catholic	
	N=	Per-cent	N=	Per-cent	N=	Per-cent	N=	Per-cent	N=	Per-cent	N=	Per-cent
High	219	29	289	12	216	56	287	77	213	6	286	16
Medium	320	13	160	6	320	34	158	17	313	20	152	30
Low	79	5	43	2	77	16	44	5	74	34	40	50

The Consumption of Alcoholic Beverages

and Suburban Religious Institutions

One of the recurrent themes in American Protestantism has been opposition to the consumption of alcoholic beverages. Rooted in segments of Puritanism, movements to restrain consumption of liquor have been common in Protestant churches. Prohibition forces, gaining strength in the nineteenth century, finally succeeded when the Eighteenth Amendment to the Constitution banning the sale of liquor was ratified in 1920. The success was short lived for the amendment was repealed in 1933.

Following the example of John Wesley, leaders in the United Methodist Church, the representative white Protestant lay group studied here, were in the vanguard of those supporting nationwide prohibition in this earlier epoch. Minor analogues of Puritanism have existed in Catholicism and Judaism, but in the main these groups had very little to do with this predominantly Protestant movement. The ceremonial use of wine in religious services was indigenous to both these groups, and both clergy and lay people had long consumed alcoholic beverages in social gatherings.

A question on drinking was included to illumine shifting styles of personal morality in American suburbia and to assess generational and intergroup differences. The findings are summarized in Table VI-6.

As the table indicates, the majority of respondents either disagreed with the statement, "Drinking is wrong" or felt it depended on circumstances. The generational contrast in Protestantism was reflected in the responses of the white Protestants, for three times as many white Protestant respondents in Satellite City, where 42 percent of the respondents were over fifty-four, felt drinking was wrong as did white Protestant respondents in New Town or Country Club Estates, where less than 15 percent of the respondents were over fifty-four. In American suburbia, mainline American Protestants have largely accommodated to the broader cultural mores on this issue. Roman Catholics and Jews have even fewer scruples about the immorality of drinking.

On this issue, Roman Catholic and NCC-affiliated Protestant clergy shared lay views (see Table IV-16, Chapter 4). In the suburban context, this issue was inconsequential in most NCC-affiliated Protestant churches; it was a live one in many black churches and many non-NCC-affiliated white Protestant churches, where the southern and frontier influences continue to be reflected.

TABLE VI-6

RESPONSE TO STATEMENT "DRINKING IS WRONG"

IN PERCENT BY COMMUNITY FOR SELECTED RELIGIOUS GROUPS

Community

Response to Statement	Satellite City			New Town		Country Club Estates		
	Black Protestant	White Protestant	Catholic	White Protestant	Catholic	White Protestant	Catholic	Jewish
Strongly agree	11	16	6	2	2	5	2	2
Agree	8	21	8	8	5	8	6	2
Mixed feelings or depends on circumstances	40	30	42	37	36	37	35	27
Disagree	26	25	32	42	42	37	43	45
Strongly disagree	9	5	8	10	13	12	14	22
No opinion	6	3	4	2	2	1	1	1
N =	65	183	145	264	198	218	197	121

Chi square = 193.75183 $p < 0.001$

Coefficient of Contingency = 0.34966

Summary

Religious institutions in American suburbia are family focused, but their members no longer broadly support the entire cluster of values sustaining the traditional image of a life-long monogamous marriage. Respondents are seeking ways to make the monogamous family possible in this day, for the vast majority of members affirmed the morality of marital sexual fidelity. At the same time, they equivocated on the immorality of premarital sexual relations, and the majority denied the immorality of divorce and first trimester abortion. Roman Catholics are most strong in the support of the traditional family, but even in this faith community a substantial proportion of its members disagreed with traditional church teaching.

It is almost impossible in the present context for religious institutions to maintain any semblance of strict discipline among their members. In every faith group substantial proportions of members rejected the idea that the church or synagogue should enforce a strict standard of moral conduct among its members. Some small sectarian groups may succeed in this type of ecclesiastical discipline, but such a style--even if it were held to be desirable--is simply not feasible in most of the large voluntary churches and synagogues.[1] Many do not think that the church or synagogue should try to do so, and those who do would find it almost impossible to agree on the form of the moral standards to be enforced.

The fragmentation of social groups in America and the pluralization of moral values conditions institutional religious life and makes it very difficult to attain a consensus on issues of faith and morals.

Small groups within larger institutions may attain a consensus, and broad non-specific consensuses may develop in large religious institutions, but the pluralism discerned here limits the possibilities. Those who believe the positive aspects of the voluntary religious institution outweigh the negative aspects are most able to live graciously in this situation.[2]

CHAPTER VII

SOCIAL AND ETHNIC SEGREGATION: SOCIAL STRATIFICATION,

ETHNICITY, AND SUBURBAN RELIGIOUS INSTITUTIONS

Introduction

Authentic religion always fosters a vision of the inclusiveness of the whole, a sense of the common good, and a concern for the well-being of all humankind. These impulses are perennially limited by the conditions of existence, for the bearers of these impulses are also bound to particular class, status, ethnic, nationality, and cultural groups.

In the American context, Protestant churches are especially fractured by ethnic and status differences, for the large number of denominations accentuates ethnic and status diversity. Judaism is more homogeneous, having very few black adherents and relatively few low status members.[1]

Catholicism, as the following section shows, is more inclusive by status and ethnicity than Protestant denominations, for most Catholic parishes are geographically based, incorporating all Catholics within a given geographical area. Ethnic and status exclusiveness in Catholicism are due primarily to the patterns of residential segregation by race, nationality, and status extant in a given geographical area.[2] As Chapter III has shown, such exclusiveness is quite marked in the suburban sector, as it is in all metropolitan areas.

The ethnic accent was still very discernible in several of the suburban Catholic parishes, but it was not as marked as it was a generation ago. It was especially evident in lower status Satellite City, where the members still identified strongly with particular nationality groups.

The most dramatic ethnic cleavages were between predominantly white and predominantly black churches. Both Protestant churches and Catholic parishes reflected the cleavages, for the residential segregation of blacks and whites directly affects the membership composition of geographically based churches. Both the much smaller number of black Catholics and the hierarchical structure of the Catholic church mitigate the problems in Catholicism. Most blacks are Protestant, so the black-white cleavage is more visible in Protestantism. The presence of predominant black denominations, such as the African Methodist Episcopal Church and the various Baptist denominations, contributed to the segregated patterns, for many black clergy prefer to participate in all-black denominations. Rooted

in the evangelical style of white southern churches, black Protestantism
has fused that style with its own indigenous heritage to produce a unique
style of church life.[3]

Socioeconomic Differentiations among All

Suburban Religious Institutions

The broad patterns of religious institution distribution were
discussed in Chapter III. The regular distribution of Catholic parishes
by geographical area contrasted with the more haphazard distribution of
Protestant churches and synagogues.

In that chapter, the distribution of Protestant churches and
synagogues was correlated with the socioeconomic status of the various
suburban communities. It was noted that synagogues and NCC-affiliated
Protestant churches were concentrated in the middle and upper status
suburbs, and non-NCC-affiliated Protestant churches were concentrated
in lower status suburbs.

Differences in the social status of churches were assessed by
discerning the clergymen's estimates of the proportion of white collar
and blue collar families in a given congregation and the percent of
members with some college education. Table VII-1 summarizes the distribution of NCC-affiliated Protestant churches, non-NCC-affiliated white
Protestant churches, and Roman Catholic parishes by percent of white
collar families in the church. Table VII-2 summarizes the same groups by
percent of members in the church with some college training.[4]

Roman Catholic parish distribution reflects closely the social
status of the various suburban communities. About a third of the parishes
had 80 percent or more white collar workers and about a quarter had 80
percent or more college trained lay people.

Protestantism showed a sharp contrast between NCC-affiliated
churches and non-NCC-affiliated churches. Sixty percent of the NCC-
affiliated churches reported 80 percent or more of their lay people were
employed in white collar jobs, and half of them reported 70 percent or
more of their lay people had some college training. In sharp contrast,
less than 15 percent of non-NCC-affiliated Protestant churches reported
80 percent or more of their memberships in white collar jobs and less than
30 percent reported 70 percent or more of their members had some college
training. The bimodal distribution among non-NCC-affiliated churches
reflects the split between lower status southern origin non-NCC-affiliated
churches and the others, such as the Lutheran Missouri Synod, which are
relatively more middle status.

Conversely, over half the non-NCC-affiliated white Protestant
churches reported 30 percent or less of their members held white collar
jobs, compared with less than 15 percent of the NCC-affiliated Protestant
churches. Similarly, half of the non-NCC-affiliated white Protestant

TABLE VII-1

PROPORTION OF WHITE COLLAR FAMILIES IN MEMBERSHIP FOR NCC-AFFILIATED

PROTESTANT CHURCHES, NON-NCC-AFFILIATED WHITE PROTESTANT CHURCHES,

AND ROMAN CATHOLIC CHURCHES IN THE SUBURBAN SECTOR

Type of Church

Percent of Membership Who Are White Collar	NCC-Affiliated Protestant	Non-NCC-Affiliated White Protestant	Roman Catholic
	N=26	N=29	N=9
90 percent or more	8	2	2
80	7	2	1
70	1	2	1
60	2	3	1
50	3	0	1
40	1	5	1
30 or less	4	15	2

churches reported less than 20 percent of their members had some college education, compared with 15 percent of the NCC-affiliated churches so reporting.

The synagogues in the south suburban sector were all located in the upper middle and upper status suburbs. As noted previously, three of the five rabbis were interviewed. All reported more than 80 percent of their members were employed in white collar occupations and more than 75 percent had had some college education. There is every reason to think the same situations existed in the other two synagogues.

Status differences were reflected in the two Reform synagogues for which data were available. Located about three miles apart, one was in upper status Country Club Estates and one was in middle status New Town. Ninety-five percent of the members of the Country Club Estates synagogue were employed in white collar occupations and the same percentage had attended college. The comparable percentages in the New Town synagogue were 80 percent and 75 percent.

TABLE VII-2

PROPORTION OF ADULT MEMBERS WITH SOME COLLEGE EDUCATION FOR NCC-
AFFILIATED PROTESTANT CHURCHES, NON-NCC-AFFILIATED WHITE PROTESTANT
CHURCHES, AND ROMAN CATHOLIC CHURCHES IN THE SUBURBAN SECTOR

	Type of Church		
Percent of Laity with Some College Education	NCC-Affiliated Protestant	Non-NCC-Affiliated White Protestant	Roman Catholic
	N=26	N=28	N=8
10 or less	2	9	0
20	2	5	0
30	2	3	2
40	4	1	0
50	2	1	2
60	1	1	1
70	2	2	1
80 or more	11	6	2

With respect to socioeconomic status, the synagogues and NCC-
affiliated Protestant churches display similar patterns, for both groups
drew disproportionately from the middle and upper socioeconomic levels.

Compared to the white Protestant denomination, the Catholic church
was much more inclusive by social status, for it more closely reflected
the social status of members living within its parish boundaries. (Protestantism as a whole is status inclusive, but particular denominations within
Protestantism and especially particular congregations within a given denomination tend toward status exclusiveness.)

This situation is a consequence of the contrasting principles of
organization discussed earlier. Catholicism, with its cultic focus and
predominantly geographically based parishes, is relatively status inclusive;
Protestantism, with its congregational focus, its heightened intentionality
and its multiplicity of churches, is relatively status exclusive.[5] At the
synagogue level, Judaism is also congregationally based, so synagogues have

to compete for members in the same fashion as Protestant churches. Because
of the relative paucity of lower status Jews, synagogue families are concentrated in the middle and upper statuses.

Socioeconomic Differentiation among the Surveyed Faith Groups

in Lower Status Satellite City, Middle Status New Town,

and Upper Status Country Club Estates

Introduction

        Data in the preceding section were based on information provided
by the clergy, so they dealt with all the churches and synagogues in the
suburban sector. Data in this section deal only with the surveyed faith
groups in the three suburban communities where they were located. Findings
on age, sex, education and income are presented.

Age Distribution

        The age of the memberships of the religious institutions is shown
in Table VII-3. The distributions reflect both the ecological processes
and demographic characteristics discussed in Chapter III and the peculi-
arities of the sampling processes used in this study.

        As observed earlier, Catholic parish mailing lists were organized
by family, and there was no way to discover either unmarried young adults
living at home or young adults away at school; consequently the under twenty
and twenty to twenty-four age groups were underrepresented in all the
Catholic parishes. This lacuna is most unfortunate, but with the limited
resources available there was no way to augment this list directly.

        The white Protestant and Catholic memberships reflected the age
distributions of the communities in which they were located, allowing
for the underrepresentation of young adults in the Catholic parishes just
discussed. The higher proportions of persons fifty-five and over in the
white Protestant church and in the Catholic parish in Satellite City were
consistent with the age composition of its white population. Young and
middle-aged white adults were moving away disproportionately, and young
and middle-aged black adults were moving in. This situation is related
to the dramatic contrasts in the percentage of members fifty-five and over
in the three Satellite City churches. Only 8 percent of the black Protestants were over fifty-five, compared to 43 percent of the white Protestants
and 33 percent of the Catholics. Unless utterly unforeseeable changes in
migration patterns occur, the white Protestant and Roman Catholic churches
in Satellite City will continue to decline in numbers and the black Protestant churches will continue to increase.

TABLE VII-3

MEMBERSHIP DISTRIBUTION IN PERCENT BY AGE

AND COMMUNITY FOR SELECTED RELIGIOUS GROUPS

	Community							
	Satellite City			New Town		Country Club Estates		
Age	Black Protestant	White Protestant	Catholic	White Protestant	Catholic	White Protestant	Catholic	Jewish
Under 20	6	2	1	9	1	5	0	10
20-24	6	10	3	8	6	9	2	19
25-29	6	4	6	7	25	10	3	5
30-34	8	6	10	11	14	15	11	4
35-44	30	19	20	27	18	25	36	29
45-54	35	18	28	25	24	26	30	24
55-64	5	21	19	9	8	10	12	10
65 and over	3	22	14	3	5	2	5	0
N=	63	189	144	267	200	219	204	123

Chi square = 327.48511   p<.001

Coefficient of Contingency = 0.43427

The much lower proportion of Catholics in the under thirty age groups in Country Club Estates than in New Town was a result of the economic situation, for high housing costs in upper status Country Club Estates effectively precluded most married couples under thirty. On the other hand, New Town, a middle status "port of entry" community, had substantial housing stock which young adults could afford.

The situation of the white Protestants in New Town and Country Club Estates requires an interpretation, for the age distributions were very similar in the two churches. The heightened intentionality of Protestant church membership is very evident in these data, for loyal United Methodists from several lower status communities belonged to the United Methodist church in Country Club Estates. As a result, more young adults belonged to the United Methodist Church in Country Club Estates than to the Catholic church there. Catholic families are much more likely to attend their geographically defined parish, so their membership patterns more closely cohered with the age distribution of New Town and Country Club Estates.

Sex Distribution

Membership by sex, shown in Table VII-4, displayed patterns common in religious institutions in America. All the religious institutions studied had more females than males, consistent with the findings reported in Chapter III. The unusually high percent of females among the Satellite City white Protestant and Catholic churches was correlated with the high proportion of older people in these churches, for females live longer than males.

An unusually high proportion of females among the black Protestants has been traditional among black Americans for a long period; possibly this can be traced to the once-posited matriarchical forms of family organization in antebellum days.[6]

In New Town and Country Club Estates, there were slightly more females than males in all the religious institutions, but these institutions were more balanced by sex than those in Satellite City.

Education and Income Distribution

The heightened intentionality of the white Protestants was also manifest in the data on years of school completed and family income level, as shown in Tables VII-5 and VII-6. There was minimal variation in the level of education between Protestant, Catholic, and Jewish lay people in Country Club Estates, but the proportion of Protestants with incomes of $25,000 and more was substantially less than for Catholics and Jews. The substantial presence of younger members in the Protestant church contributed to this situation.

TABLE VII-4

MEMBERSHIP DISTRIBUTION IN PERCENT BY SEX

AND COMMUNITY FOR SELECTED RELIGIOUS GROUPS

Community

Sex	Satellite City			New Town		Country Club Estates		
	Black Protestant	White Protestant	Catholic	White Protestant	Catholic	White Protestant	Catholic	Jewish
Female	73	66	70	58	56	55	60	59
Male	27	34	30	42	44	45	40	41
N=	67	188	145	268	200	219	197	124

Chi square = 17.11421 $p < 0.017$

Coefficient of Contingency = 0.10962

TABLE VII-5

YEARS OF SCHOOL COMPLETED IN PERCENT BY

COMMUNITY FOR SELECTED RELIGIOUS GROUPINGS

	Community							
	Satellite City			New Town		Country Club Estates		
Years of School Completed	Black Protestant	White Protestant	Catholic	White Protestant	Catholic	White Protestant	Catholic	Jewish
Some grammar school	2	1	3	0	2	0	1	0
Eighth grade graduate	2	6	12	0	2	0	2	1
Some high school	11	10	20	6	5	1	5	0
High school graduate	23	30	35	22	26	16	23	16
Some college	35	30	18	31	35	38	30	36
Four year college graduate	10	13	6	23	18	20	21	22
Post-graduate work	18	10	4	18	14	23	18	25
N=	62	188	146	268	191	218	199	123

Chi square = 232.41940   p<0.001

Coefficient of Contingency = 0.37791

TABLE VII-6

YEARLY FAMILY INCOME BEFORE TAXES IN PERCENT

BY COMMUNITY FOR SELECTED RELIGIOUS GROUPS

Community

Yearly Family Income	Satellite City			New Town		Country Club Estates		
	Black Protestant	White Protestant	Catholic	White Protestant	Catholic	White Protestant	Catholic	Jewish
Under $5000	12	13	14	3	5	2	1	0
$5000-$9,999	19	16	33	7	13	9	5	6
$10,000-$14,999	29	34	34	26	35	18	13	19
$15,000-$19,999	17	21	11	30	31	25	20	19
$20,000-$24,999	7	11	4	17	11	25	16	13
$25,000-$49,999	16	4	3	16	3	17	36	32
$50,000 and over	0	1	0	1	1	4	9	10
N=	58	172	123	257	178	211	174	78

Chi square = 361.44336   p<0.001

Coefficient of Contingency = 0.47345

Another factor related both to Jewish and Protestant intentionality of religious institutional affiliation should be noted. The Jewish synagogue studied was the largest and most prestigious in the suburban sector; it probably attracted the more affluent disproportionately.

The Protestant situation differed markedly, for there were two Protestant churches that were much larger and more prestigious than the United Methodist Church in Country Club Estates. It is highly likely that upper income Protestant families were attracted disproportionately to these institutions.

The Satellite City family income data highlight both the contrasting levels of intentionality between Protestantism and Catholicism and also real differences in income levels, for the United Methodist Church tended to be a middle status church regardless of the predominant social status of community in which it was set.

The "elitist" character of the black churches studied here is pronounced, for both the income and education levels of their respondents were markedly above the black average. Nonetheless, the greatest socioeconomic variation in membership was manifest among black Protestants.

The sample was markedly above the national averages in educational attainment, for approximately ten percent of the nations' population over twenty-five are college graduates. The Catholic parish in Satellite City approximated that average; the rest were very substantially above it.

The income distributions of members shown in Table VII-6 reflect the socioeconomic levels of the communities in which they were located. In Satellite City, 23 percent of the black Protestants, 16 percent of the white Protestants, and 7 percent of the Catholics reported family incomes of $20,000 or more. In New Town, 34 percent of the white Protestants and 15 percent of the Catholics reported incomes or family incomes of $20,000 or more. In Country Club Estates, 46 percent of the white Protestants, 61 percent of the Catholics, and 55 percent of the Jews reported family incomes of $20,000 or more.

Ethnicity and Suburban Religious Institutions

Introduction

America's religious institutions show the effects of its ethnic diversity. Immigrants cannot bring the laws and economic systems of their country of origin with them, but they can more easily transplant their religious institutions.

These institutions are transmuted in the process of transplantation, for no church or synagogue can be moved from one culture to another without modification. The emergence of the voluntary religious institution, discussed in Part I, transformed the major religious institutions, for Lutherans, Episcopalians, Presbyterians and Roman Catholics--to cite the major groups--had enjoyed special privileges in some parts of Europe. The spawning of various sectarian groups and the emergence of indigenous denominations such as the Congregationalists and the Disciples of Christ contributed to a religious pluralism unknown in any other country.

In the process of acculturation, various immigrant groups shed some of their old customs and values and appropriated some of the customs and values of their adopted land, but none of them completely assimilated the values of the new nation. To this day marks of ethnic identity can be discerned in the various Protestant denominations, in groups within Judaism, and in various nationality groups in Roman Catholicism.

This separateness is more evident among some groups than among others; in general, Protestant groups--especially Anglo-Saxon and indigeneous groups--have sensed less conflict between their religious values and the public religion of America, for the two were intertwined from an early day. Among Protestants, the Lutherans and Episcopalians-- both emphasizing liturgies and both established churches in Europe--had the greatest difficulty in adjusting to the American situation. In the case of the Lutherans, large migrations from Germany and Scandinavia after the Civil War complicated the acculturation process, for language and cultural contrasts heightened their sense of distinctiveness. (The merger of several Lutheran bodies in the past two decades indicates the lessening of old ethnic loyalties.)

The most persistent ethnic cleavage in America is between blacks and whites. Rooted in the slavery epoch and accentuated by color differences, the separation of blacks and whites is very sharp. Residential segregation is very general in the North and West. This segregation heightens the division between black churches and white churches, for almost all churches are residentially based.

The consequences of this cleavage for institutional religious life were discussed in Chapter III. The emergence of the visible black Protestant church after the Civil War provided black people with a social institution which they could control and which could speak and respond to their condition. Evolving out of the "invisible" black church of antebellum days and appropriating and modifying southern evangelical Protestantism, black Protestantism developed a unique shape and style.

As blacks migrated from the South to urban centers in other parts of the United States, they settled in segregated residential areas. In part this ethnic clustering was similar to that of European migrants, for most ethnic groups settling in urban areas sought to claim some turf and to establish urban villages in the large and diverse cities. In the black instance, this natural tendency was accentuated by racial prejudice, so the black ghetto became quasi-compulsory. Blacks were forced to live in restricted areas of the urban complex. Restrictive covenants, declared unconstitutional in the late 1940's, were legal instruments to foster ghettos. Since then, a variety of extra-legal means have been employed to sustain large ghettos of black people in northern urban centers.

This situation prevailed in the suburban sector, for, as noted in Chapter III, the black population was confined primarily to Satellite City and Shopton, the two suburban communities ranking lowest socio-economically of any of those in the sector.

All of the predominantly black churches were located here. A few churches on the fringe of the ghetto--all of them financially pre-carious--had interracial congregations. These congregations consisted primarily of young and middle-aged blacks and old whites. They gave every evidence of being churches in the process of transition from all white to all black institutions.

This distribution illumines the extreme difficulty of maintaining integrated voluntary institutions in a racially segregated society. Per-haps in no other area does the ideal of the inclusiveness of universal religious vision contrast more sharply with the exclusiveness of particular religious institutions. There were a sprinkling of middle status blacks in other suburbs, and a few of the churches in these areas reported some black members. In no instance did the percentage of black members approach 5 percent—— except in Satellite City and Shopton.[7]

Contemporary Ethnic Consciousness

The relatively greater ethnic identification of Catholics, black Protestants and Jews is illustrated in Table VII-7. As that table reveals, much higher proportions of black Protestants, Catholics, and Jews than of white Protestants identified with a particular nationality or ethnic group.

The insensitivity of many mainline Protestant leaders to ethnic groups other than the black ethnic group is related to these differentials in ethnic sensitivities, for the white Anglo-Saxon Protestant is more conscious of black ethnicity than of white ethnicity.[8]

These data illustrate the value of distinguishing between "accul-turation" and "assimilation." Members of an ethnic group are acculturated if they affirm some of the core values of their new country but maintain some values giving them a distinctive style of life. They are assimilated if they accept so many of the core values of their new country they lose their distinct identity and blend indistinguishably into the predominant group.

Using this terminology, Catholics, Jews, and black Protestants have been acculturated but not assimilated. Indeed, the genius of the American experiment is that it seeks the acculturation but not the assimilation of its diverse social, ethnic, cultural, and religious groups. The need for the appropriation of some common values by all subgroups in a complex society inevitably blurs the dividing line between acculturation and assimilation.

Responses to the question "Being a [Methodist, Catholic, Jew] makes it harder to feel a part of American society" illumined the

TABLE VII-7

ETHNIC IDENTITY IN PERCENT BY

COMMUNITY FOR SELECTED RELIGIOUS GROUPS

Community

Ethnic Identity	Satellite City			New Town		Country Club Estates		
	Black Protestant	White Protestant	Catholic	White Protestant	Catholic	White Protestant	Catholic	Jewish
Respondent identifies with ethnic group	36	19	32	14	30	12	35	26
Respondent does not identify with ethnic group	64	81	68	86	70	88	65	74
N=	61	183	145	268	200	218	204	121

Chi square = 63.19031 $p < 0.001$

Coefficient of Contingency = 0.20781

acculturation of all these groups so far as religious identification is concerned, for the overwhelming majority of the four faith groups disagreed with this statement. The actual percentages of the respondents agreeing with that statement were: white Protestants, 2 percent; black Protestants, 3 percent; Catholics, 2 percent; and Jews, 9 percent.

Some social critics have scored the idolatry of the nation implicit in such affirmations, claiming religious institutions have too closely identified with the "American way of life."[9] There is some truth in such criticisms, but these findings lend themselves to a more moderate inter- pretation. They indicate the legitimacy of the several faith groups in the context of the American experience. Without such a common affirmation by the members of the several faith groups, America would be struggling with highly volatile religious controversies.[10]

Interfaith Friendships

Interfaith friendships shed further light on the issue of religious and ethnic identity, for people do not relate closely to those with whom they have major disagreements on core values.

To assess the extent of interfaith friendships, respondents were asked to indicate the number of their four closest friends who were Protestant, Catholic, and Jewish. The variations by community area were not very great, probably reflecting the presence of substantial numbers of each faith group in each community.

Approximately one-third of the Protestant respondents reported no closest Catholic friends, and approximately four-fifths reported no closest Jewish friends. The Catholic data were almost identical, with about one-third of the Catholics reporting no closest Protestant friends and slightly over four-fifths reporting no closest Jewish friends. Slightly over half the Jewish respondents reported no closest Protestant friends, and the same proportion reported no closest Catholic friends.

Taking into account the fact that the suburban sector was less than 5 percent Jewish, more Protestants and Catholics reported closest Jewish friends than vice versa. No data on black-white friendship patterns were obtained, but it is apparent that black-white friendship patterns are less frequent than gentile-Jewish ones.

These data cohere with others suggesting an increasing rapprochement between white Protestants and Catholics in America, but they indicate persistent cleavage between Jews, white Christians, and black Protestants.

Summary

The data shown here depict substantial contrasts in social status within Protestantism. In general, NCC-affiliated Protestant churches attract middle and upper status members disproportionately, and non-NCC-affiliated Protestant churches attract lower status members disproportionately. The Catholic church is more status inclusive than particular Protestant denominations and than particular Protestant churches, for their liturgical style and geographically based parishes encourage common participation in the Mass. Because there are relatively few lower status Jews, synagogues draw disproportionately from the middle and upper social strata.

Young adults and men are less frequent participants in religious institutions than children or middle-aged and older adults and women. Relatively low young adult participation is not confined to religious institutions, for they participate less frequently in all voluntary associations.

White Protestants have the least ethnic identification and black Protestants and Catholics have the most. Friendship patterns suggest increasing white Protestant-Catholic rapprochement, but continued cleavages between blacks and whites and between Jews and the other groups.

CHAPTER VIII

THE RECEDING STORM: RELIGION AND THE QUEST FOR JUSTICE

Introduction

People motivated by religious impulses have perennially sought justice among humankind. They have not always been true to their impulses, and they have not always been clear about the nature of justice and its relation to religion. Nonetheless, a concern for the common good and a quest for social justice have been a part of the predominant religious heritages in America.

People have always disagreed about the proper relation of religious institutions to other social institutions. Some have thought religious institutions should not deal directly with matters in the public sphere, some have thought religious institutions should seek to transform and/or sustain the public sphere, and a few have thought religious institutions should seek to revolutionize the public sphere.[1]

In the American experience, race, poverty, and war have been the triad of issues around which religious professionals and lay people have centered their social concerns. Sometimes they have sought to aid directly the victims of these scourges, and sometimes they have sought to address themselves to the issues giving rise to the injustices.[2]

In the 1960's, highly visible church and synagogue leadership was in the vanguard of those seeking to advance the Civil Rights Movement. Church leaders were staunch supporters of Martin Luther King, and many responded to his call for protest marches, sit-ins, and similar activities to dramatize long-standing injustices. Concern for the plight of the poor and the dispossessed of all races was an inextricable part of this movement. Within Protestantism, many denominational and interdenominational agencies supported the Civil Rights Movement. The National Council of Churches was a particularly visible proponent of racial justice. Interfaith agencies and instrumentalities were established to promote racial and social justice.

Later in the decade many Protestant clergy, particularly in NCC-affiliated denominations, joined with some priests and rabbis to protest United States involvement in the Vietnam War. This public opposition, as subsequent data will show, received conflicting lay responses, for lay people were very divided in their attitudes toward the war. Some foresaw a gathering storm in the churches with groups polarized around alternative interpretations and actions on public policy issues.[3]

139

In the early 1970's, these movements began to ebb. The intracta-
bility of some of the problems and increased lay questioning of denominational and interdenominational programs and pronouncements combined to
diminish public involvement by religious institutions. Self-interest
among middle status lay people contributed to the disaffection, but the
lack of realism, undue optimism, and lack of balance and proportion displayed by many ecclesiastical leaders contributed to the shifting climate
of opinion.[3]

This chapter explores some of the persistent and pervasive factors
related to religious institutions' quests for social justice in order to
understand why the gathering storm some anticipated receded so gently.
The factors include: the contributions lay people think their churches
and synagogues have made to their understanding of job morality and public
policy issues; lay and clergy attitudes toward various facets of church
and synagogue programs; the views of various groups within voluntary
religious institutions both toward public policy involvement by churches
and synagogues in general and also toward specific public policy issues;
and lay people's attitudes toward American society.

Lay Evaluation of Helpfulness of Church or

Synagogue in Intergroup Morality

In addition to lay evaluation of the helpfulness of the church or
synagogue in providing guidance on interpersonal relations, lay evaluation
of the helpfulness of their church or synagogue in providing guidance in
their economic endeavors and on social and political issues was also
obtained. The findings are summarized in Tables VIII-1 and VIII-2.

The majority of respondents did not find their religious institutions helpful in these areas of intergroup morality. Only among Satellite
City's white Protestants did a majority find their church helpful in
providing guidance in the economic sphere as Table VIII-1 indicates.

In no instance did a majority of respondents report their religious
institution helpful in providing guidance on social and political issues.
As Table VIII-2 reveals, only a small percent of the respondents found
their religious institution "very helpful" in providing guidance on social
and political issues.

In the main, respondents felt their church or synagogue to have
been of little help one way or another in providing guidance for intergroup
relations. Data reported earlier revealed that a much higher proportion
of respondents reported their church or synagogue had been helpful in
interpersonal relations (see Chapter VI, pp. 112-3).

Such findings are not surprising. Clergy interviews indicated
that very few clergy had any explicit understanding of differences in the
priority of love and justice in interpersonal and intergroup relations, so

TABLE VIII-1

HELPFULNESS OF RELIGIOUS INSTITUTION FOR GUIDANCE ON THE JOB

IN PERCENT BY COMMUNITY FOR SELECTED RELIGIOUS GROUPS

	Community							
	Satellite City			New Town		Country Club Estates		
Degree of Helpfulness	Black Protestant	White Protestant	Catholic	White Protestant	Catholic	White Protestant	Catholic	Jewish
Very helpful	8	24	7	9	4	11	6	2
Helpful	31	34	34	34	30	37	35	14
Of little help one way or another	46	38	45	51	56	43	44	69
Somewhat helpful	2	1	3	2	4	1	5	2
Very unhelpful	10	2	5	2	3	4	4	7
Other	3	2	6	2	3	4	5	6
N=	59	160	126	248	192	206	189	120

Chi square = 122.03989   p<0.001

Coefficient of Contingency = 0.29295

TABLE VIII-2

HELPFULNESS OF RELIGIOUS INSTITUTION FOR GUIDANCE

ON SOCIAL AND POLITICAL ISSUES

IN PERCENT BY COMMUNITY FOR SELECTED RELIGIOUS GROUPS

	Community							
	Satellite City			New Town		Country Club Estates		
Degree of Helpfulness	Black Protestant	White Protestant	Catholic	White Protestant	Catholic	White Protestant	Catholic	Jewish
Very helpful	9	12	2	4	2	4	3	4
Helpful	34	36	23	27	18	33	21	27
Of little help one way or another	39	44	52	59	61	50	58	52
Somewhat unhelpful	5	2	6	3	7	4	6	3
Very unhelpful	8	4	10	4	7	6	7	7
Other	5	2	6	2	5	3	5	6
N=	64	165	127	249	192	209	192	121

Chi square = 79.29070   p<0.001

Coefficient of Contingency = 0.23813

they had little explicit guidance to offer to lay people on intergroup relations. In addition, theological understanding can provide more explicit guidelines for interpersonal relations than for intergroup relations. Authentic conflict exists in the social, economic, and political realms because it is so difficult to develop a consensus on the issues among the protagonists involved in social conflict. In vague and relatively inchoate ways lay people are reflecting their intuitions of this reality in their responses to these questions.[4]

Lay Attitudes toward Various Church and Synagogue Programs

Introduction

Lay respondents were asked to indicate their feelings toward personal growth groups, prayer and devotional groups, recreational and social groups, service groups, adult religious education groups, youth groups, social action groups, choir and/or liturgy groups, and administrative and policy groups.

In only two facets of local parish program did more than 10 percent of the respondents report negative feelings. In the cases of experimental growth groups and social action groups, about 20 percent of the respondents reported negative feelings. These controversial groups will be considered in more detail in the following two subsections.

Lay Attitudes toward Experimental Growth Groups

Lay attitudes toward experimental growth groups are shown in Table VIII-3. Approximately a quarter of the respondents had favorable attitudes toward such groups, and about 20 percent had unfavorable feelings. This distribution suggests that judicious clergy could promote such groups if they wanted, but there would be some internal controversy about them. Substantial proportions of the respondents had never heard of such programs, probably disproportionately including potential opponents. Allowing for the higher proportion of respondents in Satellite City who had never heard of such groups, there was no marked variation in responses by faith group or community area.

Clergy attitudes toward personal growth groups parallelled those of the laity quite closely. (See Table IV-3). In this instance, there was sufficient interest among laity for clergy desiring to initiate such programs to attract some interest.

TABLE VIII-3

ATTITUDE TOWARD EXPERIMENTAL GROWTH GROUPS

IN PERCENT BY COMMUNITY FOR SELECTED RELIGIOUS GROUPS

	Community							
	Satellite City			New Town		Country Club Estates		
Attitude towards Growth Groups	Black Protestant	White Protestant	Catholic	White Protestant	Catholic	White Protestant	Catholic	Jewish
Very favorable	10	6	3	8	9	5	2	8
Favorable	24	14	16	23	20	20	24	26
Mixed feelings	29	27	23	34	30	33	28	29
Unfavorable	5	15	11	14	13	15	14	16
Very unfavorable	10	5	10	6	7	8	8	7
Don't know or no opinion	21	35	38	15	22	19	22	13
N=	58	176	133	268	195	212	201	122

Chi square = 77.50923 $p < 0.001$

Coefficient of Contingency = 0.23180

Lay Attitudes toward Social Action Groups and

Church Involvement in Public Policy Issues

As Table VII-4 shows, there was a much greater spread in the unfavorable responses on social action groups by faith group than on experimental growth groups. Unfavorable responses ranged from a low of 5 percent among black Protestants in Satellite City to a high of 32 percent among Catholics in Country Club Estates. Eleven percent of the Jewish respondents reported unfavorable feelings toward social action groups, and about 20 percent of the respondents in the other faith groups reported unfavorable feelings toward them.

Conversely, twice as many black Protestants and Jewish respondents reported "strongly favorable" feelings toward social action groups than did the respondents of the other faith groups. As the greatest victims of social injustice and prejudice, respondents of these groups were the staunchest supporters of religiously based social action groups.

Lay-clergy contrasts in attitudes on social action groups were sharper than on personal growth groups. Three-quarters of the NCC-affiliated Protestant clergy and 55 percent of the Catholic clergy were favorably disposed toward such groups--approximately twice as many as comparable lay groups. (See Table IV-4.)

Since less than 10 percent of the respondents indicated "very unfavorable" attitudes toward local social action groups, clergy have considerable latitude in sponsoring social action groups, but they need to be especially sensitive to lay feelings on this facet of their program.

Further data on lay attitudes toward church involvement in social issues are shown in Tables VIII-5 and VIII-6.

In Table VIII-5, four levels of local involvement are distinguished: none, low, medium and high. The "none" response included those who felt the religious institution should not become involved in matters of public policy in any form. The "low" response included those who would only agree to the religious institution giving help to people to join community social action groups not identified with the religious institution. The "medium" response included those who thought the religious institution should allow its facilities to be used for social action group meetings, should sponsor discussion groups to discuss public issues, or both. The "high" response included those who thought the religious institution should take official stands on public issues, help establish informal parish social action groups, or both.

As Table VIII-5 reveals, there was substantial lay Catholic opposition to any form of local parish social action programs. Nonetheless, there was majority support in all of the surveyed religious institutions for at least a "medium" level of local religious institutional involvement in social action.

TABLE VIII-4

ATTITUDE TOWARD LOCAL SOCIAL ACTION GROUPS

IN PERCENT BY COMMUNITY FOR SELECTED RELIGIOUS GROUPS

	Community							
	Satellite City			New Town		Country Club Estates		
Attitude toward Local Social Action Groups	Black Protestant	White Protestant	Catholic	White Protestant	Catholic	White Protestant	Catholic	Jewish
Very favorable	26	12	12	14	13	8	5	24
Favorable	42	24	24	29	18	23	20	35
Mixed feelings	24	36	25	33	33	44	32	23
Unfavorable	5	13	10	10	13	13	21	7
Very unfavorable	0	7	10	8	9	8	11	4
Don't know or no opinion	3	8	21	6	14	6	11	6
N=	62	177	136	265	196	211	200	123

Chi square = 135.57767   p<0.001

Coefficient of Contingency = 0.30008

TABLE VIII-5

PROPER RESPONSE OF LOCAL RELIGIOUS INSTITUTION TO SOCIAL ISSUES

IN PERCENT BY COMMUNITY FOR SELECTED RELIGIOUS GROUPS

	Community							
	Satellite City			New Town		Country Club Estates		
Type of Response	Black Protestant	White Protestant	Catholic	White Protestant	Catholic	White Protestant	Catholic	Jewish
None	5	19	30	17	22	17	24	13
Low	23	14	14	16	19	19	18	17
Medium	35	43	38	41	32	43	37	40
High	37	25	18	26	27	21	21	30
N=	65	167	138	261	187	210	187	119

Chi square = 39.91249 $p < 0.01$

Coefficient of Contingency = 0.17050

TABLE VIII-6

ATTITUDE   TOWARD PUBLIC STANDS ON POLITICAL ISSUES

BY NON-LOCAL ECCLESIASTICAL BODIES

IN PERCENT BY COMMUNITY FOR SELECTED RELIGIOUS GROUPS

Community

Attitudes toward Public Stands on Political Issues by Ecclesias- tical Bodies	Satellite City			New Town		Country Club Estates		
	Black Protestant	White Protestant	Catholic	White Protestant	Catholic	White Protestant	Catholic	Jewish
Strongly agree	17	6	3	3	3	2	3	9
Agree	19	20	8	13	11	7	11	19
Mixed feelings	23	28	20	24	19	25	20	20
Disagree	22	27	26	34	37	37	33	33
Strongly disagree	11	13	31	22	26	27	30	16
No opinion	8	6	12	3	4	3	3	2
N=	64	176	145	263	194	214	202	122

Chi square = 122.93831   p<0.001

Coefficient of Contingency = 0.28600

Comparable clergy responses were reported in Chapter IV. (See Table IV-5.) Catholic priests had a much higher percentage of "high" responses than Catholic laity, suggesting substantial disagreements within that faith community. Such sharp contrasts did not emerge among white Protestants.

Table VIII-6 indicates that lay people were especially disenchanted with the practice of non-local ecclesiastical bodies taking public stands on political issues, a practice very widespread in the 1960's in the National Council of Churches and some of its affiliated denominations. Black Protestants were split on the issue, but pluralities or majorities of the respondents in all the other faith groups disagreed with the policy.

The fact that both local and non-local political stands by churches or synagogues are strongly opposed is related to the voluntaryism of the religions of America. This voluntaryism elevates the individual conscience to a commanding position: there is a strong tendency to reject any decisions made by the group or its representatives which seem to be "imposed" on individual members. This individualism holds for matters of morality as well, as Chapter IX will show.

The opposition to binding corporate decisions is evident in the marginal comments that the respondents were encouraged to make: an analysis of them suggests that many of the laity are concerned that their individual judgments be respected. Even in the Protestant congregations in which the principle of voluntaryism is clearly and strongly affirmed officially, lay people are concerned that their ministers are not mindful enough of the individual's responsibility for decision.

This lay negativity toward public stands on political issues by local and non-local ecclesiastical bodies does not mean lay people are unequivocally conservative or insensitive to issues involving social justice. As Table VIII-7 indicates, a sizable minority of lay people in each congregation supports the idea that "Christian (Jewish) principles can provide the basis for participating in protest movements." Indeed, in no case did the proportion who flatly opposed such an idea exceed 30 percent.

It may well be assumed that the idea of religious legitimation for protest movements would have been clearly and overwhelmingly rejected before the 1960's. There is thus a great lesson here: the decade of clerical involvement in protest movements has not only been followed by a "backlash" denial of financial support due to protests over specific corporate ecclesiastical actions, but it has also led to a widespread adoption by lay people of the idea that the individual may rightly find that his religious convictions impel him to take part in public protests.

In sum, these findings reveal the complexity of the relationship of churches and synagogues to political activity in contemporary American society. There is majority lay support for actions which may be termed "facilitating" (urging community involvement, forming discussion groups, allowing premises to be used by community groups), but strong opposition to religious leaders and groups taking actions or making pronouncements which may be considered "binding" on the individual member. It seems evident that clergy of each faith grouping need to be

TABLE VIII-7

RESPONSE TO STATEMENT "CHRISTIAN (JEWISH) PRINCIPLES CAN PROVIDE

THE BASIS FOR PARTICIPATING IN PROTEST MOVEMENTS"

IN PERCENT BY COMMUNITY FOR SELECTED RELIGIOUS GROUPS

	Community							
	Satellite City			New Town		Country Club Estates		
Response to Statement	Black Protestant	White Protestant	Catholic	White Protestant	Catholic	White Protestant	Catholic	Jewish
Strongly agree	15	8	9	5	6	2	6	11
Agree	29	24	21	36	23	27	28	28
Mixed feelings or depends on circumstances	31	32	26	28	33	32	26	26
Disagree	8	18	19	16	15	24	15	9
Strongly disagree	3	7	8	8	7	6	12	11
No opinion	15	10	17	8	16	9	12	16
N=	62	177	140	256	195	216	200	121

Chi square = 78.11957 $p < 0.001$

Coefficient of Contingency = 0.23250

much more explicit, if they wish to assure the laity that they do not speak as the oracle of God. As Robert Bellah suggests, the issue of the legitimacy of dissent within the individual church or synagogue needs and probably will receive explicit attention in the coming years.[5]

Suburban Lay People Assess Public Policy Issues

Introduction

It is apparent that there was considerable lay ambivalence about the principle of church or synagogue involvement in issues of public policy. Substantial minorities opposed local church and synagogue social action groups, and substantial majorities opposed public policy pronouncements by ecclesiastical bodies.

Respondents were also asked to respond to more specific policy matters in order to explore the substance of public policy issues. The areas examined were race, poverty, and war, the three persistent areas of social concern in American religious institutions. In addition, a question on the legalization of the sale of marijuana was included to assess perspectives on an emerging social issue. In order to permit lay-clergy comparisons these items are the same as the ones used in the clergy analyses presented in Chapter IV.

Race and Suburban Lay People

Rooted in the institution of slavery and reinforced by ethnocentric tendencies, including endogamy and limited friendships across racial lines, race relations reflect the sharpest internal contrast between the ideals of liberty and equality envisaged in the American dream and the social reality of segregation and inequality.[6]

As noted in Chapter VII, the disharmony is also a product of authentic religion, for the vision of the well being of the whole and the common good contrasts with the reality of inordinate segregation and inequality. To assess the views of members of the religions of American suburbia on racial problems, respondents were asked to indicate their responses to the statement "The suburbs should be racially integrated."

The data in Table VIII-8 illustrate the ambivalent feelings of lay respondents about racial integration of the suburbs. Black Protestants, Jews, and New Town white Protestants were the only groups in which a majority of the respondents agreed that the suburbs should be racially integrated, but no group had as many as 30 percent of respondents disagreeing with the proposition. This ambivalence, pointing to the continued presence of the racial problem in America, contrasts markedly with clergy attitudes (see Table IV-17), for all the clergy groups except non-NCC-affiliated white Protestants strongly supported the idea of racial integration

TABLE VIII-8

RESPONSE TO STATEMENT "THE SUBURBS SHOULD BE RACIALLY INTEGRATED"

IN PERCENT BY COMMUNITY FOR SELECTED RELIGIOUS GROUPS

	Community							
	Satellite City			New Town		Country Club Estates		
Response to Statement	Black Protestant	White Protestant	Catholic	White Protestant	Catholic	White Protestant	Catholic	Jewish
Strongly agree	40	8	10	11	11	4	6	18
Agree	35	21	21	45	34	27	24	36
Mixed feelings or depends on circumstances	20	39	35	29	37	40	38	36
Disagree	0	16	13	7	10	18	16	4
Strongly disagree	2	8	11	4	4	9	11	4
No opinion	3	7	10	3	3	1	4	2
N =	65	179	144	262	194	215	200	123

Chi square = 196.73288 $p < 0.001$

Coefficient of Contingency = 0.35301

of the suburbs. Responses of the non-NCC-affiliated white Protestant clergy parallel lay responses more closely than do those of any other clergy group.

The data are not unqualifiedly discouraging, for the direction of conviction is toward the desirability of racial integration. Fewer than one in ten respondents "strongly disagreed" with the proposition. These responses suggest no quick resolution of the racial problem, but only a small minority of members of suburban religious institutions were adamant in their opposition to suburban racial integration.

Poverty and Suburban Lay People

The work ethic is deeply ingrained in the American experience. Rooted in Calvinism and powerfully expressed in secular form by Benjamin Franklin in Poor Richard's Almanac, the idea that those who are not willing to work should not eat is widespread in contemporary America. Complex contemporary welfare problems obviously do not lend themselves to easy solutions, but the insistence that able-bodied welfare recipients work for their welfare benefits has received widespread acclaim.

Such views pervade both the clergy and the lay people of suburban churches and synagogues. Table VIII-9 shows the predominance of a "no-work" "no-benefit" mentality among lay respondents, for less than 5 percent of them disagreed with the statement.

A substantial proportion of lay respondents gave circumstantial responses. The four groups in which a majority of the respondents agreed with the statement were white Protestants and Catholics in lower status Satellite City, Catholics in New Town, and white Protestants in Country Club Estates. Black Protestants, who probably were better acquainted with the problems of the welfare recipient than these white respondents, had the most respondents saying it depended on the circumstances.

A higher proportion of circumstantial responses among lay people than among clergy (see Table IV-18) is due to a different wording of the item in the clergy questionnaire. In the clergy questionnaire the item read: Able-bodied welfare recipients should be put to work. At any rate, the mind set of both clergy and lay people suggests that welfare rights movements are not going to have much support from suburban lay people, be they black, white, Protestant, Catholic, or Jew.

The Vietnam War and Suburban Lay People

No public policy issue was being more intensely debated when this study was being conducted in the spring of 1972 than the issue of United States involvement in Vietnam. Many ecclesiastical bodies had issued pronouncements against the war, and many religious leaders had been out-spoken in their moral denunciation of the war.

A majority of black Protestants and a substantial plurality of Jews agreed with the statement "American involvement in the Vietnam War

TABLE VIII-9

LAY ATTITUDES TOWARD STATEMENT "WELFARE RECIPIENTS SHOULD BE PUT TO WORK"

IN PERCENT BY COMMUNITY FOR SELECTED RELIGIOUS GROUPS

	Community							
	Satellite City			New Town		Country Club Estates		
Response to Statement	Black Protestant	White Protestant	Catholic	White Protestant	Catholic	White Protestant	Catholic	Jewish
Strongly agree	12	21	29	14	17	17	22	18
Agree	14	30	24	26	38	33	26	28
Mixed feelings or depends on circumstances	69	45	43	55	40	47	47	52
Disagree	3	2	1	4	2	2	2	1
Strongly disagree	0	1	1	1	1	0	1	1
No opinion	2	1	2	0	3	1	3	1
N=	65	183	145	263	194	214	199	122

Chi square = 74.10498 $p < 0.002$

Coefficient of Contingency = 0.22521

TABLE VIII-10

RESPONSE TO STATEMENT "AMERICAN INVOLVEMENT

IN THE VIETNAM WAR HAS BEEN IMMORAL"

IN PERCENT BY COMMUNITY FOR SELECTED RELIGIOUS GROUPS

Community

Response to Statement	Satellite City			New Town		Country Club Estates		
	Black Protestant	White Protestant	Catholic	White Protestant	Catholic	White Protestant	Catholic	Jewish
Strongly agree	19	11	15	8	7	7	7	26
Agree	33	17	20	14	23	16	16	22
Mixed feelings or depends on circumstances	23	41	34	38	36	37	36	30
Disagree	8	19	15	27	20	29	26	14
Strongly disagree	5	6	2	10	5	7	8	7
No opinion	12	7	13	3	8	4	6	1
N=	64	180	143	263	191	214	203	122

Chi square = 132.66525 $p < 0.001$

Coefficient of Contingency = 0.29615

has been immoral," as Table VIII-10 indicates. Few differences emerged
between white Protestants and Catholics, but lower status Satellite City
had a higher proportion of respondents agreeing that the war was immoral
than did middle status New Town or upper status Country Club Estates.

The ambivalence of lay feelings is reflected by the fact that the
modal response for all groups except black Protestants was "mixed feelings."
Considering the multiple sources contributing to people's judgments about
public policy issues, the influence of religious leadership on people's
attitudes toward the war cannot be dismissed as inconsequential, but it
cannot be characterized as determinative.

NCC-affiliated Protestant clergy were most sharply at odds with
lay evaluations, and Roman Catholic clergy were in closest accord with lay
evaluations (see Table IV-19).

Legalizing Sale of Marijuana

Lay respondents were strongly opposed to the legalization of
marijuana, an item selected to illumine contrasts on an emerging social
issue. The Jewish group was the only one in which a substantial minority
of respondents favored the legalization of the sale of marijuana, as Table
VIII-11 shows. No Protestant-Catholic contrasts emerged. The suburban
religious groups were clearly on the conserving side of this issue, but
once again more Jews than Christians were on the "permissive" or "liberal"
side of a public policy issue.

Summary

The clergy were more supportive of racial integration of the suburbs and less certain about the morality of American involvement in the
Vietnam War than lay people. There was basically a lay-clergy consensus
on work requirements for able-bodied welfare recipients.

Small minorities of lay and clergy respondents felt marijuana should
be legalized, but except for non-NCC-affiliated white Protestant clergy
only a minority of each group strongly disagreed with the proposition.
Churches are unlikely to be in the vanguard of those urging a change in
drug laws on marijuana.

These responses indicated a more substantial contrast between the
views of the NCC-affiliated clergy and lay people on these representative
social issues than between other clergy and lay people. The non-NCC-
affiliated white clergy had responses more closely akin to white Protestants
(who were members of a NCC-affiliated church) than did NCC-affiliated
Protestant clergy.

This situation is illuminating, for it helps to explain the popularity of mass evangelists such as Billy Graham and Oral Roberts. The

TABLE VIII-11

RESPONSE TO STATEMENT "THE SALE OF MARIJUANA SHOULD BE LEGALIZED"

IN PERCENT BY COMMUNITY FOR SELECTED RELIGIOUS GROUPS

	Community							
	Satellite City			New Town		Country Club Estates		
Response to Statement	Black Protestant	White Protestant	Catholic	White Protestant	Catholic	White Protestant	Catholic	Jewish
Strongly agree	8	4	5	3	4	3	2	10
Agree	8	4	3	10	8	7	6	24
Mixed feelings or depends on circumstances	20	12	11	23	28	17	21	27
Disagree	35	37	33	37	19	32	29	22
Strongly disagree	22	40	45	25	36	38	38	15
No opinion	7	3	3	2	4	3	4	2
N=	65	186	146	264	195	217	202	123

Chi square = 152.94264 $p < 0.001$

Coefficient of Contingency = 0.31403

majority of Protestant lay people outside the southern and southwestern
Bible Belt do not share either their biblical fundamentalism or their
evangelical fervor, but they are more apt to be in sympathy with their
views on social (not private) morality than with the views of their own
NCC-affiliated clergy.

Suburban Lay People Look at American

Society and Political Parties

Introduction

In the past decade many social analysts--both within and outside
religious institutions--have been very critical of America's economic and
political institutions. They have blamed them for many of the difficulties
of American life, and they have often called for radical revisions of all
or some of them.[7]

Items dealing with people's basic view of American society were
included in the schedule to assess the extent to which people felt they
were alienated from the basic structures of American society. The items
examined in this section--lay attitudes toward America's future, America's
present economic and political systems, the principle of separation of
church and state, and lay political preference--parallel the discussion of
clergy responses in Chapter IV to permit comparisons between lay and
clergy groups.

Lay Attitudes toward America's Future

Historically Americans have entertained a basic optimism about
the future of the nation. Coupling this optimism with a doctrine of
progress--often crudely equated with an increase in wealth--they have been
motivated to push ahead to master the environment and to forge relatively
novel instruments of government.

The press of technical rationalism and its byproducts have transformed the shape of America and have undermined many traditional values.
Such transformations may have modified the traditional optimism.

Unfortunately, comparable data for earlier periods are not available,
but the responses portrayed in Table VIII-12 indicate a persistence of
optimistic attitudes, perhaps modified by the events of the past decade or
two. Respondents' attitudes were correlated with both socioeconomic status
and major faith groups.

White Protestants and Catholics were more optimistic than were black
Protestants and Jews. Black Protestants and Jews, the two groups most

TABLE VIII-12

ATTITUDE   TOWARD AMERICA'S FUTURE

IN PERCENT BY COMMUNITY FOR SELECTED RELIGIOUS GROUPS

	Community							
	Satellite City			New Town		Country Club Estates		
Attitude toward America's Future	Black Protestant	White Protestant	Catholic	White Protestant	Catholic	White Protestant	Catholic	Jewish
Very optimistic	8	14	15	19	17	24	25	15
Somewhat optimistic	23	27	23	34	31	35	39	23
Mixed Feelings	30	35	31	29	24	24	19	32
Somewhat pessimistic	8	11	7	9	18	9	8	19
Very pessimistic	9	1	1	2	1	1	1	5
Confused and uncertain	20	9	16	6	7	7	7	7
No opinion	2	3	7	1	2	1	1	0
N=	64	187	142	265	201	212	199	123

Chi square = 146.63695 $p < 0.001$

Coefficient of Contingency = 0.30881

marginal to the center of American life, expressed the most pessimism
about the future, but even among these groups less than a quarter expressed
pessimistic views about America's future.

Not surprisingly, middle and upper status people who had greater
than average economic and social recognition were more optimistic about
America's future than those who did not. This situation is reflected in
the fact that substantial majorities of Protestants and Catholics in upper
status Country Club Estates expressed optimistic views about America's
future. A smaller majority of Protestants and a plurality of Catholics
expressed optimistic views in middle status New Town, and smaller pluralities
of both Protestants and Catholics expressed optimistic views in lower status
Satellite City.

Overall, the findings reflect a tempered optimism or a muted
pessimism. In no instance did more than a quarter of the respondents
report a very optimistic attitude toward America's future nor more than
10 percent report a very pessimistic attitude. Aside from the black
respondents, only a negligible proportion of respondents reported a very
pessimistic attitude. Perhaps somewhat sobered by the events of the past
decade, the majority of lay people still rejected a pessimistic interpretation of America's future.[8]

Evaluations of Existing Economic and Political Systems

Lay responses to items seeking a broad evaluation of America's
existing economic and political systems revealed the same centralist
tendencies as reported above. In the main, respondents expressed moderately
positive evaluation of both economic and political systems, as Tables
VIII-13 and VIII-14 show. Respondents were somewhat more positive about
the political system than the economic one, and black respondents were
most critical of both economic and political systems. In this instance
the black Protestants, who are less successful economically than the Jews,
were much more critical of the economic system than were Jews.

An "Index of Societal Integration" was constructed to get an
overview of the respondents' assessment of American society and its social
institutions. This index was based on responses to three questions:
"How do you feel about America's future?" "Our present economic system
is the best form of economic organization," and "Our present form of
political organization is the best form of political organization."
Responses to the first question were scored as follows: Very optimistic--1;
somewhat optimistic--2; mixed feelings or confused and uncertain--3; somewhat pessimistic--4; very pessimistic--5. Responses to the other two
questions were scored as follows: strongly agree--1; agree--2; mixed
feelings or depends on circumstances--3; disagree--4; strongly disagree--5.

Scores were summed, and the following groupings on the index of
Societal Value Integration were made:

TABLE VIII-13

RESPONSE TO STATEMENT "OUR PRESENT ECONOMIC SYSTEM

IS THE BEST FORM OF ECONOMIC ORGANIZATION"

IN PERCENT BY COMMUNITY FOR SELECTED RELIGIOUS GROUPS

	Community							
	Satellite City			New Town		Country Club Estates		
Response to Statement	Black Protestant	White Protestant	Catholic	White Protestant	Catholic	White Protestant	Catholic	Jewish
Strongly agree	0	6	4	4	4	7	9	7
Agree	6	31	17	32	23	34	34	26
Mixed feelings or depends on circumstances	35	35	37	40	40	38	36	43
Disagree	32	11	19	11	18	8	12	16
Strongly disagree	14	3	4	4	4	4	2	5
No opinion	15	14	18	8	12	9	8	3
N=	63	178	138	263	194	217	197	121

Chi square = 112.12167 $p < 0.001$

Coefficient of Contingency = 0.27495

TABLE VIII-14

RESPONSE TO STATEMENT "OUR PRESENT POLITICAL SYSTEM

IS THE BEST FORM OF POLITICAL ORGANIZATION"

IN PERCENT BY COMMUNITY FOR SELECTED RELIGIOUS GROUPS

Community

Response to Statement	Satellite City			New Town		Country Club Estates		
	Black Protestant	White Protestant	Catholic	White Protestant	Catholic	White Protestant	Catholic	Jewish
Strongly agree	0	7	6	5	6	8	8	6
Agree	14	36	24	40	33	49	39	33
Mixed feelings or depends on circumstances	47	32	34	38	36	29	35	41
Disagree	20	11	14	9	12	10	9	16
Strongly disagree	11	3	5	3	3	2	3	3
No opinion	8	11	18	5	10	2	4	2
N=	64	183	144	262	193	217	202	122

Chi square = 127.84116 $p < 0.001$

Coefficient of Contingency = 0.29050

	Score
High:	3-6
Medium:	7-10
Low:	11-15

The percentage of white Protestants and Catholics in the three communities scoring "high," "medium," and "low" on the index are shown in Table VIII-15.

TABLE VIII-15

INDEX OF SOCIETAL INTEGRATION

IN PERCENT BY COMMUNITY FOR SELECTED RELIGIOUS GROUPS

Community

Index of Societal Integration	Satellite City		New Town		Country Club Estates	
	White Protestant	Catholic	White Protestant	Catholic	White Protestant	Catholic
High	27	18	27	23	36	35
Medium	64	69	64	63	56	61
Low	9	13	9	13	8	4
N=	143	95	228	164	188	175

Chi square = 23.72 $p < 0.01$

Coefficient of contingency = 0.15274

The majority of respondents in all groups are in the "medium" category. Though not shown here, the majority of black Protestants and Jews were also in the "medium" category.

These findings indicate most members of suburban churches and synagogues neither exalt existing forms of social and economic organization nor condemn them sharply. Lay people may be prepared to seek reform of existing social institutions, but they are not prepared to revolutionize them.

Clergy seeking to foster reform to further the manifestations of love through the form of justice in the public sphere may anticipate substantial lay support, but those radically criticizing existing social institutions may anticipate opposition.

Clergy responses to these items were discussed in Chapter IV (see Tables IV-22 through IV-24). Except for the stronger commitment to the existing economic and political system by non-NCC-affiliated white Protestant clergy, lay and clergy response patterns were similar. The clergy tended to be somewhat more critical of existing forms of economic and political organizations, but the differences were modest.

Lay Political Preferences

The quest for justice leads both to broad concerns about the shape of public policy and also to specific concerns about the implementation of policy. The latter dimension is more specifically political than the former, for the development of laws and institutions to implement public policy requires political decisions. In the American context, such decisions are directly related to political parties.

Viewed broadly, the Republican Party has tended to accentuate the principle of self-determination in shaping public policy, and the Democratic Party has tended to accentuate the principle of equality.[9] Both principles are legitimate but partially contradictory under the conditions of existence, so compromises are generally effected in the political process. Nonetheless, historically the parties have reflected differing emphases.

In the American context, there has been no close ideological relation between religious and political preference. In fact, the privatization of the religious sphere discussed in Part I effectively precludes such relations. Nonetheless, historically various status and ethnic groups have identified both with particular religious groups and also with particular political parties. The majority of blacks, Jews, and Catholics have been identified with the Democratic Party, and the majority of white Protestants with the Republican Party.

As Table VIII-16 reveals, these historic patterns, modified by social status, persist among suburban lay people. Almost three-quarters of the black Protestants and almost three-fifths of the Jews indicated a Democratic preference. Only 3 percent of the black Protestants and 16 percent of the Jews reported a Republican preference.

TABLE VIII-16

POLITICAL PREFERENCE

IN PERCENT BY COMMUNITY FOR SELECTED RELIGIOUS GROUPS

	Community							
	Satellite City			New Town		Country Club Estates		
Political Preference	Black Protestant	White Protestant	Catholic	White Protestant	Catholic	White Protestant	Catholic	Jewish
Democratic	36	9	35	5	20	5	14	17
Independent, leaning toward Democratic	34	10	18	14	21	9	15	42
Strictly independent	15	8	11	10	14	10	16	14
Independent, leaning toward Republican	0	22	5	29	16	28	18	11
Republican	3	39	6	29	7	37	21	5
American Independent	0	0	1	0	0	1	1	0
No political preference	10	12	20	11	18	10	14	10
Other	2	1	2	1	4	1	2	2
N=	61	185	143	261	195	210	199	122

Chi square = 379.81738   p$<$0.001

Coefficient of Contingency = 0.46510

At the other extreme, about three-fifths of the white Protestants indicated Republican preferences, and less than one-fifth indicated Democratic preferences.

Suburban Catholic lay people reflected their historical Democratic preferences, but these preferences are being modified by Catholic upward social mobility. Fifty-three percent of the Catholics in lower status Satellite City, 41 percent of the Catholics in middle status New Town, and 29 percent of the Catholics in upper status Country Club Estates reported a Democratic political preference. Conversely, 11 percent of the Catholics in Satellite City, 23 percent of the Catholics in New Town, and 39 percent of Catholics in Country Club Estates reported a Republican political preference.

Roman Catholic and black Protestant clergy were more strongly Democratic in their political preference than their lay people, but lay people and clergy shared the same general direction of preference (see Table IV-26). Catholic clergy were much more strongly Democratic than suburban Catholic laity, suggesting some priest-laity conflict in this area in the future.

Within Protestantism, significant contrasts existed between clergy and lay people. The non-NCC-affiliated white clergy had political preference profiles which were very similar to the sample of NCC-affiliated white lay people. However, the NCC-affiliated clergy had political preference profiles differing sharply from NCC-affiliated white lay people, for a plurality of NCC-affiliated clergy reported Democratic preferences (44 percent), but a majority of white Protestant lay people (about 60 percent) reported Republican preferences. This contrast between NCC-affiliated Protestant clergy and NCC-affiliated white Protestant lay people illumines the controversies about social action in NCC-affiliated Protestant churches.

Summary

The privatization of the religious sphere, an outgrowth partly of American personal piety and partly of a need to sustain religious liberty, tolerance, and pluralism in America, has been highlighted in this chapter. Lay people do not think their churches and synagogues have provided them with as much guidance in the public realm as in the private realm.

Given the wide range of lay responses to specific policy issues, it seems unlikely that churches and synagogues can expect to attain a consensus on most issues of public policy. In the voluntary church such diversity is scarcely surprising. Some small highly intentional and highly disciplined groups may attain considerable consensus on religious beliefs and related matters of personal and social morality, but most voluntary religious groups are more inclusive and amorphous. As has been noted the idea of the supremacy of individual judgment is widespread. Clerical actions--or even majority lay action--which do not respect this principle will encounter strong resistance.

Even as concerned clergy and lay people in the latter type of religious institutions continue to try to discern the meaning and implications of their religious heritages through worship, education, and close interpersonal relations and seek to serve in the larger community, they will continue to encounter internal diversity of belief and practice. They will never attain a full consensus on matters of faith and morals, but they may continue to sustain institutions seeking to illumine and to bear faltering witness to the Divine Presence in human life.

CHAPTER IX

SECULARIZATION AND THE PUBLIC RELIGION OF AMERICA:

CHANGING PATTERNS OF BELIEF AMONG THE RELIGIONS OF AMERICAN SUBURBIA

Introduction

Survey data are necessarily rather crude, and they tend to atomize the cluster of beliefs held by particular individuals into inordinately discrete parts. In spite of these limitations, such data do provide some insight into changing patterns of belief.

Technical rationalism epitomizes secularization. Though in our day many people affirm the autonomy and the analytic calculating nature of reason, they ignore or reject the notions that reason participates in nature, has a depth-dimension, is synthetic, and/or is intimately related to a Supreme Entity Who is, in some senses, _sui generis_. In fact, they are suspicious when others even raise philosophic questions about the nature of reason and its relation to the world. Persons affirming the supremacy of technical reason attest to a secular matter-of-factness about a world which people--at least potentially--can dominate and master. They may not themselves understand the processes by which things work, but they have confidence that someone understands or will understand such processes.

Because the United States is a technical society _par excellence_, secularization is a very powerful motif in American life. Nonetheless, technical rationalism is not the only motif in the American value complex. It coexists with secular humanism, the public religion of America, and the various religious heritages constituting the religions of America. Most people reflect values drawn from each of these facets of the American value complex, and they do not press for any strongly coherent integrated perspective. This accepted lack of coherence is the basis for the judgment that America is both very secular and very pious.

The existence of this panoply of diverse values qualifies religious beliefs, for they must be accommodated to the pluralism and tolerance of the American situation. In this chapter, the diverse ways in which the four faith groups have modified their historic religious heritages to accommodate to pluralism and tolerance are explored.

Lay assessments of the helpfulness of religious institutions in shaping their religious beliefs provide clues about the feelings of members toward the broad cluster of beliefs represented in the four faith groups. The involvement of families in their faith group is assessed by discerning the frequency of family discussion of faith and morals.

In order to assess the religious and moral perspectives of suburban lay people, the following items are examined: experience of the presence of God, views toward the Ten Commandments, expectations about moral standards in churches and synagogues, the desirability of finding peace and security in religious institutions, the interpretations of Scripture; and views on evangelism.

Lay Evaluations of the Helpfulness of Religious

Institutions in the Formation of Religious Beliefs

The majority of lay respondents in each faith group felt that their church or synagogue had been helpful in the formation of their religious beliefs, as Table IX-1 shows. About three-fourths of the Christian respondents and over half the Jewish respondents felt their religious institution had been helpful in the formation of their religious beliefs. Some might hold the question had a Catholic-Christian bias, since that faith group emphasizes the importance of doctrine more forcefully than do Protestants or Jews. However, the differences are probably pointing to authentic contrasts. As other data have revealed, more Jews have difficulty with the theological side of the religio-historical tradition than is the case with respondents from any of the other faith groups, and Protestants do emphasize aspects of the formal side of religious experience.

Respondents were also asked to evaluate the degree of helpfulness of their church or synagogue in providing guidance for their personal prayer life. As Table IX-2 indicates, a similar pattern emerged. Less than a third of the Jewish respondents reported that their synagogue had been helpful here, compared to more than half in all the Christian groups.

Christianity has probably emphasized personal piety more strongly than has Judaism, for Jews historically have tended to intertwine the personal and communal sides of religious experience. It is likely that both this situation and also the more marginal involvement of Jews in the synagogue are reflected in these differences in responses.

A comparison with responses to comparable questions dealing with family life (Table VI-1), on-the-job morality (Table VIII-1), and social and political issues (Table VIII-2) is revealing.

The highest proportion of respondents reported their church or synagogue had been helpful in providing guidance for the formation of religious beliefs, and the lowest proportion of respondents reported the church or synagogue had been helpful in providing guidance on social and political issues. The second highest proportion reported their church or synagogue had been helpful in providing guidance for family life.

This pattern agrees with the interpretation of religious life in America developed in Chapter II. In that chapter, the separation of the religious sphere from the public spheres was discussed, and the privatization

TABLE IX-1

HELPFULNESS OF RELIGIOUS INSTITUTION IN FORMING RELIGIOUS BELIEFS

IN PERCENT BY COMMUNITY FOR SELECTED RELIGIOUS GROUPS

Community

Degree of Helpfulness	Satellite City			New Town		Country Club Estates		
	Black Protestant	White Protestant	Catholic	White Protestant	Catholic	White Protestant	Catholic	Jewish
Very helpful	24	45	33	30	22	37	22	20
Helpful	40	42	48	49	48	40	50	36
Of little help one way or another	25	12	12	17	23	18	21	35
Somewhat unhelpful	2	1	2	2	4	3	4	2
Very unhelpful	8	0	4	1	2	1	0	4
Other	2	0	0	1	1	0	3	2
N=	63	172	134	255	195	211	194	122

Chi square = 112.60828 $p < 0.001$

Coefficient of Contingency = 0.27785

TABLE IX-2

HELPFULNESS OF RELIGIOUS INSTITUTION FOR

GUIDANCE IN PERSONAL PRAYER LIFE

IN PERCENT BY COMMUNITY FOR SELECTED RELIGIOUS GROUPS

Community

| Degree of Helpfulness | Satellite City | | | New Town | | Country Club Estates | | |
	Black Protestant	White Protestant	Catholic	White Protestant	Catholic	White Protestant	Catholic	Jewish
Very helpful	26	37	24	18	14	23	15	6
Helpful	29	40	42	41	42	40	44	26
Of little help one way or another	28	23	25	37	35	34	32	57
Somewhat unhelpful	5	1	2	2	4	1	6	1
Very unhelpful	11	0	4	1	4	1	1	5
Other	2	0	2	1	1	0	3	5
N=	65	168	135	250	195	211	196	121

Chi square = 152.15233   p<0.001

Coefficient of Contingency = 0.31922

of the religions of America was elaborated. In accord with that privatization, substantial majorities of respondents reported their church or
synagogue had been helpful in providing guidance in the private spheres of
religion and family life, but only minorities of respondents reported
their church or synagogue had been helpful in providing guidance in the
public spheres of work and politics.

Discussions of Meaning of Religious Faith in the Family

The majority of respondents may have felt their faith group was
helpful in providing guidance for their religious beliefs; but, as Table
IX-3 indicates, this guidance has not led families to try to discern the
implications of their faith for daily living. Less than 10 percent of the
respondents reported almost daily family discussions of the meaning of
one's religious faith for daily life, and over half reported such discussions occurred only on special occasions or almost never.

These findings accentuate the lack of impact of informing notions
drawn self-consciously from one's religious tradition for one's daily life.
No data in the entire study better illumine the diversity in levels of
involvement of lay people in their religious institutions; the majority of
members do not relate the insights of their religious heritage frequently
to their family conversations.

The responses also reflect the intermingling of piety and secularity
in the American context. In spite of the fact that a majority of the
respondents reported their religious institution had been helpful in
providing guidance in the formation of their religious beliefs, a majority
also reported that they rarely or never discussed the implications of their
faith for their daily lives.

The self-reporting of the helpfulness of churches and synagogues
on guidance in religious beliefs reveals nothing of the substance of those
beliefs. Some of them dealing with the familial, social, economic, and
political spheres have been examined in Chapters VI-VIII. In the following
section the more explicitly religious and traditionally moral views of the
laity are examined.

Religious and Moral Perspectives of Suburban Lay People

Introduction

Lay responses to five items in the questionnaire have been selected
to probe the religious and moral perspectives of the four faith groups of
suburban lay people: experience of presence of God; views of the Ten
Commandments; level of moral standards to be maintained in one's religious
institutions; peace and security in religious institutions; and interpretations of the Bible.

TABLE IX-3

FREQUENCY OF DISCUSSION OF MEANING OF ONE'S RELIGIOUS FAITH FOR

DAILY LIFE WITH FAMILY OR OTHER RESIDENTS

IN PERCENT BY COMMUNITY FOR SELECTED RELIGIOUS GROUPS

Community

Frequency of Discussion	Satellite City			New Town		Country Club Estates		
	Black Protestant	White Protestant	Catholic	White Protestant	Catholic	White Protestant	Catholic	Jewish
Almost every day	9	11	11	4	6	4	13	2
About every week	20	14	10	10	14	13	12	11
About once or twice a month	26	15	20	24	21	19	21	19
Only on special occasions	20	29	32	29	28	34	32	32
Almost never	14	21	19	30	29	28	19	34
Respondent lives alone*	9	9	7	3	2	2	4	2
N=	64	182	145	263	196	214	199	123

*Excluded in statistical tests

Chi square = 59.47250   p<0.001

Coefficient of Contingency = 0.20719

These items were chosen because they illumined foundational religious experience and salient forms and practices related to it. Such items are inadequate to plumb the depths and complexity of religious experience and its interpretation, but they do shed some light and permit suggestive inter-group comparisons.

Suburban Lay Experience of the Presence of God

Religious experience is foundational to full participation in the life of any religious institution. To assess such experience among suburban church and synagogue members they were asked "As an adult, have you ever had an experience of the presence of God?" The Protestant bias of the item was discussed in Chapter IV, where it was noted that the experiential dimension is more evenly balanced by an objectivistic one in Catholicism. Though not mentioned in that context because the discussion was dealing with Christian clergy, it should also be observed that the item is somewhat alien to classical Judaism, for the separation of a "religious" dimension from a communal one is very problematic in Judaism.

The Protestant bias of the question has probably contributed somewhat to the interfaith variations shown in Table IX-4, but their coherence with other findings on participation and beliefs suggests the differences do reflect authentic contrasts between the various faith groups. The low proportion of Jewish respondents reporting an experience of the Divine Presence coheres with the relatively high proportion who reported they felt uncomfortable in synagogue due to religious doubts, the relatively low involvement of Jews in synagogue events, and the relatively high proportion who reported belief in God was not necessary as a condition for their faith.

The high proportion of black Protestants attesting to an adult experience of God's presence is consistent with the experiential emphases in the black Protestant tradition. Substantial proportions of white Protestants questioned the actuality of such an experience, indicating many members are out of tune with classical Protestant emphases.

Lay affiliation in religious institutions in America does not depend on personal certainty about the authenticity of religious experience or agreement with salient aspects of traditional beliefs. Over a third of the white Protestants and Catholics and over two-thirds of the Jews did not think they had had a personal experience of the Divine Presence in their adult lives.

The clergy were much more certain of their adult experience of Divine Presence, for only a tiny minority of them responded "I don't think so" or "I'm sure I have not" (see Table IV-10). Such a clergy-lay contrast is scarcely surprising. The professional is by training more able to perceive an inconsistency between the lack of confirming experience and the religion he professes. As a religious leader, he focuses on this dimension of human experience to a degree matched by few lay people.

TABLE IX-4

RESPONSE TO QUESTION "AS AN ADULT, HAVE YOU EVER HAD AN

EXPERIENCE OF THE PRESENCE OF GOD?"

IN PERCENT BY COMMUNITY FOR SELECTED RELIGIOUS GROUPS

	Community							
	Satellite City			New Town		Country Club Estates		
Responses	Black Protestant	White Protestant	Catholic	White Protestant	Catholic	White Protestant	Catholic	Jewish
I'm sure I have	54	42	29	29	25	28	45	16
I think I have	32	30	28	33	28	30	23	17
I don't think so	11	20	32	29	34	32	23	40
I'm sure I have not	3	8	11	9	13	10	10	26
N=	65	180	139	262	195	218	195	121

Chi square = 107.36478   p<0.001

Coefficient of Contingency = 0.26931

Suburban Lay Views of the Ten Commandments

There have always been disputes in religious social ethics about the relation between formal and dynamic components in human conduct. Those who accentuate formal components have tended to be more "legalistic" and to seek principles, rules, and regulations to guide human decisions. Those who accentuate dynamic components have tended to be more "volitional" and to emphasize human response to the Divine Presence in the context in which one finds oneself.

In recent times, these differing emphases have given rise to major debates among Christian social ethicists. "Contextual" ethicists have suggested that <u>a priori</u> principles are unable to guide people to loving responses in specific contexts. Instead they hold people should respond in love in the context in which they find themselves. Principled ethicists have responded that rules and regulations of human conduct do, in fact, provide guidance to loving action in varying situations.[1]

In the main, contemporary proponents of a "situation" ethic have been concentrated in denominations affiliated with the National Council of Churches. Protagonists of this viewpoint would be expected to agree with the statement "There are times when it might be all right to break one of the Ten Commandments."

The vast majority of suburban lay people believed the Ten Commandments are inviolate, as Table IX-5 reveals. There was very little difference between white Protestants and Catholics in any of the three communities. Jews were somewhat less moralistic than white Protestants and Catholics, but the patterns of distribution were similar for all the religious groupings.

The concentration of "contextualist" ethicists among NCC-affiliated Protestant clergy was noted earlier. Thirty-six percent of those clergy agreed with the statement (see Table IV-8) compared with less than 20 percent of the NCC-affiliated lay people.

The strong moralistic motif present among these suburban people is part and parcel of the American religious heritage. NCC-affiliated Protestant clergy supporting a "contextual" approach to morality are in a minority. Religious moralism is most firmly entrenched in non-NCC-affiliated white Protestantism and in Roman Catholicism, but it is predominant in all faith groups.

Suburban Lay Views on Enforcement of a Strict
Standard of Moral Conduct among Church Members

Voluntaryism, and the concomitant need for suasion, have altered the established church-intentional sect dichotomy characterizing earlier European history. The intentional gathered congregation has become the norm in the American context, but the intentionality often is more habitual

TABLE IX-5

ATTITUDE TOWARD STATEMENT "THERE ARE TIMES WHEN IT MIGHT

BE ALL RIGHT TO BREAK ONE OF THE TEN COMMANDMENTS"

IN PERCENT BY COMMUNITY FOR SELECTED RELIGIOUS GROUPS

	Community							
	Satellite City			New Town		Country Club Estates		
Attitude toward Statement	Black Protestant	White Protestant	Catholic	White Protestant	Catholic	White Protestant	Catholic	Jewish
Strongly agree	2	2	4	3	3	3	2	6
Agree	9	12	17	15	20	16	21	27
Mixed feelings	20	21	18	27	18	24	18	23
Disagree	31	45	33	39	37	36	41	30
Strongly disagree	31	19	22	14	20	19	16	10
No opinion	6	2	6	2	2	2	2	4
N=	64	179	144	258	197	215	198	120

Chi square = 61.67882 $p < 0.001$

Coefficient of Contingency = 0.20720

than convictional. The American "denomination," more sectarian than the
European "church" but more churchly than the European "sect," has become
the norm of institutional religious life in America. Reformists arguing
for more strictness and discipline and for more rigid membership tests
emerge again and again in America, but their efforts are blunted in most
communions by both clergy and lay opposition.

The reluctance of suburban lay people to support ecclesiastical
enforcement of strict standards of moral conduct is shown in Table IX-6.
In this instance, a plurality of black Protestants and Catholics thought
the church should enforce a strict standard of moral conduct among its
members. Even in these cases, the majority of respondents reported either
mixed feelings or disagreement. The white Protestant and Jewish cases are
striking, for less than 20 percent of them concurred. The older white
Protestant congregation in lower status Satellite City had the most supporters of the enforcement of a strict standard of moral conduct, but even
here only 36 percent of the respondents supported such a view.

Only a plurality of respondents in each religious group strongly
agreed with the proposition. In the American context, even the Catholic
lay people, whose tradition most strongly supports the enforcement of a
strict standard of moral conduct for its adherents, were not strongly
enthusiastic about such a viewpoint.

NCC-affiliated Protestant and Catholic clergy paralleled the
responses of their laity (see Table IV-9). Non-NCC-affiliated white
Protestant clergy and black Protestant clergy were the only clergy groups
having majorities favoring enforcement of strict standards of moral conduct
among their members.

Some of the small black Protestant and non-NCC-affiliated white
Protestant churches can probably enforce moral standards which their
pastors desire, for informal means of social control may function
effectively in these small churches that insist on strict standards of
belief and conduct. Such enforcement is a practical impossibility in the
larger NCC-affiliated Protestant churches, in Catholic churches, and in
the larger synagogues.

Thus, in personal morality, as well as in matters of public policy,
most lay people do not grant religious institutions the authority to bind
or to control their consciences. Lay people in all groups do see a
role for their religious institution in moral improvement, for they gave
overwhelming support to the proposition that after a good worship service,
they resolve to improve their relations with their fellow humans. Marginal
comments on the questionnaires strongly confirmed that the laity wishes to
be persuaded, inspired, and "converted" to better actions, rather than to
be disciplined or coerced into them.

TABLE IX-6

RESPONSE TO STATEMENT "THE CHURCH (SYNAGOGUE) SHOULD ENFORCE A

STRICT STANDARD OF MORAL CONDUCT AMONG ITS MEMBERS"

IN PERCENT BY COMMUNITY FOR SELECTED RELIGIOUS GROUPS

					Community			
	Satellite City			New Town		Country Club Estates		
Response to Statement	Black Protestant	White Protestant	Catholic	White Protestant	Catholic	White Protestant	Catholic	Jewish
Strongly agree	16	9	12	2	6	3	8	4
Agree	23	27	31	11	27	12	34	13
Mixed feelings	23	24	19	21	26	24	17	15
Disagree	23	28	23	42	26	42	26	46
Strongly disagree	8	6	5	18	8	14	9	22
No opinion	8	5	10	6	8	5	6	0
N=	62	176	145	265	195	214	197	123

Chi square = 174.87236   p<0.001

Coefficient of Contingency = 0.33569

Suburban Lay Views on Religious Institutions

as Places of Peace and Security

As noted in Chapter IV, one of the byproducts of authentic religion is a profound sense of peace and security which people experience from time to time under the conditions of human existence. Sometimes this experience has been trivialized,evoking criticism from some theologians and other social critics, but it is a legitimate expectation.

This expectation is deeply felt by suburban lay people, as Table IX-7 indicates.[2] Overwhelming majorities of lay people in every community and in every faith group agreed that religious institutions should be places where one can go and find peace of mind and security. No group had more than 8 percent disagreeing with the statement.

Lay-clergy contrasts on this item were very sharp among NCC-affiliated Protestant and Roman Catholic clergy (see Table IV-11). Only 27 percent of the NCC-affiliated Protestant clergy and 47 percent of the Roman Catholic clergy agreed with the statement.

The dimension of "Divine discontent" probably reflected in clergy responses was the justification frequently offered in marginal comments on the questionnaire by the minority of lay people who responded with disagreement or mixed feelings. However, the "peace of mind" motif is certainly the predominant lay expectation. This expectation forms part of the basis of opposition to religious institutional involvement in contro-versial issues, for lay people are seeking a tranquil and harmonious religious institution.

Suburban Lay Interpretations of the Bible

Christianity and Judaism have always been book religions, and Scripture has occupied an important place in both traditions. Varying views of Scripture were discussed briefly in Chapter IV. In that context, various clergy views on Scripture were examined.

Significant contrasts in interpretation were reported there. All clergy attached importance to Scripture, but the agreement ended there. The majority of non-NCC-affiliated white Protestant and black Protestant clergy, reflecting a common southern rootage, believed that Scripture was literally true (see Table IV-12). Only a tiny minority of NCC-affiliated Protestants were biblical literalists, but two-thirds of them felt the Bible was the most important way of knowing about God. There were no Catholic clergy who were biblical literalists, and their responses agreed generally with their church's teaching.

Lay responses contrasted most suggestively with clergy responses, as Table IX-8 indicates. A plurality of white Protestants in Country Club

TABLE IX-7

RESPONSE   TO STATEMENT "THE CHURCH (SYNAGOGUE) SHOULD BE A

PLACE WHERE ONE CAN GO AND FIND PEACE OF MIND AND SECURITY"

IN PERCENT BY COMMUNITY FOR SELECTED RELIGIOUS GROUPS

	Community							
	Satellite City			New Town		Country Club Estates		
Response to Statement	Black Protestant	White Protestant	Catholic	White Protestant	Catholic	White Protestant	Catholic	Jewish
Strongly agree	55	37	59	30	37	35	34	38
Agree	38	47	33	48	53	51	50	53
Mixed feelings	8	9	4	12	4	8	9	3
Disagree	0	6	2	6	5	3	5	2
Strongly disagree	0	1	0	2	1	1	0	2
No opinion	0	1	2	1	1	1	1	2
N=	64	180	147	264	198	214	203	123

Chi square = 75.45116   p<0.001

Coefficient of Contingency = 0.22667

TABLE IX-8

ATTITUDE TOWARD SCRIPTURE

IN PERCENT BY COMMUNITY FOR SELECTED RELIGIOUS GROUPS

Community

Attitude toward Scripture	Satellite City			New Town		Country Club Estates		
	Black Protestant	White Protestant	Catholic	White Protestant	Catholic	White Protestant	Catholic	Jewish
Scripture is literally true	31	14	14	8	6	14	11	2
Scripture is not literally true, but it is the most important way of knowing about God	13	21	10	30	25	37	23	26
Scripture is one of many equally important ways of knowing about God	55	52	60	53	56	38	55	47
Scripture is less important than other ways of knowing about God	0	1	2	4	3	2	5	12
Scripture is of very little importance	0	0	2	1	3	2	1	5
Other*	0	13	12	4	7	8	5	7
N=	67	180	144	267	197	218	202	121

*Omitted in statistical tests

Chi square = 132.34444   p<0.001

Coefficient of Contingency = 0.30484

Estates and a majority in every other group felt that Scripture was one
of many equally important ways of knowing about God.

Such a response by itself might be considered "orthodox" among
Catholics, but it certainly is not a predominant view among Protestant
theologians. Suburban Protestant lay people have qualified a classical
Protestant particularistic emphasis to fit the basic tenets of religious
pluralism and religious tolerance of the religion of America. The Catholic
situation is unclear on the basis of the responses to this question, but
their ambivalence about evangelism, which will be discussed below, suggests
they have also accommodated their traditional beliefs to the public religion
of America. The scientific world-view associated with technical rationalism
undoubtedly limited their affirmation of biblical literalism.

Because no non-NCC lay group was included in the sample, only a few
respondents espoused biblical literalism. The relatively high proportion
of black Protestants affirming literal understanding of Scripture is
related both to the higher proportion of lower status respondents in this
group and also to the southern evangelical roots of the black churches.
It is safe to assume the majority of the members of the non-NCC-affiliated
Protestant churches whose pastors were biblical literalists were also
biblical literalists, for there was strong pressure for doctrinal consensus
among members of these churches.

Suburban Lay Views on Evangelism

Christianity has traditionally been evangelistic, and many clergy
still espouse proselytism. In the American context, interest in evangelism
has been accentuated by religious voluntaryism, for persons must be persuaded
to affiliate with a religious institution. This situation is, however,
ambiguous, for this voluntaryism is balanced by the values of religious
pluralism and religious tolerance.

The Jewish presence highlights the problem. Insofar as clergy and
laity recognize the legitimacy of differences in religious style and
substance, the claims to universalism and inclusiveness of various religious
groups are limited.[3] This limitation is aided by the religious indifference
associated with technical rationalism and secular humanism.

To explore the impact of these partially conflicting facets of the
public faith of America on the religions of American suburbia, respondents
were asked to indicate their reactions to the statement "We should seek to
make all men Christians" ("Jews" for Jewish respondents).[4] As Table IX-9
reveals, only a minority of lay Christians thought one should seek to make
all men Christians. Only among black and white Protestants in lower status
Satellite City did the majority of respondents agree with the statement
"We should seek to make all men Christians." These responses reflect the
special circumstances of these two Satellite City congregations. The
southern influence is evident in the black Protestant responses, for the
evangelical emphasis is much stronger in southern Protestantism. The older

TABLE IX-9

RESPONSE TO STATEMENT "WE SHOULD SEEK

TO MAKE ALL MEN CHRISTIANS (JEWS)"

IN PERCENT BY COMMUNITY FOR SELECTED RELIGIOUS GROUPS

Community

Response to Statement	Satellite City			New Town		Country Club Estates		
	Black Protestant	White Protestant	Catholic	White Protestant	Catholic	White Protestant	Catholic	Jewish
Strongly agree	34	23	23	6	6	13	6	0
Agree	31	33	24	17	21	18	22	1
Mixed feelings	15	19	17	22	26	23	26	3
Disagree	12	17	19	36	29	31	29	31
Strongly disagree	5	5	6	16	13	13	12	64
No opinion	3	3	10	3	5	2	4	0
N=	65	176	145	264	195	215	201	122

Chi square = 426.34619 $p < 0.001$

Coefficient of Contingency = 0.48542

median age of the white Protestant congregation in Satellite City is
reflected in their responses, for responses to this item were strongly
correlated with age. Less than a third of the Catholic and white Protestants
in middle status New Town and upper status Country Club Estates concurred
with this evangelical emphasis.

The ambivalent feelings about this tenet of classical Christianity
are most revealing, for they reflect the American experience in both its
secular and religious dimensions. The emergence of alternative interpretations of reality may undermine the interest in evangelism, for the church
member may be less than fully persuaded about the validity of his particular
religious tradition. Such a secular reason for the diminution of this
evangelical thrust is reinforced by the tenets of religious tolerance,
religious pluralism, and religious liberty embodied in the public religion
of America.

For more than a millennium Jews have shown minimal interest in
winning converts to their faith group. This traditional view is reinforced
by values embodied in the religion of America and in secularism, so it is
scarcely surprising to find Jewish respondents overwhelmingly rejecting
evangelism.

Summary

The findings reveal the intermingling of influences shaping the
religious and moral perspectives of lay people in American suburbia.

The majority of participants reported a foundational religious
experience. Even granting the Protestant-Christian bias of the item, the
low proportion of Jews responding affirmatively illumines the ambivalence
of the Jewish religious situation. Disproportionate numbers of Jews, while
desiring to participate in the communal side of their religio-historical
heritage, have difficulty with the religious side. Since the two dimensions
are inextricably interrelated in Judaism, many suburban Jews display very
ambivalent feelings toward the synagogue and their involvement in it.

Most lay respondents think the Ten Commandments are inviolate, but
they resist the idea of enforcing a strict standard of moral conduct among
the members of their church or synagogue. This reticence is best understood
as a widespread lay affirmation of the primacy of the individual conscience
over the authority of the corporate religious institution. It also shows
the appropriation of the public religion of America and the anti-traditionalism
rooted in technical rationalism and secular humanism.

Lay attitudes toward Scripture and evangelism also indicate the
way in which the American experience has modified traditional views. Lay
respondents qualify the exclusiveness and particularity of their own
traditions by seeing Scripture as one of many equally significant ways of
knowing about God and by displaying great ambivalence about the merits
of evangelism.

At the same time, fewer than 10 percent of the lay people showed patterns of response sharply rejecting the historic norms of their tradition. This is partly a result of the fact that those moving too far away from traditional values are apt to dissociate themselves from their faith community altogether and thus are beyond the purview of this study. Traditional beliefs of the religions of American suburbia have been tempered but not eliminated by secular humanism, technical rationalism, and the public religion of America.

PART IV

SUMMARY AND CONCLUSION

CHAPTER X

A CONSTRUCTIVE INTERPRETATION: AUTHENTIC RELIGION,

AMERICA'S PUBLIC FAITH AND THE RELIGIONS OF AMERICAN SUBURBIA*

Introduction

The interplay between and intermingling of human religious experience and its institutional manifestations in contemporary American suburbia have been traced in the preceding chapters. People must appropriate the cultural forms and the social institutions they have inherited to communicate their religious experience.

In their evaluation of these forms and institutions, people are guided partly by their broad understanding of the nature of authentic religion and its relation to culture, partly by their view of the relation between love, justice, and forms of social organization, and partly by their assessment of the degree of harmony of life with life possible under the conditions of existence.

Many of the assessments of the religious situation in America in the past two decades have been negative to a greater or lesser degree. Peter Berger, Harvey Cox, Roy Eckardt, Will Herberg and Gibson Winter, for example, have all made cultural analyses the basis for sharp critiques of the salient forms of religious life in the United States.[1]

Some interpreters have developed more positive evaluations of the predominant forms of religious life in contemporary America: James Dittes, James Gustafson, John Courtney Murray, and H. Richard Niebuhr, for example.[2]

Although these contrasting interpretations cannot be examined in detail here, it is necessary to address the problems common to all interpretations: the nature of "authentic" religion, the relation of "authentic" religion to other religions and to culture, the relation between love, justice, and forms of social organization, and the degree of harmony possible in human life. Views on these matters shape the evaluation of the relation between authentic religion, the public faith of America, and the religions of American suburbia.

---

*This chapter has been written by W. Widick Schroeder. The interpretative dimension is substantial in this chapter, and the other authors do not necessarily subscribe to the understanding of "authentic" religion and its relation to the other "religions" developed here.

The understanding of authentic religion is the most critical component in this assessment, for all else is an outgrowth of this foundational interpretation. A constructive view of authentic religion permits an assessment of the adequacy of the public faith of America and the religions of American suburbia. The empirical data presented in this study contribute only indirectly to the understanding of authentic religion, but they contribute directly to an evaluative interpretation of America's public faith and the religions of American suburbia.

In the following section, a constructive view of authentic religion is elaborated and contrasted with the public faith. The concluding section contrasts authentic religion with the public faith of America and the religions of American suburbia.

Authentic Religion and the Public Faith of America

Authentic Religion[3]

The Bases of Authentic Religion

Religious experience--more fundamental and elemental than its rational interpretation--is rooted in the human experience of harmony, aesthetic sensitivity, and intensity of feeling. In this experience formal and dynamic components are synthesized into a harmonious unity. The true, the good, and the beautiful are interrelated, so that rational, moral, or aesthetic experiences may elicit religious experience. It is grounded in the Divine Reality, a Reality Who, in a qualified sense, is sui generis. In religious experience, humans intuit a sense of a basic harmony embodied in the Divine nature.

Before humans rationalized their religious experiences, they fostered them through ritual and emotion.[4] In connection with acts and feelings, they developed beliefs to interpret the meaning of the rituals in which they engaged. Particular traditions and patterns of acting and feeling became important for a given group, and thus reinforced the significance of a given religious tradition for its adherents.

These beliefs, somewhat inconsistent and only partially rationalized, were later elaborated into more coherent and inclusive schemata by specialized theologians seeking to interpret the rituals, feelings, and beliefs incorporated in their particular religious tradition. No high religion has been without its interpreters, seeking to rationalize its practices, feelings, and beliefs.

In the American context, Christianity is the predominant bearer of religious rituals, feelings, and beliefs. It is interpreted differently by representatives of various historic groups and is qualified by the public faith embodied in the religion of America and in the technical rationalism and secular humanism predominant in many facets of social and cultural life.

Authentic religion involves a sense of the inclusiveness of life and the unity of the whole. As one responds to the solitariness of his experience of harmony and intensity of feeling, authentic religion elicits world loyalty. Authentic religion also involves a sense of the insistent particularity and exclusiveness of life and the significance of the parts for the whole. It leads to an appreciation of the contributions of people to each other, to the life of humankind, and to the Divine Life.

This contrast between the universal and the particular contributes to human awareness of the discrepancy between what is and what ought to be. Grounded in finitude and ignorance, this contrast accentuates the limits of the harmony of life with life that can be achieved in human existence. Differences in fundamental understanding and in temperament contribute to varying assessments of what is desirable and practicable in corporate and personal life.

A human religious experience incorporates both formal and dynamic components. The formal component--forms of definiteness, the objectification of others and the Divine, the reality of societies with recognizable defining characteristics--is intrinsic to religious experience, so the distinction sometimes made between form and substance in authentic religion is spurious. Forms contribute to substance, so a more adequate interpretation of religious experience may deepen such experience.[5] "Forms of definiteness," including such senses as "greenness" and such geometric objects as "roundness," are comparable to the Platonic "ideas" and the Whiteheadian "eternal objects."

The dynamic component--the creative advance, the surpassing of the past in the present, and the evolving synthesis by an emerging creature of feelings and forms of definiteness embodied in other creatures and in God--is also intrinsic, so life cannot be embalmed in forms. Life is a bid for freedom in the vivid immediacy of present experience.[6] Without the dynamic side of religious experience, rituals, beliefs, and rational interpretations become stale and outworn.

The dynamic growth toward aesthetic satisfaction is guided by the attraction for order, harmony, and intensity of feeling inherent in God's subjective aim. In this sense, creatures are dependent on God's grace for their satisfaction. He is immanent in creatures through His overpowering rationality and His desire for harmony and intensity of feeling, whether or not the creatures can or do acknowledge His presence in their lives.

The elaborations developed in this sub-section are set forth in diagrammatic form in Figures X-1 and X-2.

Religious Experience, Religious Institutions, and Principles of Justice

The reality of religious experience and the social character of existence combine to bring forth religious institutions. Because rituals, feelings, beliefs, and rational interpretations related to religious experience are universal, religious institutions will emerge in any culture; but the particular forms which religious institutions evolve will

Human experience of

a) Harmony
b) Aesthetic satisfaction
c) Intensity of feeling

Divine subjective aim
←—lures forth these experiences
in the creative process

evokes

Human religious experience

involving

Unification of formal and dynamic components of experience embodying harmony, aesthetic satisfaction, and intensity of feeling. Decision, involving deliberation and self-determination is inherent in this unification.

Provisionally primary basis for aesthetic experiences related to the beautiful.

Because the components are three-in-relation, the locus of and distinction between the true, the good, and the beautiful are preliminary and provisional; experience of any one may elicit any of the others.

three-in-relation

Formal components, involving forms of definiteness, the objectification of others and the Divine in the emerging experience of the creature, and societies with recognizable defining characteristics; these are the permanent aspects of experience.

Provisionally primary basis for rational experiences related to the true.

Dynamic components, involving advance in the grip of creativity, the surpassing of the past in the present, and the emerging subject's evolving synthesis of subjective feelings and forms of definiteness embodied in other creatures, including God; these are the changing aspects of experience

Provisionally primary basis for moral experiences related to the good.

FIGURE X-2

PHASES OF HUMAN EXPERIENCE GIVING RISE TO RITUAL,

EMOTION, BELIEF, AND INTERPRETATION SEQUENCE IN HUMAN

RELIGIOUS EXPERIENCE

The phases are interrelated. Beliefs and interpretations qualify rituals and emotions and vice versa.

Ritual ←→ Emotions ←→ Beliefs ←→ Interpretations

More elemental in experience ────────→ More derivative in experience

"Physical" or originative phase involves objectification in an emerging subject of forms and feelings embodied in events in causal past.

"Conceptual" or supplemental phase involves influx of forms and relates feelings not necessarily in the causal past of the emerging subject.

Movement from more particularistic to more universalistic aspects of human religious experience. The particularity of the feelings embodied in rituals and in emotions makes them more difficult to communicate beyond groups sharing a common history and liturgy than beliefs and interpretations.

depend on the cultural context in which they emerge. Worship, education, and the cultivation of sociability are the visible marks of a religious institution.

Worship is the constitutive event in the life of religious institutions. Rooted in human responses to the Divine Presence, acts of worship accentuate the aesthetic dimensions of existence and the unifying aspect of experience. Education, including the recall of one's own and other religious traditions, the examination of human reflections on the Divine nature, and explorations of the implications of these analyses for human life, accentuates the rational dimension of existence and the formal aspect of experience. Sociability, including the cultivation of concerned groups related to interpersonal and intergroup relations, accentuates the inextricably social character of existence and the dynamic aspect of experience.

Since authentic religion includes formal components and induces world loyalty, the question of the relation of religious experience to justice is an inevitable one. Implicit in this question is the issue of the proper relation of religious institutions to other social institutions.

The quest for justice includes the quest for principles of justice to guide moral decisions and to suggest desirable forms of social organization, for justice necessarily entails the formal dimension of human experience.

The unification of form and dynamics in human experience provides the basis for the development of principles of justice. Love, implying order, peace, and harmony, is reflected in the unification of formal and dynamic components of experience. Order thus constitutes the first principle of justice.

The formal principle of equality appropriate to form constitutes the second principle of justice. Equality is grounded in human recognition of congruence and correspondence. Equality implies that the law should be applied in like manner to all for whom it is applicable. Beyond legal principles, equality conveys the idea that creatures should have equal access to some of the earth's resources. The phrase "appropriate to form" qualifies equality, for principles should be applied equally only to those creatures with comparable defining characteristics. Age, sex, and social position illustrate various factors qualifying equality among humans.

The dynamic principle of self-determination informed by excellence constitutes the third principle of justice. Self-determination is rooted in internal freedom, for creatures possess the capacity to choose between alternatives and to place the stamp of individuality on that which they appropriate as they become. The phrase "informed by excellence" qualifies self-determination, for "excellence" suggests the concern for the common good and the harmony of the parts in a whole.

Self-determination informed by excellence and equality appropriate to form can not be harmonized perfectly, for finitude, ignorance, sloth, and lethargy combine to produce limitations on self-determination and equality, resulting in some discord between them. Some disharmony-- and some injustice--are perennial and inevitable in human life.

The development of more adequate rules and regulations of justice, embodiments of the principles of justice in the life of living communities, may increase harmony in the future, but all disharmony cannot--and should not--be eliminated within or between states.

The elaborations developed in this subsection are summarized in Figure X-3.

Principles of Justice and Normative Forms of Social Organization

The principles of equality appropriate to form, self-determination informed by excellence, and order, coupled with a consideration of the characteristics of human beings, guide the elaboration of forms of social organization normatively most desirable for humans. These forms of social organization foster but do not insure the development of harmonious life with intensity of feeling enhanced by depth and breadth of experience.

The family is rooted in biological and social necessity. The forms shaping the family are the predominantly diadic character of human sexuality, the prolonged nature of human infancy and childhood, and the human needs for intimacy, companionship and shared history. Though limited by these forms, humans may have considerable latitude in selecting marriage partners. Once such choices are made, factors over which humans have less conscious control assert themselves. Consequently, the human family is an especially good example of the interplay of freedom and destiny manifest in all aspects of human existence.

Within this framework, the monogamous family is most apt to harmonize self-determination informed by excellence (one's actions are shaped by concern for the whole family) and equality appropriate to form (one may sensitively take age and sexual differentiations and special circumstances into account as one seeks to deal "equally" with the various members of the primary group).

Closely related to the familial sphere is the social sphere, associated with ethnicity, race, and status. It is a product of biological and social necessity and human creating capacities especially related to self-determination informed by excellence, for humans create the symbols, styles of life, and sense of shared history and interpret the common physical characteristics that give identity to ethnic, status, and racial groups.

The need for some contrasts to produce the breadth necessary for intensity of feelings and the principle of self-determination informed by excellence suggest that a "good" society will have a multiplicity of ethnic, racial, and status groups. The precise range of desirable pluralism cannot be discerned except in a given context. "Equality appropriate to form" in this context implies the legitimacy of varied social, ethnic, and racial forms. Order involves the unifying of the various groups into a harmonious whole, fostering mutual respect and tolerance.

Human rational shaping capacities and biological necessity combine to produce an economic sphere. An economic system must seek to harmonize (order) the demands for goods and services (self-determination) with available resources and responsible growth (equality). Some pricing mechanism based on supply and demand is necessary, but the "best" form of economic organization cannot be discerned except in a given context.

FIGURE X-3

THE RELATION OF RELIGIOUS EXPERIENCE, RELIGIOUS INSTITUTIONS,

PRINCIPLES OF JUSTICE, AND NORMATIVE FORMS OF SOCIAL ORGANIZATION

Religious experiences

and

Social character of existence

elicit

Religious institutions

characterized by

1) Worship, in response to Divine Presence (unification provisionally paramount)

2) Education, involving the historical appropriation of rituals and beliefs and the elaboration of alternative modes of interpretation (form provisionally para-mount)

3) Sociability, involving the cultivation of various forms of fellowship (dynamics provisionally paramount)

Include formal components (see Figure X-1) and elicit world loyalty which raises questions of justice, focused on the formal rational dimension of experience involving

normative desirable forms of social organization

--and--

principles of justice rooted in

Principles and human characteristics guide elaboration (see Figure X-4)

Unification → Love implying order, peace or harmony as a principle of justice

Form involving equality appropriate to form as a principle of justice

Dynamics involving self-determination informed by excellence as a principle of justice

Human rational shaping capacities and social necessity combine to produce a political sphere. The principles of equality appropriate to form and self-determination informed by excellence cannot be perfectly harmonized, but the government, which is the organizing center of the society, must seek a reasonably satisfactory balance of the two principles of justice manifest in the individuals and groups in a society. Democracy is the form of political organization best able to harmonize these partially contradictory principles, for the principle of self-determination is inherent in the democratic process. The involvement of large numbers of citizens in the political processes fosters the principle of equality appropriate to form; in a large society, a federated form of democracy balances equality and self-determination, inducing the emergence of some elites.

Human rational shaping capacity and the play of imagination combine to produce a cultural sphere: education, science, and art. As was the case with the social sphere, cultural diversity and pluralism are desirable and for the same reasons. There are limits to the degree of pluralism a given society can sustain without disintegrating, but the limits cannot be discerned except in a given situation.

Human experience of the Divine Presence combines with rational shaping capacity to produce a religious sphere. As people are rooted in particular religious traditions, religious meaning and feeling are mediated to them by one or a small number of traditions. This legitimate pluralism and human capacity for self-determination, coupled with finitude and ignorance, lead to the desirability of religious liberty and religious pluralism in the context of some overarching unity.

In sum, monogamy, an economic organization permitting rational allocation of resources through a supply-demand mechanism, some risk-taking and responsible growth, democracy, social, ethnic, racial, and cultural pluralism, and religious pluralism and liberty are desirable in a "good" society. The elaborations developed in this subsection are summarized in Figure X-4.

The Public Faith of America

The public faith incorporates a panoply that includes the religion of America, predominant principles of justice, the values sustaining the actual forms of social organization, technical rationalism, and secular humanism.

In Chapter I the outstanding dimensions of the religion of America were characterized. The notion that a transcendent God judged America was included in this characterization. This God is *sui generis* and is to be worshipped and respected.

Closely related to this notion of a transcendent God is the ideal of liberty, equality, and brotherhood in a democracy under God. To be sure, the ideals sometimes are rather inchoate and often disregarded,

FIGURE X-4

BASES FOR NORMATIVE FORMS OF SOCIAL ORGANIZATION

Sphere of social order	Bases	
	Dynamic, self-determining process side / Formal, rational or conceptual side rooted in the Divine / "Physical" side rooted in biological necessity, characteristics of body / "Center" of human experience unifies formal and dynamic sides	Human being / social necessity, rooted in multiplicity of people in society / Human being
Familial	Biological and social necessity, rooted in the predominantly diadic nature of sexual relations, the nature of human infancy and childhood, and the need for intimacy and shared experiences	Monogamy
		Normative form of social organization most apt to enhance harmony of self-determination informed by excellence and equality appropriate to form (rooted in cultural sphere)
Social, including ethnic, racial, and status group-ings	Biological necessity, social necessity, and human creating capacities especially related to self-determination informed by excellence	Multiplicity of ethnic, racial, and status groups harmonized in a complex unity

(continued on next page)

Economic	Biological necessity and human creating capacities related to technical reason	No single form. Economic system must seek to harmonize demand for goods and services with available resources and responsible growth; some pricing mechanism based on supply and demand is necessary
Political	Human rational shaping capacity and social necessity	Democracy
Cultural	Human rational shaping capacity and free play of imagination	Cultural pluralism and diversity, giving rise to multiplicity of institutions in educational, scientific, and artistic realms
Religious	Human religious experience and rational shaping capacity	Institutions informed by notions of religious liberty, religious tolerance, and religious pluralism. Religious institutions should articulate principles of justice, but should be wary of direct involvement in other spheres of social order

but they are a central part of the integrative values in America's panoply of core foundational values.

The shift of the religions of America from the public realm to the private realm was discussed in Chapters I and II. The emergence of the principles of religious voluntaryism, religious liberty, and religious tolerance into central positions was necessary to insure the hegemony of the principle of the separation of church and state. If separatism were to be established as the norm for church-state relations, these core values had to be affirmed by a substantial majority of the people.

In the course of events, the predominantly Protestant nation began to extend its religious pluralism by incorporating substantial numbers of Catholics and Jews within its religious framework. The basic tri-partite faith structure--Protestant, Catholic, and Jewish--became predominant in the twentieth century.

The accompanying competition for members primarily within and sometimes between major faith groupings reflects another central core value in America--the doctrine of multiplication of factions. Forcefully developed by James Madison in The Federalist Papers and incorporated in the Constitution, it reflects a checks and balance view of social life. Madison had a rather pessimistic view of man, for he advanced this doctrine to prevent any person or group from gaining too much power. This more negative assessment of human nature, accentuating the necessity for coercion to complement suasion in human societies, was also a part of the value complex induced by the American experience.

The democratic principle embodied in the ideals "liberty, equality, and brotherhood in a democracy under God" has been institutionalized in a federated form and shaped by the balance-of-power doctrine just noted. Citizens have voice in giving direction to the society, but they delegate the responsibility for giving directives to smaller bodies.

The history of racial, social, and ethnic groups in America has reflected the duality of inclusiveness and factions. The "melting pot" theory of acculturation evolved during the periods of great immigration contrasts with "the unmeltable ethnics" theory of the 1970's.[7] Actually both the unity inherent in the former theory and the diversity inherent in the latter are almost inevitable in the context of the American experience, for no society has sought to integrate so many diverse groups into a unity in so short a time.

The multiplicity of centers of initiative in American life has produced pluralism in the cultural realm. The numerous schools of art, drama, and literature reflect this pluralism at the creative level. The mixture of public and private education and the variety of types of schools, colleges, and universities reflect this cultural pluralism at the institutional level.

In contrast with the solemnity and piety manifest in the religion of America is the matter-of-factness and secularity of technical rationalism. It is the backbone of the urbanization, bureaucratization, industrialization complex discussed in Chapters I and II.

Technical rationalism has enhanced human life in numerous ways, but it has also contributed to many of the tensions and dislocations in American life. The social and psychological consequences of urban, industrial, bureaucratic life discussed in Chapter II are often hard on individuals. Pragmatism and activism, also a part of America's core values, are informed by technical rationalism and contribute to its saliency.

The relative inclusiveness of the state is both good and evil. Insofar as it sustains values and coordinates and integrates diverse interests and groups, the state is good. Insofar as it seeks absolute allegiance, makes inordinate claims, and blocks the vision of a more inclusive whole, it is evil.

The ambiguity of the religion of America is rooted in this duality. It affirms the reality of a transcendent God, generally tolerates prophetic criticisms by shifting and unstable minorities, seeks to embody principles of justice cohering with the principles of justice of authentic religion, and fosters some of the forms of social organization permitting the partial realization of the principles of justice. At the same time, it sometimes thwarts the realization of higher principles of justice, inordinately supports social institutions that need reform, expresses undue faith in process and progress, legitimates imperialistic tendencies, and obscures loyalty to a whole more inclusive than the nation.

The relation of authentic religion to the public faith of America is thus a complex one. According to the criteria developed here, America's public faith is assessed in an ambivalently positive way. Unqualified criticism of the public faith of America in the name of authentic religion is as inappropriate as unqualified support of the public faith of America in the name of authentic religion.

Authentic Religion, the Public Faith of
America, and the Religions of American Suburbia

Introduction

The relations between authentic religion, the public faith of America, and the religions of American suburbia are even more ambiguous than the relation between authentic religion and the public faith.

The findings and interpretations developed in the preceding chapters illumine the complex and variegated interplay between these components. White Protestantism, Catholicism, black Protestantism, and Judaism participate commonly in important aspects of the public faith of America, but they also differ on significant components.

Traditionally cultic and traditionally directive in the public sphere, Roman Catholicism has undergone the most significant transformation of any of the religions of American suburbia. Its increasing emphases

on lay participation and decentralized decisionmaking has brought it into
closer agreement both with the ideas of religious liberty, religious
tolerance, and religious pluralism and also those of the separation of
church and state embodied in the religion of America.[8]

To be sure, Roman Catholicism still had more adherents affirming
traditional familial values than any other groups and had more respondents
believing the church should uphold a strict standard of moral conduct.
Nonetheless, only pluralities or small majorities of lay people affirmed
traditional church norms on many issues. Such patterns were especially
evident in New Town, the suburb with the highest proportion of young
parishioners.

If present trends persist--and this study has found no evidence
to suggest any dramatic changes--the Catholic church will continue to
increase its emphasis on lay participation and more democratic decisionmaking.
The church will have to rely increasingly on suasion and consensus-formation
on moral issues, for decreasing proportions of lay people are apt to follow
church teachings because they are told to do so.

In contrast to an emphasis on the authority of the church, facets
of Protestantism have emphasized the authority of the Scriptures. Fundamentalists, insisting on the literal truth of Scripture, were more prevalent
among black clergy and black laity than among clergy and laity of any
other group studied, as revealed in Chapters IV and IX.

It would be a mistake to over-emphasize this formalistic and
authoritarian dimension in black Protestantism, for it is counterbalanced
by a dynamic fluidity--albeit a stylized one--in worship and expression.
Black Protestants were not as moralistically rigid as were Catholics, for
they were less firmly affixed to traditional views on sexual mores, family
values, and abortion.

White Protestant churches not affiliated with the National Council
of Churches were also apt to be traditional and authoritarian. Unfortunately, lay responses from such a church were not available in this
study, but clergy responses were obtained. As reported in Chapter IV,
they were much more moralistic than NCC clergy on every item exploring
morality.

White Protestants (as represented by the United Methodists) were
least certain about the validity of clear-cut moral principles to inform
conduct in the familial sphere. They were more attracted to a contextual
approach to decisionmaking in this sphere.

The Familial Sphere

Jews were the least traditional of any major faith group in values
related to the familial sphere. The large majority rejected extramarital
sexual relations, but they were most permissive with regard to premarital

sexual relations. They were strongly supportive of first trimester abortion,
and they did not question the morality of divorce.

The relation of these familial values manifest in the religions
of American suburbia to authentic religion and the public faith of America
is ambivalently positive. All three, in varying degrees, sustain values
associated with the monogamous family, but the qualification of some
traditional values by the secularity fostered by technical rationalism
has undercut some traditional family values. Divorce, abortion, and
premarital sexual relations were either condoned by majorities or substantial minorities in each major faith group, suggesting the dissolution
of many of the norms traditionally contributing to family stability. This
situation heightens the intentionality of marriage and contributes to
the increased instability of life-long monogamy in American society. In
this instance, destiny is minimized, and freedom is accentuated. At
the same time, the vast majority of respondents affirmed marital fidelity.
Such responses indicate strong efforts to sustain the monogamous family
in spite of the powerful pressures which are modifying traditional norms.

The Public Sphere

There was much greater consensus on family values among the four
faith groups than there was about values in the political and economic
spheres. In part this diversity reflects the realities of the situation,
for power is more important in intergroup relations than in interpersonal
relations. This emphasis on power makes it more difficult to attain a
tolerable harmony between the principles of equality appropriate to form
and self-determination informed by excellence. Consequently, naked power
is more likely to be exercised in intergroup relations than in interpersonal ones, and the principles guiding forms of association change
more rapidly in these relations. In addition, vested interests, peoples'
limited visions, and human propensities to overvalue one's nation or
significant social groups are accentuated in intergroup relations.[9]

For all these reasons, the development and the application of moral
principles in intergroup relations is more difficult and less clear than
in interpersonal relations. Representatives of religious institutions
may be expected to articulate and to seek a consensus on principles of
justice and forms of social organization that will foster these principles,
but due to the factors just noted it is very unlikely they will be able
to attain a consensus on particular rules and regulations of justice or
particular issues of public policy.

At present, this discussion of the role of religious institutions
in the public sphere is inchoate and confused. Every lay group in every
religious institution studied displayed a substantial range of judgments
on policy issues ranging from the Vietnam War to racial integration in the
suburbs. In many ways, they reflected the disharmonies manifest in the
larger society.

Traditional political loyalties seemed to influence lay views in the public realm. Catholics, Jews, and black Protestants had Democratic preferences, and white Protestants had Republican preferences. The low correlations between orthodoxy, devotionalism, and issues of public policy reflect the lacuna of principles or middle axioms by which lay people discerned the implications of their experience and understanding of the Divine for justice in the public sphere.

Lay people did support the basic political and economic systems in the United States. Nonetheless, only small minorities supported them in an unqualified way. Their stance coheres with the evaluation developed earlier in this chapter in the discussion of authentic religion. Given the importance of self-interest in human affairs, it is scarcely surprising to find that the more privileged Christians in Country Club Estates were most supportive of the present forms of economic and political organization and the least-privileged black Protestants in Satellite City were least supportive.

The most important single finding in this area was the "centralist" tendencies of all groups. Few people either "strongly agreed" or "strongly disagreed" with statements about the quality of institutions in the economic or political spheres. Lay people sustaining the religions of America were prepared to support efforts to improve the quality of American economic and political institutions, but they were not prepared to support efforts to overhaul them radically.

Based on criteria derived from authentic religion and the characteristics of human beings, American forms of economic and political organization were interpreted in an ambivalently positive manner. Consequently, a rough coherence exists between the evaluation of existing forms of economic and political organization based on normative criteria and on the judgments of suburban lay people. Even so, most suburban lay people did not offer a theological reason for their assessments. The coherence between authentic religion and the religions of American suburbia is grounded in facets of the public faith of America.

There was one exception to these patterns warranting some emphasis. Pastors of non-NCC-affiliated Protestant churches were most uncritically supportive of existing forms of economic and political organization, most equivocal about the desirability of racial integration in the suburbs, and most supportive of the morality of the Vietnam War. Piety, economic and political conservatism, and support of officially sanctioned foreign policy were thus intertwined among these clergy.

On the issues of the Vietnam War and racial integration of the suburbs, these clergy were closer to the American majority than the other clergy. (On some items, they were closer to the NCC Protestant laity than were the NCC clergy.) Such a coherence illumines the popularity of many mass evangelists, such as Billy Graham and Oral Roberts, for they help legitimate controversial values by over-simplification, and/or exclusion of complex policy issues in their public statements.

With the exception of these clergy, the other groups in the study blended conservation and innovation in their attitudes toward the public spheres.

The very wide distribution of responses to religious institutional involvement in the public sphere highlights the complexity of the situation and the difficulties religious groups have developing positions with regard to many issues of public policy. Such diffuseness, according to the interpretation advanced here, reflects the realities of the actual situation.

The Religious Sphere

Historical interfaith prejudices persisted to some extent, but the majority of lay people were reasonably tolerant or indifferent toward other faith groups, about which they knew relatively little. They were understandably somewhat critical of groups with strong evangelical emphases, such as Jehovah's Witnesses, for such exclusiveness runs counter to the notions of religious pluralism and religious tolerance inherent in authentic religion and partially embodied in the religion of America.

The acceptance of the principle of the separation of church and state, a necessary corollary of religious tolerance, religious liberty, and religious pluralism, was very general among the members of all the major faith groups, but there were some suggestive intergroup differences. Jews were most staunchly supportive of church-state separation, white Protestants second, Catholics third, and black Protestants fourth. (See Tables I-1 and II-1.)

As a people suffering much persecution over the centuries, the Jewish community in America has sensed the importance of church-state separation and religious tolerance, pluralism, and voluntaryism for its own well-being. Such self-interest has accentuated its support of these tenets on other grounds. White Protestants struggled with the problems of church-state relations in the eighteenth and nineteenth centuries, and they generally accepted church-state separation by the time of the Civil War.

The Catholic support of church-state separation has emerged later in the context of the acculturation of vast numbers of Catholic immigrants coming to America between 1865 and 1920. Coming from areas not sustaining church-state separation, these immigrants responded by constructing their own institutions and remaining in relative isolation from the dominant culture.

The Catholic church has appropriated many values in the broader society over the past fifty or seventy-five years. The parochial school and separate social institutions seemed less crucial than in earlier times, and a substantial majority of Catholics affirmed church-state separation.

This situation does not preclude some conflict when self-interest and matters of faith and morals are at stake. The issues of public aid

to private schools and abortion are especially salient loci of conflict
in the present period.

The black Protestants were also _relatively_ less supportive of
church-state separation and government neutrality in religious affairs.
Such views are rooted in the black experience in America, especially in
the reconstruction era following the Civil War. As E. Franklin Frazier
has shown, the black church emerged in this era as an inclusive black
social institution, performing economic and political as well as religious
functions. The presence of black clergy in political office and economic
life today has its roots in this era in the history of the black church
in America.

The voluntaryism of religious institutions in America necessi-
tates the development of various fund-raising activities and accentuates
the consensus-formation nonauthoritarian style of church life and professional religious leadership. The round of social activities and fund-
raising ventures associated with almost every local religious institution
is necessary in the American context for institutional maintenance as
well as for fellowship.

As noted earlier, this central cultural yalue makes the "gathered"
congregation the norm for ecclesiastical organization in the United States,
regardless of the type of polity formally established in a particular
tradition. It is the basic reason why the church-sect typology, developed
in the context of the European experience, is of limited usefulness in
interpreting the American religious situation.

The realities of the current situation suggest some modifications
and qualifications of the historic tri-partite structure of American
religious institutions. For historical and sociological reasons, black
Protestantism has developed in relative isolation from white Protestantism,
reflecting a somewhat distinctive style and form of religious expression.

Insofar as these developments foster legitimate ethnic, cultural,
and religious pluralism, they are good; insofar as they isolate people
inordinately one from another and destroy a sense of the unity of the
whole, they are evil.

During the past fifty years under the influence of the American
experience, white Protestantism and Catholicism have undergone considerable
rapprochement. A predominantly white centralist Christianity seems to be
emerging, with conservative Catholics accentuating Catholic identity and
conservative Protestants accentuating Protestant identity. In the center
are moderate Protestants and moderate Catholics, accentuating Christian
identity.

Inevitably, white Protestants, black Protestants, Catholics, and
Jews share salient facets of the religion of America. Without such common
shared values, they would not be able to affirm the voluntaryism, tolerance,
and pluralism permitting the cooperative coexistence of the religions of
American suburbia.

Another facet of this shared public faith is the technical rationalism
which is so powerful in American life. It influences all faith groups and

modifies the religious dimension. Because of the diffuseness of explicit theological understanding, this secularism coexists with the piety of the religious heritage.

Technical rationalism contributes to the physical well-being of people and enhances excellence in some dimensions of life. It also disrupts inclusive and wholistic human relations, fosters inordinate acquisitiveness, and upsets the balance of nature. This compounds the ambiguity inherent in the relation between authentic religion, the public faith, and the religions of American suburbia. The supportive and contra- dictory interrelations of the components considered in this chapter preclude a simple evaluation of the relation of authentic religion to the public faith, and the religions of American suburbia. In light of the understanding of authentic religion suggested here, these relations are interpreted in an ambivalently positive manner.

The Voluntary Religious Institution in America

Voluntary religious institutions, which are attuned to authentic religion, the religion of America, and the religions of American suburbia, will probably make few dramatic or radical contributions to the life of the larger society. Clergy and lay people are engaged in mutual explora- tions centered in the experiences of worship, education, and sociability, which are at the heart of religious institutions. Some participants are deeply involved in the ongoing life of the religious institution, many are moderately involved, and some are only peripherally involved.

Except for a few very small groups, no highly self-conscious and intentional religious communities were found in the suburban sector. The impact of such groups and of especially creative leaders associated with them cannot be assessed through the instruments used in this study, but this methodological stricture is certainly not sufficient justification to exclude the contribution of such groups and individuals from a discussion of authentic religion, the public faith, and the religions of American suburbia.

The words and deeds of small groups and outstanding individuals affect the shape and substance of the dialog in which participants in local religious institutions engage. These innovative and creative efforts emerging from more highly intentional communities and from people associated with theological schools and other innovative centers are modified in the context of local religious institutional life, but they do contribute indirectly to the lives of such institutions and to the broader society.

The efforts to attain a moral consensus among members of religious institutions are slow, undramatic, and often not very successful. Since creative innovators and social and religious critics often seek to impose their wills and views on people in an authoritatian manner, it is not sur- prising that they are usually not particularly successful in the short run. Many such innovators and critics would find it almost impossible to serve as religious leaders in most local churches and synagogues, for a relatively non-authoritarian style of pastoral direction is more appropriate in these situations.

Those committed to a non-authoritarian style of religious leadership and able to interpret the findings reported here in an ambivalently
positive manner will be able to serve those institutions best. They
can respond to the needs of American religious institutions with inner
integrity and with a sense of cause, a sense of proportion, and a sense
of responsibility. They can share in the efforts of people who voluntarily
support churches and synagogues to discern the Divine Presence in our
lives and to enhance our lives together.

NOTES

Introduction

1. Religious institutions are present in all literate societies, and their more or less formalized precursors have existed in all pre-literate human societies. Scholars have differed in their basic interpretations of the ubiquity of religious institutions in human societies. Some have held religious institutions arise in response to authentic religious experience of a Divine Reality Who is in some sense _sui generis_. Some have distinguished between authentic and inauthentic religious institutions, assigning priorities based on some criteria related to a particular tradition.

There are scholars who have questioned the authenticity of religious institutions altogether; they have distinguished between the secondary interpretations offered by the adherents of particular religious traditions and the primary interpretation offered by the scientist who really understands the basic reasons for the emergence and persistence of religious institutions. Still other scholars, distinguishing between scientific and confessional studies, incorporate two perspectives within the same investigation.

It is not necessary to delineate extensively alternate modes of interpretation in the present context, but it is necessary to sketch briefly in the body of the text the mode of interpretation employed here.

For a systematic discussion of these alternatives, see Schroeder, 1970, pp. 145-162.

2. Throughout this volume the term "ambiguous" is used in a special sense. It is employed to designate a situation in which the finite actualization of the harmony of the potentiality of forms occurs. Because actualization requires limitations and exclusions, the contrast between the "perfect" harmonization of potentiality and the "imperfect" (in the sense of "limited") harmonization of experience in a definite actual creature results in "ambiguity."

The term "ambiguously positive" is used to designate an enhancement of harmony and intensity of feeling in existence. The term "ambiguously negative" is used to designate the attenuation of feeling and/or the enhancement of disharmony in existence.

3. For three evocative discussions of the latent and manifest church within Christian thought, see Niebuhr, 1956; Gustafson, 1961; and Tillich, 1963, pp. 138-245.

There is some legitimacy to critiques suggesting that the substance and form of religion are derived from American culture; but this constitutive act of worship embodies symbols, evokes feelings, and stimulates thoughts surpassing cultural forms and societal substance. This type of critique of "culture" religion has been fashionable in the past two decades. Marty, 1959, Berger, 1961, and Winter, 1961, are representative of this type of sociological and theological analysis.

4. For a suggestive discussion of this phenomenon, see Niebuhr, 1958.

5. For a useful discussion of historical trends, see Gaustad, 1962. For a summary of recent data, see George Gallup, Jr., and John O. Davies, III, 1971.

6. For a somewhat exaggerated but illumining study of these trends, see Hadden, 1969. For historical comparisons, see Hopkins, 1940, and May, 1949.

7. This study differs considerably in design from Lenski, 1961, and Herberg, 1955. Nonetheless, it utilizes the major faith groupings Lenski used in his study, and it shares Herberg's interest in integrative common values unifying Americans and in differentiated faith groups separating them. Herberg's failure to consider black Protestants is a lacuna in his very suggestive work. For an interpretation of contemporary faith identities, see Mueller, 1971.

8. According to the 1972 Yearbook of American Churches, the United Methodist Church had 10,700,000 members. The Southern Baptist Convention, concentrated in the South, reported 11,600,000 members. The next largest Protestant denomination was the National Baptist Convention, with 5,500,000 members.

9. For an excellent portrayal of the South's distinctive cultural and religious ethos, see Hill, 1968.

10. In this study causal model building and associated statistical techniques are rejected in favor of the examination of correlates using the simple chi-square test of significance and the related contingency coefficient. This approach was taken because some members of the research team were informed by a more contextual, wholistic, and dynamic interpretation of social existence than causal model building presupposes. See Schroeder, 1970, pp. 141-144, for a discussion of these problems.

Chapter I

1. For a most perceptive discussion of the impact of immigration on American society, see Handlin, 1957.

2. For extensive discussions of these developments see Ahlstrom, 1972; Littell, 1962; and Mead, 1963.

3. For a detailed exploration of these matters, see Hudson, 1953.

4. The classic church-sect distinctions were made by Troeltsch, 1931. Though appropriate for the European situations, such distinctions were not directly applicable to the American context. The "denomination" is intermediate between the church and the sect. For a discussion of this area, see Yinger, 1970. The classic sociocultural analysis of the emergence of denominations in the American context is Niebuhr, 1957.

5. See Robertson, ed., 1966. The essays "The Voluntary Principle in Religion and Religious Freedom in America" by Robert T. Handy and "The Voluntary Church: A Moral Appraisal" by James M. Gustafson are especially pertinent.

6. On the issue of the coexistence of pious and secular motifs in America, see Niebuhr, 1958, and Clebsch, 1968.

For perceptive analyses of the development of technical rationalism, see Weber, 1930, and "Science as a Vocation," "Politics as a Vocation," and "Bureaucracy" in Gerth and Mills, eds., 1946; Little, 1969; and Tawney, 1920, 1926.

For a discussion of the religion of America, see "Civil Religion in America," Bellah, 1970. For related discussions, see Warner, 1949; Luckmann, 1967; and Williams, 1970.

7. In the development of this section, the following works have been especially helpful: Ellul, 1964; Kornhauser, 1959; Moore, 1963; Stein, 1960; Taylor, 1953; Vidich and Bensman, 1958; W. Lloyd Warner, ed., 1967; Weber, 1958; Williams, 1970; and Wirth, 1938.

8. See Winter, 1968. For an analysis of some of the implications of this growth of the ecclesiastical bureaucracy, see Hadden, 1969. For an illuminating case study of one Protestant ecclesiastical bureaucracy, see Harrison, 1959.

Chapter II

1. Luckmann, 1967, informed by a Durkheimian perspective, makes much of the privatization of particular religious groups. For further references see Note 6 in the notes for Chapter I.

2. The term "America's public religion" is used here to designate a commonly shared public religion held by people in the United States. It is comparable to the term "civil religion" coined by Jean Jacques Rousseau and recently popularized by Robert N. Bellah. The "public faith" of America is used here to refer to technical rationalism, secular humanism, and the public religion as aspects of common and partially contradictory core values shared by most Americans. (See "Civil Religion in America," in Bellah, 1970.) For related discussions, see

Warner, 1949, and Luckmann, 1967. For a suggestive analysis, albeit one accentuating inordinately the dimensions of technical rationalism and non-theistic humanism, see Wilson, 1969. Because Wilson's interpretative perspective does not incorporate the notion of a Divine Reality Who is, in some sense sui generis, his discussion of classical Christianity is critical and external.

3. Some of the authors reject Durkheim's interpretation of reality, but we all think his discussion of the rhythm of societal life is very suggestive (Durkheim, 1915). Similarly Warner, 1949, 1961, is suggestive.

4. For an illuminating study replete with historical documentation, see Burns, 1957.

5. See Cousins, ed., 1958, and Gabriel, 1940.

6. See Trueblood, 1973.

7. The reemergence of ethnic self-consciousness in the 1960's and 1970's is evidence of both the success and failure of the melting pot imagery.

8. In this context it is suggestive to speculate on the symbolic significance of the life and death of Martin Luther King, Jr. In his quest for social justice, he frequently appealed to the ideas of liberty, equality, and brotherhood in a democracy under God, notions deeply embodied in America's public religion. If America's quest for racial justice is partially successful in the coming decades, King may well join Washington and Lincoln among the high personages of the religion of America. Since "destiny" is always a factor in the emergence of persons constituting central figures in a public religion, it is too early to be clear on this development.

9. It is not coincidental that renewed interest in America's public religion developed in the late 1960's, for controversy about race and about the Vietnam War were accentuating conflict and the diversity of the American experience. America's public religion, emphasizing unity and harmony, partly balanced these disintegrative tendencies. This situation reflects the perennial political problem of seeking to avoid both tyranny and anarchy in the body politic.

10. The classic interpretation of this phenomenon is found in Herberg, 1955.

11. This matter is discussed extensively in Chapter III.

12. On this issue, see Mueller, 1971.

13. For a valuable interpretation of this process see Wakin and Scheuer, 1966.

Chapter III

1. The following works were especially useful in the preparation of this discussion: Douglass, 1925; Hoover and Vernon, 1962; Mumford, 1938; Park and Burgess, 1925; Weber, 1958; and Wirth, 1938.

2. Membership data are correlated with type of suburban community in this section. Most of the data were obtained from religious professionals serving institutions in the suburban sector. In the dozen or so instances when the religious professional serving an institution refused to provide membership data, estimates were made. With one exception, the institutions where membership was estimated were small. Estimates were based on information provided by other clergy, the physical size of the church or synagogue, and the number of people and/or automobiles observed at worship services. These institutions could not have a combined membership of more than 2000 members at the very most, so even a 15 or 20 percent error in estimate would not affect significantly the patterns illuminated here.

The problem of estimating the number of members of Jewish synagogues and Roman Catholic parishes was more serious. Reflecting the principles of institutional organization discussed in Chapter I, these institutions reported membership by number of families rather than by number of individual members.

This problem was compounded by the fact that different institutions had different criteria on age and intentionality for membership. In Roman Catholic parishes children seven and above were counted as confirmed members. In many Protestant churches and in the Jewish synagogues, children were not considered confirmed members until about puberty. In all groups, the membership status of children moving away from their family of origin was murky. Most religious institutions considered children of members to be members related to their family of origin until they married or took jobs and moved out of their parents' homes. The marginal position of the college student, even living away from home, is reflected here.

To resolve these membership data problems, the Protestant data given by clergy were used and a conversion factor of 2.2 was employed to convert the Catholic and Jewish data from number of families to number of "adult" members. The figure is somewhat arbitrary, but it does permit reasonably accurate membership comparisons.

Since this section is concerned primarily with examining broad patterns and trends, the minor inaccuracies caused by these estimate procedures are inconsequential. The membership data were accurate enough to illimine general tendencies and configurations.

The patterns traced here are manifest in almost all major metropolitan areas, and the study is concerned primarily with these broad patterns. The very large size of the Midwest City metropolitan area accentuates the intensity of the patterns outlined here, but they are apparent in every American metropolitan area.

3. See Kincheloe, 1938.

Chapter IV

1. Will Herberg, 1955, has analyzed this phenomenon.

2. Three Reform synagogues and two Conservative synagogues were located in the studied suburban sector. There were no Orthodox synagogues in the sector. Orthodox strength is greater in the East than in the Midwest. Roughly half of the approximately 6,000,000 Jews in the United States belong to a synagogue.

3. For the classic study of the sociohistorical factors contributing to this division, see Niebuhr, 1957.

4. See Jacquet, 1972, Table 1-A (pp. 220-228) and Table 1-E (p. 231). Religious membership data are not very accurate, so these figures should be taken to be merely indicative of the situation. Unevenness of reporting is compounded by the fact that some groups consider children to be members and others do not.

5. These contrasts appear clearly in the data on the clergy presented in this chapter. Unfortunately financial restrictions prevented the study of the lay members of a non-NCC church. The lay data in this study, as observed in the Introduction, are based on responses from lay questionnaires sent to members of three United Methodist Churches. This church is the centralist Protestant church outside the South, so it was selected for study here.

6. It is beyond the scope of this discussion to delineate inner struggles within these broad groupings. The focus here is on the general turn of mind leading to a relatively static, formal view, or a rather dynamic innovating view. The important sociological issue is the degree of diversity present within a major faith grouping, for such diversity or lack of diversity shapes the faith identity issue.

7. So far as the research team could determine, none of these clergy were college graduates. Most of their churches were "store front" institutions.

8. The findings are summarized in Gallup and Davies, 1971, pp. 1-7.

9. The relation between fellowship and institution is implicit in the sect-church dichotomy elaborated by Ernest Troeltsch and still the topic of frequent scholarly discussions. In our judgment, the most evocative discussions of this issue in recent times have been advanced by H. Richard Niebuhr and James Gustafson, both of whom insist the church is both fellowship and institution. See Niebuhr, 1956, and Gustafson, 1961, 1970. Dittes, 1967, also provides a very helpful treatment of aspects of the life of the voluntary church.

10. A large number of studies of clergy roles and job satisfaction have been conducted in the past decade. Among the more significant
are: Bartlett, 1971; Fukuyama, 1972; Greeley, 1972; and Jud, Mills, and
Burch, 1970.

For a variety of reasons rooted in the American experience, the
problem of clergy satisfaction is more acute in Catholicism and Judaism
than in Protestantism. The fact that the findings of this study agree
with national findings increases one's confidence in the case-study approach
employed here to illumine salient facets of suburban religion in America.

11. See, for example, Cox, 1967, and Hadden, 1969. For a case
study of this phenomenon at a local level, see Lee and Galloway, 1969,
and Cutting, 1972.

12. See, for example, Drake and Cayton, 1945, and Frazier, 1963.

13. The travail of the National Council of Churches, which is
short of funds, is undergoing much criticism from various groups that hold
sharply contrasting views on matters of public policy, and is considering
reorganization, illustrates the shape of the conflict among interdenominational agencies. The most direct influence lay people and local clergy
can have on an ecclesiastical bureaucracy is the withholding or reduction
of funds, and they have done so in recent years.

An Associated Press dispatch reporting the establishment of a
fifteen-member NCC task force to consider reorganization concluded:

> In setting up the task force, the church representatives
> said it should develop its plans for a redesigned organization
> in line with several "tests of obedience" to member churches,
> including its ability to register their real concerns and
> enlist their financial backing and energies in carrying out
> its work.
> One of the chief problems in the present setup, as
> highlighted at the meeting here, is that it frequently
> authorizes programs--particularly on such issues as peace and
> race--that the churches decline to finance or push in their
> own ranks.
> As a suggested solution, some churchmen here advocate
> that an overhauled organization should provide an inclusive
> form for Christian interchange, study and service, both with
> specific action projects undertaken only by those favoring
> them. (Chicago Sun-Times, January 24, 1970, p. 34)

Delegates to this conference were well aware of the sharp divergence
that had developed between the staff members of the National Council of
Churches and delegates to meetings sponsored by the National Council, on
the one hand, and constituent churches, on the other hand. The suggested
separation of Christian interchange, study and service from specific action
projects is an implicit acknowledgement of the lack of unanimity on those
matters among clergy and lay people.

Most major denominations are encountering comparable financial
pressures. In 1970, national leaders of the United Presbyterian Church
reported a 33 percent reduction in buying power in the past three years,
based on a 15 percent decline in income and an 18 percent inflationary
factor. (Reported in the <u>Chicago Sun-Times</u>, November 14, 1970, p. 37)
The National Conference of Catholic Bishops confronted a $2,000,000 deficit
in 1970 in a total budget of slightly over $11,000,000. (Reported in the
<u>Chicago Sun-Times</u>, November 17, 1970, p. 52)

The financial situation was better at the local level, for overall
contributions increased from $7,930,000,000 in 1969 to $8,200,000,000
in 1970 (a 3.5 percent increase). This increase did not keep pace with
inflation; secondary agencies dependent on local churches suffered disproportionately. (See Jacquet, 1972, pp. 238-239.) By 1974 the very sharp
declines of the late 1960's have moderated, but most major denominations
have fewer staff and initiate fewer programs than in the 1960's.

14. Fletcher, 1966, represents one version of a contextualist
social ethic. Ramsey, 1967, represents one version of a principled social
ethic. This debate has been a center of much interest and controversy
in some Protestant circles in the past decade or so. Differences in the
understanding of "law-gospel" and "faith-works" were at the heart of
Protestant-Catholic conflicts during the Reformation era.

15. It is beyond the scope of this study to explore subtypes of
these major groups. For example, the question used here could not distinguish between the non-fundamentalist biblically focused neo-orthodox
theology of Karl Barth and the philosophical neo-orthodox theology of
Paul Tillich.

16. As noted, the limited research budget prevented an analysis of
lay people in a non-NCC-affiliated Protestant church. Other data suggest
a much greater coherence in values between clergy and laity in this group.

Chapter V

1. See Gaustad, 1962, Littell, 1962, and Gallup and Davies, 1971.

2. See, for example, Greeley, 1969. Interpreters also disagreed
in their assessment of religious involvement in the 1950's. See, for
example, Lipset, 1959, and Herberg, 1959.

3. See, for example, Cox, 1965; Luckmann, 1967; Demerath and
Hammond, 1968; and Wilson, 1969.

4. See, for example, Kelley, 1972. This book has been widely read.
It presents an erroneous picture of the relative strength of NCC- and
non-NCC-affiliated Protestant churches. Kelley completely ignores the
impact of the changing age composition of the American people on religious
institutional life and does not discuss adequately the effects of regionalism
on numerical growth. The most rapid growing <u>large</u> conservative churches

are the Southern Baptist Convention, predominant in the South, and the Mormons, predominant in Utah. The strong social sanctions of these sub-cultures for church participation counter the impact of the family life cycle on church participation patterns noted in the body of this chapter and in Note 8.

As a result, the Kelley volume seriously distorts the contemporary situation. The issue of meaning Kelley addresses is certainly important, but so are demographics. It is very difficult to see how many religious institutions could grow numerically when the number of people in the age groups (thirty-five to forty-nine and ten to fourteen) from which loyal members are drawn is contracting and the number of people in the age group from which members frequently defect (fifteen to twenty-nine) is expanding dramatically.

As a device to sell books to liberal clergy who are experiencing modest declines in the membership of their churches, the sensationalist character of the Kelley volume is understandable. As an analysis of the factors contributing to the present situation, the book is gross.

5. As noted in the text, no emergent religious group had developed de novo in the suburbs, so far as the study team could discover. New religious groups almost invariably develop under the auspices of a char-ismatic leader and subsequently become institutionalized. The method of investigation employed here did not permit an adequate treatment of an emerging religious group. Participant observations, interviews, and the use of archival data are necessary to study such groups. For a broad survey of the literature of sectarian movements, see Yinger, 1970. Two excellent studies of sectarian movements are Wilson, 1961, 1967. Other representative studies of sects, relying substantially on archival and/or interview data, include the following: Braden, 1963; Clark, 1949; Fauset, 1971; O'Dea, 1957; Pike, 1954; Pope, 1942; and Whitley, 1959.

6. According to pastors' estimates, 58 percent of the NCC-affiliated churches compared to 14 percent of non-NCC-affiliated churches had 80 percent or more of white collar laity. Sixty-nine percent of the non-NCC churches compared to 19 percent of NCC-affiliated churches had 60 percent or more blue collar laity.

7. See, for example, Greeley and Rossi, 1966, and Lenski, 1961.

8. Data on age in the state where Midwest City and its suburbs are located--a state with substantial inmigration--illumine the magnitude of the fluctuations. Between 1950 and 1970 the number of people between thirty-five and thirty-nine decreased by almost 10 percent, and the number of people between ten and fourteen more than doubled. Comparable increases occurred in the five to nine and fifteen to nineteen year age groups. Assuming no migration and no changes in the death rate, there will be more than 70 percent more people between thirty-five and forty-nine in Midwest City's state in the year 2000 than in 1970. Such demographics augur well for the future numerical vitality of American religious institutions. Broadly speaking, the period between 1965 and 1980 is the time period with the least desirable age mix for religious institutional membership.

9. For a perceptive discussion of the changing Catholic Church in America, see Wakin and Scheuer, 1966.

10. On this matter, see Stark and Glock, 1968. Because they did not break their data down by congregation or parish and did not deal in depth with the capacity of individuals to live graciously with diversity, they overemphasized the divisiveness of internal contrasts in beliefs.

Chapter VI

1. Proponents of the strongly disciplined and highly intentional religious institution are apt to decry this situation. See, for example, the special issue of The Chicago Theological Seminary Register on "The Believers' Church Conference, 1970" (Vol. X, No. 6 [September, 1970]). Rosemary Reuther, Carl D. Bangs, Arthur Foster, Dale W. Brown, Franklin Littell and Donald Durnbaugh are the contributors to this issue.

For a more moderate view of the situation, see Dittes, 1967.

2. For sensitive and generally supportive interpretations of the voluntary church, see Nelson, 1971; Niebuhr, 1956; and Gustafson, 1961.

Chapter VII

1. Gerhard Lenski was unable to examine statistically low status Jews in his study in the Detroit area because there were so few low status Jews in his sample. See Lenski, 1961.

2. For a discussion of the ethnic flavor of the Roman Catholic Church see Chapter 2 of Wakin and Scheuer, 1966.

3. For a very perceptive analysis of the black church, see Frazier, 1963.

4. Because so many black pastors serving non-NCC-affiliated black Protestant churches were not interviewed, data on the black churches have not been presented in tabular form here. Considering the lower educational and occupational levels of the black segment of the suburban population, these churches would certainly have lower proportions of white collar workers and college educated people than the white non-NCC-affiliated Protestant churches.

5. The literature on religious institutions and social stratification is extensive. See Demerath, 1965; Gallup and Davies, 1971; Lenski, 1961; Pope, 1942; Schroeder and Obenhaus, 1964; Vidich and Bensman, 1958; Warner, 1949.

For one constructive assessment of the implications of social stratification for religious institutions, see "Perspectives on Social Stratification" in Schroeder, 1970.

6. For a discussion of these patterns two generations ago, see Drake and Cayton, 1945. For a controversial contemporary discussion of the Negro family, see Daniel Moynihan, "The Negro Family," in Rainwater and Yancey, 1967. The familiar picture of slave families as disorganized and matriarchal must be modified by the recent findings of Fogel and Engerman, 1974.

7. Those affirming the value of some diversity in the style and shape of religious institutions cannot foresee an easy resolution of the problems this divisiveness evokes. Any simple integration of the parts-- assuming such were possible--would produce a hybrid institution which might be less satisfactory than the present multiple institutions. For the moment contacts among representatives of the various groups in regional, national, and international contexts may best symbolize the unity and diversity of human religious experience. Symbolic occasions bringing together diverse social, ethnic, nationality, and religious groups may help humankind intuit its common bonds and its legitimate diversity. Certainly no simple-minded unity in which the integrity of the various component parts is violated is desirable. In any case, concerned professionals cannot effect the unity of voluntary religious institutions by fiat, for lay members have a substantial voice in policy formation.

8. This insensitivity has not been confined to Protestant religious leaders, but it has also been reflected by some political leaders Such attitudes have evoked reactions by those identified with other ethnic groups. See, for example, the evocative analyses by Novak, 1972, and Greeley, 1971.

9. Herberg, 1955, takes such an approach.

10. For a distinguished philosopher's effort to discern a common unity amid the diversity of the American experience, see Dewey, 1934. It is not coincidental this book was written toward the end of the great Catholic migrations.

Chapter VIII

1. For typologies of Christian ethics addressing the relation of religious institutions and believers to the public sphere, see Long, 1967, and Niebuhr, 1951. For a discussion including both analytic and constructive elements, see Chapters XI and XII in Schroeder, 1970.

2. For historical discussions of social concerns in American religious institutions, see Hopkins, 1940, and May, 1949.

3. For a perceptive analysis of the contrasting religious, social, economic, and political views of some clergy and most lay people, see Hadden, 1969. Hadden foresaw a more dramatic confrontation between clergy and lay people than, in fact, developed. He underestimated the distance between ecclesiastical bureaucrats and local churches and the subtle ways in which voluntary churches often defuse controversy by the withdrawal

of fiscal and personal support from unpopular programs and projects. Local
clergy, more sensitive to lay expectations than members of ecclesiastical
bureaucracies, muted the direct criticisms of lay people.

4. For two contrasting theological interpretations of the relation
of love, power, and justice, see Ryan and Boland, 1940, and Tillich, 1954.
For a discussion including both analytic and constructive dimensions, see
Chapters XI and XII in Schroeder, 1970.

5. Bellah, 1970.

6. The most widely known interpretation seeing the racial situation
as a problem rooted in the causal past, and potentially remediable is
Myrdal, 1944. In current times, views indicting American racial relations
have become more fashionable. Carmichael and Hamilton, 1967, offer such
an interpretation.

7. See, for example, Cox, 1965; Illich, 1973; Kraemer, 1973;
Marcuse, 1964; and Winter, 1970.

8. These questionnaires were collected in the spring of 1972,
prior to the Watergate scandal or the "energy crisis." The degree of
alienation from the structures of American society has increased substantially since then, according to a Harris survey reported in the
Chicago Tribune on June 27, 1974. (Section 1, p. 18)

Harris has trend data on four items dealing with the political
system, the fairness of the American economic system, and the individual's
role in the social order. According to this survey, the largest increase
in alienation has taken place among suburban residents and among young
people. Among suburbanites, the disaffected have increased from 22 percent
in 1966 to 58 percent in 1974; among those under thirty, from 24 percent
in 1966 to 62 percent in 1974. Overall, the increase was from 29 percent
in 1966 to 59 percent in 1974.

This massive disaffection poses serious problems for America's
economic and political institutions. Whether the sources of the alienation are systemic or episodic is moot. Probably both sources are involved.
At any rate, economic and political events are combining to temper
Americans' traditional affirmations of a doctrine of progress.

9. This broad generalization obviously is subject to many
qualifications. Neither party has a monopoly on either principle. In
the American experience, a pragmatic non-ideological style is predominant
in both parties, so these principles are more implicit than explicit and
are manifest in varying degrees by members of both major parties. For a
discussion of the meaning of these principles, see Chapter XII in Schroeder,
1970.

Chapter IX

1. The primary intent here is to provide a framework from which the data on the Ten Commandments can be interpreted. Ramsey, 1967, develops a principled approach. Lehmann, 1963, elaborates a contextual approach. Fletcher, 1966, and Sittler, 1958, also develop versions of situation ethics.

2. For a study of the persistence of this motif in American folk culture, see the study of religious "best-sellers" reported by Schneider and Dornbusch, 1958. In differing ways, both Norman Vincent Peale and Billy Graham emphasize this motif.

3. There was much concern over the recent Protestant evangelism campaign--Key 73--among the Jewish leadership, for the campaign raised again the issue of the definition of the basic "ground-rules" of American religious pluralism.

4. Unfortunately the item was not included in the clergy questionnaire, so comparable clergy data are not available.

Chapter X

1. See Berger, 1961; Cox, 1965; Eckardt, 1958; Herberg, 1955; and Winter, 1961.

2. See Dittes, 1967; Gustafson, 1961, and "The Voluntary Church: A Moral Appraisal" in D. B. Robertson, ed., 1966; Murray, 1960; and Niebuhr, 1956.

3. For a more extended discussion of the issues addressed in this section see Schroeder, 1970, pp. 180-191.

4. For a fuller statement of the views inherent in this description, see Whitehead, 1926.

5. This formulation implies a rejection of the Protestant doctrine of justification by grace through faith. By their good works--intellectual, moral, and aesthetic--humans may elicit religious experience. Finitude and ignorance preclude ultimate perfection in the moral and intellectual realms, but progress is possible in both intellectual and moral realms. Art objects and aesthetic experiences are timeless and final in a unique way, for they embody the love for harmony and intensity of feeling which are rooted in the Divine Life.

6. This notion involves the rejection of the static ontology of classical Roman Catholicism. The form-dynamic relation suggested here places

a greater emphasis on formal elements than neo-orthodox Protestantism but a lesser emphasis than classical Roman Catholicism.

7. For a discussion of the assimilation theory, see Herberg, 1955. For a discussion of the pluralistic theory, see Novak, 1972.

8. For studies employing different styles of analyses but coming to comparable conclusions, see Greeley, 1967, and Wakin and Scheuer, 1966. For more extended analyses of the Catholic situation based on data gathered in connection with this study, see Sweetser, 1974, forthcoming.

9. For theological analyses of these problems see John XXIII, "Mater et Magistra," 1963; Niebuhr, 1944; and Tillich, 1954. For an illumining historical study of Christians seeking to apply their under-standing of Christianity to politics, see James, 1962.

REFERENCES

Ahlstrom, Sydney E.
    1972 A Religious History of the American People. New Haven:
          Yale University Press.
Bartlett, Laile E.
    1971 The Vanishing Parson. Boston: Beacon Press.
Bellah, Robert N.
    1970 Beyond Belief. New York: Harper and Row.
Berger, Peter
    1961 The Noise of Solemn Assemblies. Garden City: Doubleday
          & Co.
Braden, Charles S.
    1963 Spirits in Rebellion: The Rise and Development of New
          Thought. Dallas: Southern Methodist University Press.
Burns, Edward McNall
    1957 The American Idea of Mission. New Brunswick: Rutgers
          University Press.
Carmichael, Stokely and Charles V. Hamilton
    1967 Black Power. New York: Random House.
Clark, Elmer T.
    1949 The Small Sects in America. New York: Abingdon-Cokesbury
          Press.
Clebsch, William A.
    1968 From Sacred to Profane America. New York: Harper and Row.
Cousins, Norman, ed.
    1958 "In God We Trust": The Religious Beliefs and Ideas of the
          American Founding Fathers. New York: Harper and Row, Pub.
Cox, Harvey
    1965 The Secular City. New York: Macmillan.
    1967 "The 'New Breed' in American Churches: Sources of Social
          Activism in American Religion." Daedalus 96 (Winter):
          135-150.
Cutting, Thomas
    1972 "A Presbytery Considers Project Equality." Chicago Theo-
          logical Seminary Register LXII (September): 31-39.

Demerath, Nicholas J., III
     1965 Social Class in American Protestantism. Chicago: Rand
           McNally and Co.
Demerath, N. J., III, and Phillip E. Hammond
     1968 Religion in Social Context. New York: Random House.
Dewey, John
     1934 A Common Faith. New Haven: Yale University Press.
Dittes, James E.
     1967 The Church in the Way. New York: Charles Scribners Sons.
Douglass, H. Paul
     1925 The Suburban Trend. New York: The Century Co.
Drake, St. Clair and Horace R. Cayton
     1945 Black Metropolis. New York: Harcourt, Brace and Company.
Durkheim, Emile
     1915 The Elementary Forms of the Religious Life. London: George
           Allen and Unwin, Ltd.
Eckardt, A. R.
     1958 The Surge of Piety in America. New York: Association Press.
Ellul, Jacques
     1964 The Technological Society. New York: Knopf.
Fauset, Arthur H.
     1971 Black Gods of the Metropolis. Philadelphia: University
           of Pennsylvania Press.
Fletcher, Joseph
     1966 Situation Ethics. Philadelphia: Westminster Press.
Fogel, Robert W. and Stanley L. Engerman
     1974 Time on the Cross: The Economics of American Negro Slavery.
           Boston: Little, Brown.
Frazier, E. Franklin
     1963 The Negro Church in America. New York: Schocken Books.
Fukuyama, Yoshio
     1972 The Ministry in Transition. University Park, Pennsylvania:
           Pennsylvania State University Press.
Gabriel, Ralph H.
     1940 The Course of American Democratic Thought. New York:
           The Ronald Press Co.
Gallup, George H., Jr. and John O. Davies, III
     1971 Religion in America. Princeton: Gallup International, Inc.
Gaustad, Edwin S.
     1962 Historical Atlas of Religion in America. New York: Harper
           & Row.
Gerth, Hans and C. Wright Mills, eds.
     1946 From Max Weber: Essays in Sociology. New York: Oxford
           University Press.
Greeley, Andrew
     1967 The Catholic Experience. Garden City: Doubleday & Co.
     1969 Religion in the Year 2000. New York: Sheed and Ward.
     1971 Why Can't They Be Like Us? New York: E. P. Dutton.
     1972 Priests in the United States. Garden City: Doubleday & Co.
Greeley, Andrew, and Peter Rossi
     1966 The Education of Catholic Americans. Chicago: Aldine
           Publishing Co.

Gustafson, James
    1961 Treasure in Earthen Vessels. New York: Harper and Row.
    1970 The Church as Moral Decision Maker. Philadelphia: Pilgrim
          Press.
Hadden, J. K.
    1969 The Gathering Storm in the Churches. Garden City: Doubleday
          & Co.
Handlin, Oscar
    1957 Race and Nationality in American Life. Boston: Little,
          Brown.
Harrison, Paul
    1959 Authority and Power in the Free Church Tradition. Princeton:
          Princeton University Press.
Herberg, Will
    1955 Protestant, Catholic, Jew. Garden City, New York: Doubleday
          & Co.
    1959 "There Is a Religious Revival!" Review of Religious Research
          1 (Fall): 45-50.
Hill, Samuel S., Jr.
    1968 Southern Churches in Crisis. Boston: Beacon Press.
Hoover, Edgar M. and Raymond Vernon
    1962 Anatomy of a Metropolis. Garden City: Doubleday & Co.
Hopkins, Charles H.
    1940 The Rise of the Social Gospel in American Protestantism,
          1865-1915. New Haven: Yale University Press.
Hudson, Winthrop
    1953 The Great Tradition in the American Churches. New York:
          Harper & Brothers.
Illich, Ivan
    1973 Tools for Conviviality. New York: Harper and Row.
Jacquet, Constant H., Jr.
    1972 Yearbook of American Churches 1972. New York: Abingdon Press.
James, Arthur
    1962 The Christian in Politics. London: Oxford University Press.
John XXIII
    1963 "Mater et Magistra" in Seven Great Encyclicals. Glen Rock,
          New Jersey: Paulist Press.
Jud, Gerald, Edgar Mills, Jr., and Genevieve Burch
    1970 Ex Pastors. Philadelphia: Pilgrim Press.
Kelley, Dean M.
    1972 Why Conservative Churches are Growing. New York: Harper
          and Row.
Kincheloe, Samuel C.
    1938 The American City and Its Church. New York: Friendship
          Press.
Kornhauser, William
    1959 The Politics of Mass Society. Glencoe: The Free Press.
Kraemer, Paul
    1973 Awakening from the American Dream. Chicago: Center for the
          Scientific Study of Religion.
Lee, Robert and Russell Galloway
    1969 The Schizophrenic Church. Philadelphia: Westminster Press.

Lehmann, Paul
    1963 Ethics in a Christian Context. New York: Harper and Row.
Lenski, Gerhard
    1961 The Religious Factor. New York: Doubleday & Co.
Lipset, Seymour
    1959 "Religion in America: What Religious Revival?" Review of
          Religious Research 1 (Summer): 17-24.
Little, David
    1969 Religion, Order and Law. New York: Harper and Row.
Littell, Franklin H.
    1962 From State Church to Pluralism. Garden City: Anchor Books,
          Doubleday & Co.
Long, Edward, Jr.
    1967 A Survey of Christian Ethics. New York: Oxford University
          Press.
Luckmann, Thomas
    1967 The Invisible Religion. New York: Macmillan.
Marcuse, Herbert
    1964 One-Dimensional Man. Boston: Beacon Press.
Marty, Martin E.
    1959 The New Shape of American Religion. New York: Harper and Bros.
May, H. F.
    1949 Protestant Churches and Industrial America. New York:
          Harper & Brothers.
Mead, Sidney E.
    1963 The Lively Experiment. New York: Harper and Row.
Moore, Wilbert E.
    1963 Social Change. Englewood Cliffs, New Jersey: Prentice-Hall.
Mueller, Samuel A.
    1971 "The New Triple Melting Pot: Herberg Revisited." Review
          of Religious Research 13 (Fall): 18-33.
Mumford, Lewis
    1938 The Culture of Cities. New York: Harcourt, Brace & Co.
Murray, John Courtney
    1960 We Hold These Truths. New York: Sheed and Ward.
Myrdal, Gunnar
    1944 An American Dilemma. New York: Harper and Brothers.
Nelson, James B.
    1971 Moral Nexus. Philadelphia: Westminster Press.
Niebuhr, H. Richard
    1951 Christ & Culture. New York: Harper and Bros.
    1956 The Purpose of the Church and Its Ministry. New York:
          Harper and Bros.
    1957 The Social Sources of Denominationalism. New York: Meredian
          Books.
Niebuhr, Reinhold
    1944 The Children of Light and the Children of Darkness. New York:
          Charles Scribner's Sons.
    1958 Pious and Secular America. New York: Charles Scribner's
          Sons.
Novak, Michael
    1972 The Rise of the Unmeltable Ethnics. New York: Macmillan.
O'Dea, Thomas
    1957 The Mormons. Chicago: University of Chicago Press.
Park, Robert E., and E. W. Burgess
    1925 The City. Chicago: University of Chicago Press.

Pike, E. Royston
    1954 Jehovah's Witnesses. London: Watts.
Pope, Liston
    1942 Millhands and Preachers. New Haven: Yale University Press.
    1948 "Religion and the Class Structure." The Annals 256 (March):
          84-91
Rainwater, Lee, and William L. Yancy
    1967 The Moynihan Report and the Politics of Controversy.
          Cambridge: MIT Press.
Ramsey, Paul
    1967 Deeds and Rules in Christian Ethics. New York: Charles
          Scribner's Sons.
Robertson, D. B., ed.
    1966 Voluntary Associations. Richmond: John Knox Press.
Ryan, John A. and Francis J. Boland
    1940 Catholic Principles of Politics. New York: Macmillan.
Schneider, Louis, and Sanford M. Dornbusch
    1958 Popular Religion. Chicago: University of Chicago Press.
Schroeder, W. Widick
    1970 Cognitive Structures & Religious Research. East Lansing:
          Michigan State University Press.
Schroeder, W. Widick, and Victor Obenhaus
    1964 Religion in American Culture. New York: The Free Press.
Sittler, Joseph
    1958 The Structure of Christian Ethics. Baton Rouge: Louisiana
          State University Press.
Stark, Rodney, and Charles Y. Glock
    1968 American Piety: The Nature of Religious Commitment.
          Berkeley: University of California Press.
Stein, Maurice
    1960 The Eclipse of Community. Princeton: Princeton University
          Press.
Sweetser, Thomas P.
    1974 The Catholic Parish: Shifting Membership in a Changing
          Church. Chicago: Center for the Scientific Study of Religion.
    Forthcoming American Catholic Survival. Washington: Consortium
          Press.
Tawney, R. H.
    1920 The Acquisitive Society. New York: Harcourt, Brace and
          Howe, Inc.
    1926 Religion and the Rise of Capitalism. New York: Harcourt,
          Brace and Co.
Taylor, Carl C.
    1953 The Farmers' Movement, 1620-1920. New York: American Book Co.
Tillich, Paul
    1954 Love, Power, and Justice. New York: Oxford Press.
    1963 Systematic Theology, Vol. III. Chicago: University of
          Chicago Press.
Troeltsch, Ernst
    1931 The Social Teachings of the Christian Church. London:
          George Allen and Unwin, Ltd.
Trueblood, Elton
    1973 Abraham Lincoln: Theologian of American Anguish. New York:
          Harper and Row.

Vidich, Arthur J., and Joseph Bensman
    1958   Small Town in Mass Society.   Princeton: Princeton University
           Press.
Wakin, Edward, and Joseph F. Scheuer
    1966   The De-Romanization of the American Catholic Church.   New
           York: Macmillan
Warner, W. Lloyd
    1961   The Family of God.   New Haven: Yale University Press.
Warner, W. Lloyd, ed.
    1967   The Emergent American Society.   New Haven: Yale University
           Press.
Warner, W. Lloyd and Associates
    1949   Democracy in Jonesville.   New York: Harper and Bros.
Weber, Max
    1930   The Protestant Ethic and the Spirit of Capitalism.   London:
           George Allen and Unwin, Ltd.
    1958   The City.   Glencoe: The Free Press.
Whitehead, Alfred North
    1926   Religion in the Making.   New York: Macmillan.
Whitley, Oliver R.
    1959   The Trumpet Call of Reformation.   St. Louis: Bethany Press.
Williams, Robin, Jr.
    1970   American Society.   New York: Knopf.
Wilson, Bryan
    1961   Sects and Society.   London: Heinemann.
    1967   Patterns of Sectarianism.   London: Heinemann.
    1969   Religion in Secular Society.   Baltimore: Penguin Books.
Winter, Gibson
    1961   The Suburban Captivity of the Churches.   Garden City:
           Doubleday & Co.
    1968   Religious Identity.   New York: Macmillan.
    1970   Being Free.   New York: Macmillan.
Wirth, Louis
    1938   "Urbanism as a Way of Life."   American Journal of Sociology
           XLIV   (July): 1-24.
Yinger, J. Milton
    1970   The Scientific Study of Religion.   New York: Macmillan.

APPENDIX A

Comparative Data on Respondents and Non-Respondents

The following tables summarize salient data on respondents and non-respondents to the lay questionnaires.

TABLE A-1

SUMMARY DATA ON THE CATHOLIC LAITY BY COMMUNITY

Summary Data	Community					
	Satellite City		New Town		Country Club Estates	
	N=	Percent	N=	Percent	N=	Percent
Questionnaires mailed out	310	100	311	100	323	100
Dropped from sample (moved, died, in-competent, etc.)	8	3	13	4	10	3
New totals	302	100	298	100	313	100
Questionnaire respondents	149	50	201	67	205	65
Telephone respondents	19	6	25	9	30	10
Explicit refusals	67	22	25	9	36	12
Other non-respondents	67	22	47	15	42	13

TABLE A-2

SUMMARY DATA ON THE WHITE PROTESTANT LAITY BY COMMUNITY

Summary Data	Community					
	Satellite City		New Town		Country Club Estates	
	N=	Percent	N=	Percent	N=	Percent
Questionnaires mailed out	305	100	428	100	319	100
Dropped from sample (moved, no longer members, mentally incompetent)	41	13	47	11	39	12
New totals	264	100	381	100	280	100
Questionnaire respondents	189	72	270	71	219	78
Telephone respondents	36	13	54	14	29	10
Explicit refusals	26	10	39	10	27	10
Other non-respondents	13	5	18	5	5	2

TABLE A-3

SUMMARY DATA ON THE BLACK PROTESTANT LAITY

Summary Data	N=	Percent
Questionnaires mailed out	307	100
Dropped from sample (moved; no longer members)	42	14
New totals	265	100
Questionnaire respondents	67	25
Telephone respondents	42	16
Non-respondents	156	59

TABLE A-4

SUMMARY DATA ON THE JEWISH LAITY

Summary Data	N=	Percent
Questionnaires mailed out	300	100
Dropped from sample (moved; no longer members)	29	10
New totals	271	100
Questionnaire respondents	124	46
Telephone respondents	47	17
Non-respondents	100	37

TABLE A-5

FREQUENCY OF MASS ATTENDANCE OF CATHOLIC QUESTIONNAIRE

RESPONDENTS AND TELEPHONE RESPONDENTS IN PERCENT

Frequency of Attendance	Questionnaire Respondents (N=552) Percent	Telephone Respondents (N=74) Percent
Almost every week or more	72	61
Two or three times a month	7	10
Once a month	6	12
Two or three times a year	6	10
Never or almost never	9	8
Totals	100	101

TABLE A-6

FREQUENCY OF CHURCH ATTENDANCE OF WHITE

PROTESTANT RESPONDENTS AND NON-RESPONDENTS IN PERCENT

Frequency of Attendance	Respondents (N=669) Percent	Non-Respondents* (N=233) Percent
Almost every week or more	41	10
Two or three times a month	22	23
Once a month	13	12
Two or three times a year	16	19
Never or almost never	9	36
Totals	101	100

$x^2 = 136.9$ $p < .001$

*Based on telephone responses and data provided by pastors or others.

TABLE A-7

FREQUENCY OF CHURCH ATTENDANCE OF BLACK UNITED METHODIST
PROTESTANT RESPONDENTS AND NON-RESPONDENTS IN PERCENT

Frequency of Attendance	Respondents (N=35) Percent	Non-Respondents* (N=123) Percent
Almost every week or more	29	19
Two or three times a month	31	14
Once a month	20	10
Two or three times a year	11	13
Never or almost never	9	45
Totals	100	101

*Based on telephone interviews and data supplied by the pastor or others.

TABLE A-8

FREQUENCY OF SYNAGOGUE ATTENDANCE OF JEWISH
RESPONDENTS AND NON-RESPONDENTS IN PERCENT

Frequency of Attendance	Respondents (N=124) Percent	Non-Respondents* (N=128) Percent
Almost every week or more	6	3
Two or three times a month	11	4
Once a month	21	23
Two or three times a year	52	64
Never or almost never	10	7
Totals	100	101

*Based on telephone interviews and data provided by synagogue staff
person or others.

TABLE A-9

SEX OF CATHOLIC QUESTIONNAIRE RESPONDENTS

AND TELEPHONE RESPONDENTS IN PERCENT

Sex	Questionnaire Respondents (N=542) Percent	Telephone Respondents (N=73) Percent
Male	39	47
Female	61	53
Totals	100	100

TABLE A-10

SEX OF WHITE PROTESTANT RESPONDENTS AND NON-RESPONDENTS IN PERCENT

Sex	Respondents (N=675) Percent	Non-Respondents* (N=241) Percent
Male	41	54
Female	59	46
Totals	100	100

$x^2 = 14.0$ $p < .001$

*Based on telephone interviews and data supplied by pastors or others.

TABLE A-11

SEX OF BLACK UNITED METHODIST PROTESTANT

RESPONDENTS AND NON-RESPONDENTS IN PERCENT

Sex	Respondents (N=35) Percent	Non-Respondents* (N=123) Percent
Male	26	39
Female	74	61
Totals	100	100

*Based on telephone interviews and data supplied by pastor or others.

TABLE A-12

SEX OF JEWISH RESPONDENTS AND

NON-RESPONDENTS IN PERCENT

Sex	Respondents (N=124) Percent	Non-Respondents* (N=129) Percent
Male	41	51
Female	59	49
Totals	100	100

*Based on telephone interviews and data supplied by synagogue staff person or others.

TABLE A-13

EDUCATIONAL LEVEL OF CATHOLIC QUESTIONNAIRE

RESPONDENTS AND TELEPHONE RESPONDENTS IN PERCENT

Highest Year of School Completed	Questionnaire Respondents (N=544) Percent	Telephone Respondents (N=74) Percent
Non-high school graduate	15	13
High school graduate	27	37
Some college	28	28
College graduate	16	11
Graduate work	13	11
Totals	100	100

TABLE A-14

EDUCATIONAL LEVEL OF WHITE PROTESTANT QUESTIONNAIRE

RESPONDENTS AND TELEPHONE RESPONDENTS IN PERCENT

Highest Year of School Completed	Questionnaire Respondents (N=674) Percent	Telephone Respondents (N=115) Percent
Non-high school graduate	8	8
High school graduate	22	31
Some college	33	29
College graduate	19	23
Graduate work	18	9
Totals	100	100

TABLE A-15

EDUCATIONAL LEVEL OF BLACK PROTESTANT QUESTIONNAIRE

RESPONDENTS AND TELEPHONE RESPONDENTS IN PERCENT

Highest Year of School Completed	Questionnaire Respondents (N=62) Percent	Telephone Respondents (N=42) Percent
Eighth grade or less	3	21
Some high school and high school graduates	34	50
Additional education beyond high school	63	29
Totals	100	100

TABLE A-16

EDUCATIONAL LEVEL OF JEWISH QUESTIONNAIRE RESPONDENTS

AND TELEPHONE RESPONDENTS IN PERCENT

Highest Year of School Completed	Questionnaire Respondents (N=123) Percent	Telephone Respondents (N=47) Percent
Eighth grade or less	1	0
Some high school and high school graduates	16	13
Additional education beyond high school	83	87
Totals	100	100

TABLE A-17

AGE DISTRIBUTION OF CATHOLIC QUESTIONNAIRE

RESPONDENTS AND TELEPHONE RESPONDENTS

Age	Questionnaire Respondents (N=548) Percent	Telephone Respondents (N=74) Percent
Under 25	4	8
25-34	24	23
35-54	53	53
55 and over	19	16
Totals	100	100

TABLE A-18

AGE DISTRIBUTION OF WHITE PROTESTANT

RESPONDENTS AND NON-RESPONDENTS

Age	Respondents (N=675) Percent	Non-Respondents* (N=233) Percent
Under 25	14	8
25-34	18	16
35-54	47	52
55 and over	21	24
Totals	100	100

*Includes telephone responses and data provided by pastor or others.

Major Differences between Respondents and Non-Respondents

The data reveal differences between respondents and non-respondents by sex, status, and involvement in religious institutions for most groups. Differences were most marked among black Protestants and least marked among Jews. The greater differences among blacks are related to greater internal differences in the black churches, and the lesser differences among Jews are related to the greater homogeneity of the Jewish synagogue selected for study. Generally, respondents were more involved in the life of their religious institution and were better educated than non-respondents. Women were also overrepresented among the respondents.

The bias toward middle and upper status respondents and toward more highly involved respondents enhances the significance of the differences reported between the four faith groupings, for status differences and institutional marginality are minimized by the selective response patterns noted here.

The Questionnaire

The questionnaire used with Catholic lay people is reproduced in this appendix. Comparable questionnaires were employed with Protestant and Jewish lay people. In these instances, the items on the Mass were deleted and some minor changes in wording were made to fit the different traditions. In the interests of economy, those schedules and the clergy schedules, which were very comparable to the lay schedules, have not been reproduced here.

LAY QUESTIONNAIRE

Please check the proper line, circle the proper number, or fill in the proper blank. Feel free to write comments in the margin if you want.

I. Religious activities and attitudes

1. What is your present religious membership?

_____1) Catholic from birth _____4) Jewish
_____2) Protestant   _____5) None
_____3) Catholic Convert (Please _____6) Other (please
   specify previous religion.)   specify)

_____ _____

1a. Name of church or local parish to which you belong: _____ _

_____

2. What is the present religious membership of your spouse?

_____1) Catholic from birth _____4) Jewish
_____2) Protestant   _____5) None
_____3) Catholic Convert (Please _____6) I am not married.
   specify previous religion.) _____7) Other (please specify

_____ _____

3. Approximately how often do you attend Mass?

_____1) Almost every week or more _____4) About two or three
_____2) About two or three times a   times a year
   month   _____5) Almost never
_____3) About once a month

4. Compared with five years ago, how often do you attend Mass now?

    ____1) Much more often now   ____4) Less often now
    ____2) More often now   ____5) Much less often now
    ____3) About the same

5. Compared with five years ago, how much money do you contribute to your parish now (excluding school tuition)?

    ____1) Much more now   ____4) Less now
    ____2) More now   ____5) Much less now
    ____3) About the same

6. Compared with five years ago, how much time do you spend in parish activities, programs and projects now?

    ____1) Much more time now   ____4) Less time now
    ____2) More time now   ____5) Much less time now
    ____3) About the same

7. A number of parishes have activities such as those specified below. Please indicate your feelings about such activities, whether your parish has them or not. For each activity circle the number under the heading which best expresses your feelings.

	Very Favorable	Favorable	Mixed Feelings	Unfavorable	Very Unfavorable	Don't Know Or No Opinion
1) Fund raising groups (Bake sales, bazaars, paper sales, etc.)	1	2	3	4	5	6
2) Experimental personal growth groups (Marathons, encounter groups, sensitivity groups, etc.)	1	2	3	4	5	6
3) Prayer and devotional groups (Pentecostal meetings, prayer meetings, etc.)	1	2	3	4	5	6
4) Recreational and social groups (Sports, potluck dinners, etc.)	1	2	3	4	5	6
5) Adult religious educational groups (Scripture study, adult discussion, etc.)	1	2	3	4	5	6
6) Service groups (Holy Name Society, women's club, etc.)	1	2	3	4	5	6

7) Social action groups
    (Community education,
    peace groups, civil   1   2   3   4   5   6
    rights groups, etc.)

8) Liturgy (Choir,
    Commentators, etc.)   1   2   3   4   5   6

9) Youth groups (CCD,
    Teen Club, etc.,--not   1   2   3   4   5   6
    including parish school)

10) Administrative and
    policy making groups   1   2   3   4   5   6
    (Parish Council,
    School Board, etc.)

11) Other groups
    (Please specify)   1   2   3   4   5   6

_____

8. Are you a member of any groups or do you participate in any activities
    in your church? 1) Yes____   2) No____

8a. If yes, please list the group(s) or activity(ies).

Name of Group or Activity

_____

_____

_____

9. Have you ever taught CCD (Confraternity of Christian Doctrine) or been
    an advisor or teacher to a parish youth group? 1) Yes____   2) No____

    9a. If yes, what ages?

        ____1) Pre-school   ____4) Grades 10-12
        ____2) Grades 1-6   ____5) Adult
        ____3) Grades 7-9
    9b. If yes, for how many years altogether? ____years

10. About how far do you live from your church? ____miles

11. Do you frequently go to another church? 1) Yes____   2) No____

    11a. If yes, why? _____

    _____

12. Did you attend any church-related retreats, workshops, etc. in the last
    year? 1) Yes____ 2) No____

12a. If yes, approximately how many? _____

13.   Did you attend any church-related personal growth groups, such as
      sensitivity groups, encounter groups or marathons in the last year?

      1) Yes____   2) No____

      13a. If yes, approximately how many? ____

14.   Have you had religious devotions or observances (such as prayers at
      meals or at night, Bible reading, etc.) in your home?

      1) Yes____   2) No____

      14a. If yes, check as many of the following as apply.

              ____1) Within the last year, special seasonal devotions at
                      Advent, Christmas, Lent or Easter
              ____2) Within this past week, prayers at meals
              ____3) Within this past week, prayers at other times
              ____4) Within this past month, Bible reading
              ____5) Within this past month, other religious reading
              ____6) Within this last year, Masses in your home
              ____7) Other (please specify) _____

15.   Approximately how often does your family or those with whom you live
      discuss the meaning of your faith for your daily lives?

      ____1) Almost every day   ____4) Only on special occasions
      ____2) About every week   ____5) Almost never
      ____3) About once or twice a month ____6) I live alone.

16.   During the past year, do you think your parish has engaged in any
      especially creative programs or activities?

      1) Yes____   2) No____   3) Don't Know____

      16a. If yes, please specify._____
            _____

17.   What is your present attitude toward changes in the American Catholic
      Church? (Please check only one.)

              ____1) I was satisfied with the pre-Vatican II Church.
              ____2) I would like a slower rate of change.
              ____3) I am satisfied with the Church's present rate of change.
              ____4) I would like a more rapid rate of change in the future.
              ____5) I feel radical change is necessary in the Church.
              ____6) I am confused and uncertain about changes in the Church.
              ____7) I have no opinion one way or the other.

              Make any comments here:_____
      _____
      _____

18. What is your present general attitude toward the local parish?

_____1) Very favorable   _____4) Unfavorable
_____2) Favorable   _____5) Very unfavorable
_____3) Mixed feelings   _____6) No opinion

      Make any comments here:_____
_____
_____

18a. What is your present attitude toward the local parish school?

_____1) Very favorable   _____4) Unfavorable
_____2) Favorable   _____5) Very unfavorable
_____3) Mixed feelings   _____6) No opinion

      Make any comments here:_____
_____
_____

19. What is your feeling about the beliefs and practices of the following religious groups? (Circle the number under the heading most closely reflecting your attitude.)

	Very Favorable	Favorable	Mixed Feelings	Unfavorable	Very Unfavorable	Don't Know Or No Opinion
1) Catholic	1	2	3	4	5	6
2) Episcopalian	1	2	3	4	5	6
3) Lutheran	1	2	3	4	5	6
4) Jehovah's Witnesses	1	2	3	4	5	6
5) Judaism	1	2	3	4	5	6
6) Methodist	1	2	3	4	5	6
7) Presbyterian	1	2	3	4	5	6
8) Southern Baptist	1	2	3	4	5	6
9) United Church of Christ	1	2	3	4	5	6
10) Zen Buddhism	1	2	3	4	5	6

20. Excluding Catholics, which two religious groups listed in the preceding question do you think have beliefs and practices most like the Catholic Church?
1)_____   2)_____

Excluding Catholics, which two groups have beliefs and practices least like the Catholic Church?
1)_____   2)_____

21. Consider for a moment the religious affiliation of your <u>four</u> closest friends.

    ____1) How many are Catholic?
    ____2) How many are Protestant?
    ____3) How many are Jewish?
    ____4) How many are not members of a church or synagogue?

22. Approximately what proportion of the relatives whom you see once a month or more are Catholic?

    ____1) All or almost all   ____4) About one-third
    ____2) About two-thirds   ____5) None or almost none
    ____3) About half   ____6) I don't see any relatives once a month or more.

23. Listed below is a series of statements dealing with moral and religious matters. Indicate your reaction to each statement by circling the number under the heading which best expresses your feelings.

	Strongly Agree	Agree	Mixed Feelings	Disagree	Strongly Disagree	No Opinion
1) Priests today spend too much time talking about how people should behave and not enough about God and religious matters.	1	2	3	4	5	6
2) Being a Catholic makes it harder for me to feel I am part of American society.	1	2	3	4	5	6
3) Many Christians seem to think they are superior to other people.	1	2	3	4	5	6
4) There is no longer much difference between Catholic and Protestant churches.	1	2	3	4	5	6
5) The people I know who are faithful church members are less selfish than most other people I know.	1	2	3	4	5	6

6) Changes in the Mass make it harder for me to worship.   1   2   3   4   5   6

7) One should act as loving toward everyone as one does toward his family and close friends.   1   2   3   4   5   6

8) Catholic priests should be allowed to get married and still function as priests.   1   2   3   4   5   6

9) There are times when it might be all right to break one of the Ten Commandments.   1   2   3   4   5   6

10) Priests spend too much of their time condemning people for their sins.   1   2   3   4   5   6

11) We should make every effort to include all races and social classes in each local parish.   1   2   3   4   5   6

12) When I attend a good liturgy, I leave church resolved to try to improve my relations with my fellow men.   1   2   3   4   5   6

13) The Church should support Women's Liberation.   1   2   3   4   5   6

14) The Church should enforce a strict standard of moral conduct among its members.   1   2   3   4   5   6

15) The Church should be a place where one can go and find peace of mind and security.   1   2   3   4   5   6

16) The Church should take special note of major national holidays (Memorial Day and the Fourth of July).   1   2   3   4   5   6

17) The American Catholic Church should take public stands on political issues.   1   2   3   4   5   6

18) Jesus Christ is the necessary foundation for my religious faith.   1   2   3   4   5   6

19) We should seek to make all men Christians.   1   2   3   4   5   6

20) God changes as the world evolves.   1   2   3   4   5   6

23a. Indicate your feeling about the following types of parish religious activities

	Very Favor- able	Favor- able	Mixed Feelings	Unfavor- able	Very Unfavor- able	Never Heard of it
1) Quiet Mass with no responses	1	2	3	4	5	6
2) Mass with responses; no singing	1	2	3	4	5	6
3) Participation Mass with singing	1	2	3	4	5	6
4) Guitar Mass; Contemporary hymns	1	2	3	4	5	6
5) Informal Masses in homes	1	2	3	4	5	6
6) The "Kiss of Peace" in Mass	1	2	3	4	5	6
7) Laymen receiving Communion in the hand	1	2	3	4	5	6
8) Baptisms during Mass	1	2	3	4	5	6

9)	Communal Penance services	1	2	3	4	5	6
10)	Prayer Groups	1	2	3	4	5	6
11)	Benediction; Evening devotions	1	2	3	4	5	6
12)	Laymen distributing Holy Communion	1	2	3	4	5	6
13)	Other (please specify)	1	2	3	4	5	6

_____

24. Please indicate the amount of help the Church has given you through sermons, study groups, counseling, etc. on the topics listed below. Circle the number under the heading most closely reflecting your experience.

	Very Helpful	Helpful	Of Little Help One Way or Another	Somewhat Unhelpful	Very Unhelpful	Other (please specify)
1) Guidance in personal prayer life	1	2	3	4	5	6
2) Guidance for family and marital relations	1	2	3	4	5	6
3) Guidance for conduct on the job	1	2	3	4	5	6
4) Guidance on social and political issues	1	2	3	4	5	6
5) Guidance in forming my religious beliefs	1	2	3	4	5	6

25. If your parish priests took a public stand in their sermons on each of the following topics, what would your reactions be? Circle the number in each column most closely expressing your feelings.

Topic	Strongly Approve	Approve	Mixed Feelings	Dis-approve	Strongly Dis-approve	Depends on Circum-stances	No Opinion
1) Business ethics	1	2	3	4	5	6	7
2) Problems faced by welfare recipients	1	2	3	4	5	6	7

3) Pollution of our
    environment   1   2   3   4   5   6

4) School busing   1   2   3   4   5   6

5) Giving to
    charity   1   2   3   4   5   6

6) Vietnam War   1   2   3   4   5   6

7) Upbringing of
    children   1   2   3   4   5   6

8) Women's Liberation   1   2   3   4   5   6

26. Local churches react in different ways to social, economic, and politi
     issues. In which of the following ways do you feel the local parish
     should respond to these issues? If you wish, you may check more than

     ____1) Encourage individuals to form parish discussion groups on
             public policy issues
     ____2) Take official stands on public policy issues
     ____3) Allow church facilities to be used by social action groups
     ____4) Encourage individuals to form unofficial parish social
             action groups
     ____5) Encourage individuals to participate in community social
             action groups
     ____6) None of the above
     ____7) Other (please specify)_____

27. Please check the statement which comes closest to your understanding
     of the Bible.

     ____1) Scripture is literally true.
     ____2) Scripture is not literally true but is the most important
             way of knowing about God.
     ____3) Scripture is one of many equally important ways of knowing
             about God.
     ____4) Scripture is less important than other ways of knowing about
             God.
     ____5) Scripture is of very little importance.
     ____6) Other (please specify) _____

28. Please check any of the following which you think are sacred. If
     you wish, you may check more than one.

     ____1) The Ten Commandments   ____ 7) Christmas
     ____2) The Eucharist   ____ 8) Easter
     ____3) Freedom   ____ 9) Memorial Day
     ____4) A church sanctuary   ____10) Sunday
     ____5) Love   ____11) A human being
     ____6) The Bible   ____12) Other (please specify
                                                  _____

29. As an adult, have you ever had an experience of the presence
    of God?

    _____1) I'm sure I have.   _____3) I don't think so.
    _____2) I think I have.   _____4) I'm sure I have not.

30. Check those activities in the following list which you would consider
    to be worship. If you wish, you may check more than one.

    _____1) A religious discussion group   _____ 7) Sunday service in
    _____2) A group hymn sing   church
    _____3) Personal devotions   _____ 8) Performance of
    _____4) Communion with nature   great music
    _____5) Devotions connected with a   _____ 9) A prayer group meeting
             church program or activity   _____10) Study and reflection
    _____6) Sharing common concerns   _____11) An outdoor church service
             with a caring group   _____12) Other (Please specify)
                                                       _____

31. Some people say that they do not really feel comfortable in church.
    Do you ever feel uncomfortable for any of the following reasons?
    If you wish, you may check more than one.

    _____1) I have religious doubts (for example about prayer or about
             God).
    _____2) I do not feel comfortable with the other members; they
             are not the kind of people I would pick as my friends.
    _____3) I do not agree with what the priest(s) preaches or tries
             to do.
    _____4) Changes have taken away many of the things the Church
             has stood for.
    _____5) Church rituals and liturgies are outmoded.
    _____6) Church creeds and doctrines are outmoded.
    _____7) Other (please specify)_____
    _____8) I never feel uncomfortable in church.

II. Social Attitudes and Activities

1. Are you a member of any voluntary organizations besides church groups?

    1) Yes_____ 2) No_____

    1a. If yes, please list the groups and indicate the approximate
         number of hours per month you spend in connection with the group.

                                                  Approximate
              Name of Group   Hours per Month

    _____   _____
    _____   _____
    _____   _____
    _____   _____
    _____   _____

2. What is your opinion of the neighborhood in which you live?

_____1) Very favorable   _____4) Unfavorable
_____2) Favorable   _____5) Very unfavorable
_____3) Mixed feelings   _____6) No opinion

3. How do you feel about America's future?

_____1) Very optimistic   _____5) Very pessimistic
_____2) Somewhat optimistic   _____6) I am confused and
_____3) Mixed feelings   uncertain
_____4) Somewhat pessimistic   _____7) No opinion

4. What is your political preference?

_____1) Democratic   _____5) Republican
_____2) Independent, leaning toward   _____6) Independent, leaning
         Democratic   toward Republican
_____3) Strictly independent   _____7) No political preference
_____4) American Independent Party   _____8) Other (please specify)
         (Wallace)   _____

5. In general, which of the following ways of making family decisions
    do you think is most desirable?

_____1) The husband should make the major decisions.
_____2) The wife should make the major decisions.
_____3) The husband and wife together should make the major decisions.
_____4) The parents should jointly make the major decisions, but
         only after consulting the children.
_____5) The whole family, parents and children, should make the
         major decisions.
_____6) Other (please specify) _____

6. In terms of morality, do you believe that life today is getting
    better or worse?

_____1) Better
_____2) Worse
_____3) About the same
_____4) Don't know

7. Which of the following is the most important thing for a child to
    learn to prepare himself for life? (Please check only one.)

_____1) To obey
_____2) To be well-liked or popular
_____3) To think for himself
_____4) To work hard
_____5) To help others when they need help

8. How often do the following statements apply to you? Circle the number under the heading which best describes your experience.

	Very Often	Often	Some- times	Not Very Often	Never
1) I find myself so pressed for time that I do not stop and help someone when I know I should.	1	2	3	4	5
2) I trade help and favors back and forth with my friends and neighbors.	1	2	3	4	5
3) On my own I spend time helping the less fortunate members of the parish or community.	1	2	3	4	5
4) I borrow money from relatives or friends rather than from a bank or other financial institution.	1	2	3	4	5
5) I ask myself "What is the morally right thing for me to do in this situation?"	1	2	3	4	5
6) I give money to charitable causes outside the church.	1	2	3	4	5

9. Indicate your reaction to the following statements by circling the number under the heading which best expresses your feelings.

	Strongly Agree	Agree	Mixed Feelings	Disagree	Strongly Disagree	Depends on Circum- stances	No Opinion
1) It is wrong for people to have pre-marital sexual relations.	1	2	3	4	5	6	7
2) It is wrong for married people to have sexual rela- tions with persons other than their husbands or wives.	1	2	3	4	5	6	7
3) Divorce is wrong.	1	2	3	4	5	6	7
4) It is wrong for a woman who wants an abortion in the first three months of pregnancy to have one.	1	2	3	4	5	6	7

5) Drinking is wrong. 1   2   3   4   5   6   7

6) Christian princi-
   ples can provide
   the basis for   1   2   3   4   5   6   7
   participating in
   protest movements.

7) Welfare reci-
   pients should be   1   2   3   4   5   6   7
   put to work.

8) Our present econ-
   omic system is the
   best form of   1   2   3   4   5   6   7
   economic organiza-
   tion.

9) American involve-
   ment in the Viet-
   nam War has been   1   2   3   4   5   6   7
   immoral.

10) Divorces in which
    neither party has
    to give grounds   1   2   3   4   5   6   7
    for divorce should
    be legalized.

11) The suburbs should
    be racially inte-   1   2   3   4   5   6   7
    grated.

12) Communes with
    more than one
    husband or wife   1   2   3   4   5   6   7
    are acceptable
    forms of family
    life.

13) The   sale of
    marijuana should   1   2   3   4   5   6   7
    be legalized.

14) Our   present
    political system
    is the best form   1   2   3   4   5   6   7
    of political
    organization.

15) The government
    should give money
    to church-   1   2   3   4   5   6
    sponsored schools.

16) Ideas of self-sacrificing service and love toward others cannot be practiced in business and politics.

   1   2   3   4   5   6   7

17) Young people these days are too idealistic and not in touch with the real world.

   1   2   3   4   5   6   7

18) Some day men will solve most of their problems on earth and live in a peaceful world.

   1   2   3   4   5   6   7

19) The government should be neutral toward religious institutions.

   1   2   3   4   5   6   7

20) Air and water pollution is not as big a problem as newspapers and TV would lead one to believe.

   1   2   3   4   5   6   7

III. General Information

Now we would like to ask you a few personal questions about yourself. Most of these answers can be checked very quickly.

1. What is your age? (Check)

   ____1) Under 20   ____4) 30-34   ____7) 55-64
   ____2) 20-24   ____5) 35-44   ____8) 65 or over
   ____3) 25-29   ____6) 45-54

2. What is your sex? 1) Female____   2) Male____

3. What is your race?

   ____1) Black
   ____2) White
   ____3) Other (please specify) _____

4. Do you think of yourself as belonging to a particular nationality or ethnic group, such as German, Irish, etc.?

   1) Yes____ 2) No____

   4a. If yes, which one?_____

5. Were you born in the United States? 1) Yes____ 2) No____

6. What is your marital status?

   ____1) Married   ____4) Divorced
   ____2) Single   ____5) Separated
   ____3) Widowed

7. Do you have any children? 1) Yes____ 2) No____

   7a. If yes, how many? _____

   7b. If yes, how many live at home? _____

   7c. If yes, how many now attend a Catholic grade school? _____
                                     Catholic high school? _____
                                     Catholic college?   _____

8. How many of your <u>four</u> closest friends live within a mile of you? _____

9. What is the highest year of school you have completed?

   ____1) Some grammar school   ____4) High school graduate
   ____2) Eighth grade graduate   ____5) Some college
   ____3) Some high school   ____6) 4-year college graduate
                                   ____7) Post-graduate work

10. What is your present occupational status? (Check as many as apply.)

    ____1) Employed full-time   ____5) Student full-time
    ____2) Employed part-time   ____6) Homemaker full-time
    ____3) Unemployed at present   ____7) Other (please specify)
    ____4) Retired   _____

11. What kind of work does the major wage earner in your family do? (If retired, please answer on the basis of previous occupation.) Please be as specific as possible, such as plumber, electrician, insurance agent, electrical engineer, secretary, etc.

    _____

12. What is your present yearly total family income before taxes?

    ____1) Under $5,000   ____4) $15,000 to 19,999
    ____2) $5,000 to 9,999   ____5) $20,000 to 24,999
    ____3) $10,000 to 14,999   ____6) $25,000 to 49,999
                                        ____7) $50,000 and over

Please feel free to make any additional comments on this page.

_____

_____

_____

_____

_____

_____

_____

      Thank you for your time and patience. Please go over the questionnaire to make sure you have answered every question. Place the questionnaire in the pre-addressed envelope and mail it to us. If you have any questions about any part of the questionnaire, do not mail the questionnaire now. Wait for a member of the Center for the Scientific Study of Religion staff to telephone you. The staff member will explain any such questions.

                         The pastor and the CSSR